Expanding the American Dream

SUNY Series in the New Cultural History

William R. Taylor, Editor

Expanding the American Dream

Building and Rebuilding Levittown

Barbara M. Kelly

State University of New York Press

Published by
State University of New York Press, Albany

For information, address State University of New York Press,
State University Plaza, Albany, N.Y. 12246

Production by M. R. Mulholland
Marketing by Bernadette LaManna

Library of Congress Cataloging-in-Publication Data

Kelly, Barbara M.
    Expanding the American dream : building and rebuilding Levittown /
Barbara M. Kelly.
        p.   cm. — (SUNY series in the new cultural history)
    Includes bibliographical references and index.
    ISBN 0-7914-1287-3. — ISBN 0-7914-1288-1 (pbk.)
    1. Suburban homes—New York (State)—Levittown.   2. Planned
communities—New York (State)—Levittown.   3. Architects and housing
developers—New York (State)—Levittown.   4. Architecture and
society—New York (State)—Levittown.   I. Title.   II. Series.
NA7571.K44   1993
307.3'3616'09747245—dc20   91-46676
                                                                                                CIP

10 9 8 7 6 5 4 3 2 1

Now, a new house standing empty, with staring
    window and door,

Looks idle, perhaps, and foolish, like a hat
    on its block in the store.

But there's nothing mournful about it; it cannot
    be sad and lone

For the lack of something within it that it has
    never known.

But a house that has done what a house should
    do, a house that has sheltered life,

That has put its loving wooden arms around a
    man and his wife,

A house that has echoed a baby's laugh and
    held up his stumbling feet;

Is the saddest sight, when it's left alone,
    that ever your eyes could meet.[1]

1. Joyce Kilmer, "The House With Nobody In It." *Trees and Other Poems.*
(Garden City, NJ: Doubleday, Doran & Company, Inc., 1914).

CONTENTS

FIGURES

Foreword

When the first tenants began moving into the Levitt Cape Cods at Island Trees in 1947, they were beginning a new chapter in the development of American suburbia. William Levitt, a new kind of producer of domestic housing—with fresh experience from wartime construction—was opening a market in individual houses for a new segment of the society. The circumstances that brought about Levitt's initiative, its meaning in the postwar years and some of the interesting consequences of this development are the subject of Dr. Kelly's book.

A number of circumstances, according to her, lay behind Levitt's decision to build on Long Island. A general housing shortage, especially for returning veterans, legislation that led to the Veteran's Emergency Housing Program of 1946, the acquisition by Levitt of a tract of land in Hempstead, and the possibility for economies in construction through cement slab foundations and on-site construction were the most important factors. With a market assured, Levitt set about building an initial 2000 rental units and, eventually, still other units for sale at monthly costs between $52 for a mortgage and $60 rent. Some 6000 units were built at the Long Island site by 1948; by 1951 Levitt had completed a total of 17,500 units.

Levitt's Island Trees development was phase one in the immense expansion of tract housing by Levitt and others in the decade following the war. Kelly, in the chapters that follow, has tried to assess the full social and cultural significance of the Island Trees tract, both for the Levittowners themselves and for their generation and the generations to follow. She has looked carefully at the tract house development and tried to determine the extent to which it was, and was not, a planned community.

Levittown, for her, represents "the reduction of the American Dream to a practical and affordable reality." It meant that a group on the lower edge of middle-class life—in effect, a prewar tenant class with a median income of a little over $3000, was able to move into individual villa housing that had previously been available to higher-income groups in society. It also initiated a new kind of "instant community" that initiated the new dwellers into a postwar climate of "conformity and privatization." Within their own community, Levittowners were confronted with restrictive covenants that inhibited fences and prohibited laundry lines. From the outside, Levittown met with hostility and criticism—a fear by neighboring towns of instant ghettos, for example—and a dense mythology that lasted throughout the generation. Part of Kelly's task has been to examine and repudiate some of these myths.

Two kinds of analysis have added depth and further substance to Kelly's account. First, she has also tried to place the Levitt kind of community in the context of historical planned communities in America. She has also tracked down newspaper and magazine accounts both of Levittown and of suburban growth more generally, and tried to assess the climate of opinion about housing and house design in these crucial years. She has provided a fresh analysis of the image of suburbia that was projected on television and movie screens during the 1950s. Also at the macro level, she has examined the discussion of housing by the Women's Congress in 1950 and compared its recommendations for designing houses to the plans of Levitt houses.

Her interviews with the original Levittown "pioneers," as they call themselves, and her detailed studies of some of the changes they have made in the original houses, will interest readers concerned with the evolution of middle-class domestic housing since the war. The modifications made by owners in the original houses, especially the ranch house design, are extensive enough for Kelly to call them "coproducers" of a lower middle-class housing revolution. Other observations qualify her as an astute observer and critic of American popular culture and folkways.

This book joins important works by Gwendolyn Wright and Dolores Hayden in the expanding historical examination of American domestic architecture and culture.

William R. Taylor
State University of New York
at Stony Brook

Preface

In the history of the postwar American suburb, Levittown, Long Island, has long had a preeminent place.[1] Its sheer size—17,500 houses—makes it a suitable laboratory for the study of community development, and its duration—over 40 years—has made it a convenient sample for the study of suburban life. Yet, although the owner-generated redesign of individual houses has frequently been the subject of media attention, the significance of the patterns of change both individually—to the homeowner—and collectively—as an aspect of American social history—has been largely ignored.

By focusing on the homeowner as coproducer of the domestic environment, this study is intended to broaden the dialogue on the social history of American architecture. It explores the owner-generated redesign of the mass-produced houses in Levittown. Building on Le Corbusier's belief that houses are machines for living, it examines the houses of Levittown as dwelling places and sets them into a matrix of the prevailing cultural norms in the years following World War II.[2] The primary focus is on the dialectic relationship between the deliverer-designed housing and the owner-redesigned homes. Underlying this is an examination of the process by which the suburban house form was transmitted to a new socioeconomic constituency as a direct result of government programs.

When the study began, there was very little scholarly material that dealt with nonacademic residential architecture, and even less which dealt with domestic space. Dolores Hayden, now the acknowledged dean of the field, had just published her *Seven American Utopias*; Gwendolyn Wright—the heir apparent—had not yet released her first book.

Following the lead of the new social history, urban and architectural history experienced an explosion of interest in the common people and their houses, in housing and communities.[3] Within that broad spectrum of interest, several approaches to the study of the built environment of the American suburbs developed which offered new insights into the social implications of the domestic environment. Urban historians, on the one hand, focused on the suburban community, on the interaction of infrastructure with housing, and on the consequences of the suburbanization process for the larger society. In these studies domestic architecture served largely as a barometer of change. The architectural historians, on the other hand, emphasized the home and its functions in society. Focusing on the product and the providers—the designers, reformers, and builders—who generate the housing, they examined the social implications of changes in the built forms.

As this body of literature grew, the evidential basis of most of the research remained firmly rooted in the traditional archival sources. That is, the scholars focused on what had been written about houses and housing, rather than on the houses themselves; on what had been said about the houses, rather than on what had been done with them. One learned much more about what the providers—planners, reformers, developers, and designers—thought about creating housing for their constituents than about how the residents interacted with the finished houses.[4] This emphasis was reflected in the illustrations in the new architectural histories in which architects' drawings and woodcuts of "model" houses and streetscapes, largely drawn from the pages of the housing advocates, predominate.

At the same time the social historians were warning us that what the literate classes said and wrote, the stuff of archival sources, was of limited value and even distorted our understanding of the past. They held that one must move beyond the words of the leaders and find new methods for examining the actions of the followers in order to fully understand the past.

Viewed from this perspective, the reformers' or builders' views of what a home should be are only half the story. They tell us little about how the inhabitants received their homes—what they believed about them, how they lived in them. Houses that have served as homes, on the other hand, could reveal the lives and values of the people, if only we were able to read them. It is the underlying premise of this study that, by asking the proper set of questions, we are reading their meaning. Did the reformers' message trickle down to the man in the street or his wife in the parlor? Did real people build houses to match the published recommendations? Did they use the houses they built as the reformers intended? Did they alter them? If so, was there a pattern to their changes?

This essay thus shifts the emphasis from form to floorplan, from house-as-architecture to house-as-domestic-space, from container to contained. In so doing, it applies questions usually associated with the study of vernacular architecture to a more contemporary form of domestic space.[5] How do the houses work? How do they change over time? What elements persist? Which are omitted? How does the design of the house mesh with social values of the time? The technology? If the design lags behind technology, what is the cause of that lag? In short, what do these houses mean?

Whereas history is, at its essence, the study of change over time, culture is derived from those elements that persist through time. Thus, although the focus of the essay is on change over time, it also takes note of certain spatial relationships and themes that have remained constant in the middle-class American home. Whether the dwelling is located in an arcadian setting like Llewelyn Park, a suburban community like Garden City, or a six-family apartment house in Manhattan, there are persistent arrangements of space. Production areas are treated as private or semiprivate space. The kitchen, for example, is separated from the gathering room, whether that room is called parlor, hall, living room, or front room. Workshops are set apart in garages or basement areas. Separate sleeping quarters for parents and offspring and for male and female children are also constant at the middle class level. Size and style may vary, but the separations persist and are found in the floor plans of housing styles as disparate as town houses, apartments, and suburban villas.

The study traces a number of these cultural artifacts—room layout, dominance, articulation, and relative size—as they were abstracted and reinterpreted in the postwar tract houses of the GI Bill.[6] Although it is not uniquely American to specialize space in this way, it was in postwar American housing that the trickle-down process was institutionalized so that these middle-class elements were included in the design of the low-cost, government-sponsored houses of the subdivision suburbs even while the form of the house around the space was being scaled down to house workers and their families. As a result, the state-delivered, low-cost houses built at Levittown did not replicate the tenement flat, the dogtrot, or the log cabin of the nineteenth-century worker class, but rather reduced the essence of the middle-class suburban villa to an affordable level.

Initially, the study was limited to the impact of the domestic geography of a low-cost, mass-produced house on the family life of its residents. In this phase the findings suggested a Marxian argument rooted in environmental determinism: "The capitalist builder imposed a way of life on a hapless proletariat through the deliberate design of domestic space." Given that the houses in question were not only mass-produced but funded by an essentially capitalist government, the social-engineering theory did not seem to be too revolutionary a model to follow. However, as the study evolved, the class-conflict model was clearly insufficient. The story of Levittown is far more complex. It is less one of conflict than of consensus; yet there are clear issues of class.[7]

The houses of Levittown did not remain as they had been designed and delivered in 1947. Indeed, by the end of its first decade, the visual landscape of Levittown—both interior and exterior—had been almost totally redesigned, not by the builder, but by the homeowners. It became apparent that the domestic space of the Levittown houses would not stand still for any meaningful analysis of a static, deliverer-designed environment. The houses no longer fit into such a neat category of analysis. The redesigned environment was far more 'vernacular' than the original subdivision had been, and the residents far more autonomous. Yet, the underlying structure of the houses was still that which had been designed and built for the mass market—commercial, if not academic, in design. The history of the built environment of Levittown therefore had an important, multi-leveled dimension that transcended the original question. New questions began to surface that touched on this nexus between individual and societal needs in the production and design of domestic space.

The substantive issues arose first out of the changes that had been made by the homeowners. How free were the homeowners to restructure their environment? Was there a tension between the desires of the homeowner and the restrictions imposed by the original design and construction of the houses? If so, was it intended? To what degree did the homeowners subsume individualism to community harmony when they renovated their houses? To what degree were they constrained to do so by local regulations?

The interaction between government-sponsored domestic space and family life began to suggest wider implications concerning the role of domestic space in society. The significance of the do-it-yourself homeowner's redesign of the dwelling place led logically to questions about the social, economic, and political effects of a housing program on its target constituency—young, lower-income veterans. In whose interest was the housing originally built? How were those interests expressed in the spatial organization of the houses? How was the housing itself received by its target group? How and to what end was it modified? What was the social and political milieu in which Levittown and its houses grew and prospered? And, finally, to what degree did the programs that sponsored the housing succeed?

The research revolved around several themes: the physical evolution of the houses themselves; the experiences and perceptions of the homeowners; the planning that led to the original housing; and the cultural and temporal context into which it was set. As a result, there is a rather mixed bag of source material and methodology used throughout the study, which ranges from the traditional government documents to visual examination in the field.[8]

The methods developed within the field of material culture have proven to be extremely useful to the analysis, which relies heavily on the evidence provided by the houses themselves, the homeowners' explanatory commentaries on their remodelings, oral history, and the popular culture of the period to illuminate the significance of those changes in reaffirming traditional American domestic values.[9]

Underlying these are methods borrowed from several fields— cultural and intellectual history (What is the meaning of house and home in America in 1950?); material culture (What was where in the house and how did it work?); textual analysis (Why are socially weighted terms such as 'nursery' and 'parlor' used to designate space in a four-room house?); and to a lesser degree, semiotics (What was the significance of a central hearth in a low-cost house centrally heated with copper tubing in the floors? Why were chamber candles carved into the stairrail of a twentieth-century worker's house? Why, when fencing was forbidden, was each house decorated with a short, open length of fence?).[10]

The design and use of the Levittown houses was not only consistent, but in harmony with the dominant values of the period. Having said that, it is important to point out there is no attempt to argue here for a causal relationship. Both the houses and the consensus appear to have emerged from the same cultural and temporal roots. There is no evidence that the houses were designed to control or manipulate the working-class population in any way that would have been recognizable by the environmental determinists of the Progressive Era. Nor did the subdivision suburbs impose an alien value system on the residents. Rather, the design and location of the houses reinforced a value system that was not only acceptable, but desirable to the lower-income market for which the housing was produced. As a result, the postwar delivery of single-family houses in suburbia to this new constituency served to reduce the potential for class conflict by expanding the parameters of the middle class—a process of inclusion, rather than coercion.

Acknowledgments

In the writing of a book like this, one amasses many debts. I would like to acknowledge all those whose support and help made this work possible. The list is very long, and I beg the indulgence of those whose help I may have taken for granted.

It was Ruth Schwartz Cowan who suggested Levittown as a research topic in a seminar too many years ago.

William R. Taylor provided the enriched intellectual environment in which to pursue the research, and guided the development of the dissertation on which this book is based. Nancy Tomes, Eric Lampard, and Michael Schwartz read the dissertation with keen and patient eyes. Their suggestions were invaluable and any failure to profit from them is clearly my own.

Millie DeRiggi, Mollie Keller, and Seymour Mandelbaum read the manuscript and forced me to make explicit certain concepts which I too readily took for granted.

There is also an enormous debt to those who have encouraged me and listened patiently as I worked out thorny problems along the way. In particular I would like to thank Floris Cash, Marie Fitzgerald, Ann Geneva, Jane Gover, Doris Halowitch, Mark Hessler, Ruth Markowitz, Margaret Schrage, and Mark Stern.

Dean Charles Andrews of Hofstra University's Joan and Donald E. Axinn Library generously provided me with professional time in which to complete the dissertation, and my captive audience at Hofstra's Long Island Studies Institute, Irene McQuillan and Connie Rein, heard more about houses and renovations than either of them needed to hear.

Special thanks are due to Camille Costanzo who energetically opened the doors of Levittown to me. Many of the people of Levittown have graciously opened their homes to me. Others recorded their renovations in photographs, house-tours, and photo-essays which have been carefully preserved by Janet Sparr, Curator of the Levittown Collection in the Levittown Public Library. The faculty and staff of the Axinn Library made the research infinitely easier as did Richard Winsche of the Nassau County Museum Reference Library. In every instance these kind colleagues were exceedingly generous with their time and their collections.

Clay Morgan and Megeen Mulholland of SUNY Press were able to negotiate a wonderful balance—keeping my production on time without resorting to nagging.

Larry O'Connell took time from his busy life to produce—frequently on short notice—the floor plans and camera-ready copy necessary to a production of this nature.

I would also like to thank my children who generously welcomed me back into the fold when my years of scribbling in the attic were done. Jim walked his mother through the intricacies of a computer so that the phrase "scribbling woman" became just a literary device. Mike renovated my own home during the writing process and explained in detail the meaning and function of chase walls, joists and rafters. Amy kept my home fires burning; Debbie kept the hearth clean. Joe kept his father "otherwise occupied" that I might work through the wee hours. Meanwhile, Katie and Paul kept me from taking myself too seriously. Most of all, I thank my husband, Larry, who cheerfully encouraged and supported my endeavor, and continually reminds me that the best is yet to come. Without his support and confidence, his trips to computer supply stores, photography studios and take-out restaurants, this book might never have come to an end.

Introduction

There is a process through which a house becomes a 'home.' It is—even in a mass-produced tract house—an ongoing relationship between people and their space, in which the lives of the people are affected by their space as much as the space is affected by the presence of the people.

The physical arrangement of domestic space begins as a tacit statement of the values and lifestyles of those for whom it was designed and built. When an architect designs a house for a client, an interrelationship between the needs and desires of the residents and the various elements of the floor plan is built into the design. The relative location and size of various areas reflect the clients' social class, age, and stage of life, the size and lifestyle of the family, and the number of residents—such as servants—who are not members of the unit.

When houses are constructed for a mass market, the structural elements are tailored instead to a projected market: i.e., the needs and desires of a "typical"—or composite—client as those needs and desires are interpreted by the deliverers: the architect, the builder, and the lending agencies that funded the construction.

It is particularly instructive when the government intervenes in the designing of residential architecture to examine the nature of the domestic space it delivers and the cultural values it, in effect, imposes on family life through the physical arrangement of that space.[1] Government-delivered housing in a democracy further reveals the collective values and assumptions of the dominant social group to whom the elected officials are most responsive.[2]

In the years following World War II, the American government encouraged the production of large-scale suburban housing projects that were intended primarily for lower-income veterans and their families. The postwar suburbs that resulted were typically large, mass-produced, economically and socially stratified, and almost exclusively residential in nature. The single-family tract houses of these subdivision suburbs, funded by mortgages underwritten by the FHA and the GI Bill, proliferated to such a marked degree that by 1960 suburban residents in single-family houses outnumbered either rural or urban residents. In design, the houses were a reduction of the prewar middle-class house to a culturally acceptable minimum that made it affordable for a market which was younger and less affluent than its prewar home-owning counterpart.[3]

The houses were generally well-received by their target population; veterans and their newly established families flocked to the housing tracts, which were usually located in outlying areas around America's major cities. The positive reception was no doubt intensified by the postwar housing shortage, which made any and all shelter desirable. Nevertheless, the young couples whose opinions were recorded in the media gave every indication that they were pleased with the houses.[4]

Aimed at a lower socioeconomic level, the architectural and spatial elements of the houses built in the FHA-sponsored subdivision suburbs of the 1940s were reduced in size and complexity. The floor plans provided only the essential rooms—two bedrooms, living room, kitchen, and bath. Gone were the formal dining room, the sun porch and den, the pantry and guest room of the nineteenth-century suburban villa. In reducing the house to an affordable minimum, the designers had eliminated the more obviously symbolic artifacts of domestic life that had become standard in the nineteenth century and prewar middle-class home. Yet in their own way, the decisions—conscious or unconscious—to retain certain elements as essential to basic housing while eliminating others as expendable or superfluous provide a text for the values of the postwar period. Reading this text requires an inversion of the analytical method; instead of an examination of the content of those elements which society chose to *add* to basic shelter, the postwar houses force an examination of the cultural significance of those elements that were retained when the houses were stripped of what was deemed unnecessary.

Despite their rudimentary nature, the houses succeeded on several levels. At the personal level they provided veterans with the most important emblem of the American Dream—the privately owned house and lot. The new suburban homeowners generally found their houses and their suburban communities to be satisfactory. Ignoring the warnings of impending slumhood, they invested both energy and effort into physical improvements to their houses through structural additions, landscaping, and cosmetic redesign. As a result of their efforts, these communities today are more likely to resemble the lush suburbs of the rural ideal (such as those advocated by nineteenth-century housing reformers Andrew Jackson Downing and Gervase Wheeler) than a shanty town.[5]

0.1

Aerial view of Island Trees prior to construction of first Levitt units, c. 1946. (NCM) (a) First Levitt acquisition, c. 1946, Island Trees, New York. (b) Levittown, c. 1948, after construction of first 6000 units. (c) Levittown, c. 1960, all construction completed.

(a)

(b)

(c)

The homeowners' investments of time and energy—"sweat equity" in today's housing parlance—provided the fulfillment of the
second aspect of the dream, the opportunity to earn one's upward
mobility through hard work and dedication. In the first decade of
home ownership much of the expansion and redesign of the houses
was done through a combination of do-it-yourself labor and intra-
community barter. The nostalgia expressed by many of the informants in this study frequently referred to the pleasures of their shared
efforts with their neighbors as they enclosed carports, added dormers and ells, and traded tools and supplies.[6]

The residents' ability to effect the transition from tract housing to rural ideal was strongly related to the nature of the housing
that was provided under the terms of the housing programs. It was
basic shelter, affordable at the entry level; yet it was new and easily
maintained, and it offered room for expansion as needs and income
dictated. But most important, it was proprietary housing, which reflected and reinforced traditional American values and the opportunities for upward mobility they implied. A young couple was able
to buy the house before it became the home of their dreams, rather
than afterward. Their monthly payments reduced the mortgage and
increased their equity in the house; the equity in turn provided the
collateral for funding future expansion and remodeling of the house,
which would further increase their equity.

In addition, the subdivisions—really instant communities—provided the residents with a political *tabula rasa*. Erected on recently
vacated potato and corn fields, the new suburbs existed in a political
vacuum. The older communities that surrounded them were neither
prepared nor inclined to include them. As a result, the new suburbanites were not only enabled, but required, to establish a myriad of
institutions tailored to their own needs and lifestyle. In the absence
of an entrenched power structure, the young and politically inexperienced residents were able to rise to positions of influence while
still testing their organizational skills.[7] Thus, by providing simple,
proprietary housing for young workers, the housing programs of
the 1930s and particularly of the 1940s, which brought the government into a new partnership with the housing industry, succeeded
in expanding the numbers of those who could be expected to have
both an economic and a political stake in American society.[8]

Suburbia and the single-family house became the dominant
setting for family life, not only in reality, but in the popular culture
as well. Home ownership was literally in the air; it was more than a
policy, it was a creed—an idea whose time had come.

A wide range of media paid tribute to the suburban setting, from school books to magazines to television. Basal readers, designed to establish cultural norms as well as to teach children to read, reflected the suburban shift in both their illustrations and their story lines. As late as 1938 the "Alice and Jerry" reading series had set its story lines in "Friendly Village," a rural community with small, variegated houses, unpaved roads, and a grade level railroad crossing. The first reader located "Jack's House" somewhere "down a lovely country road," and featured adventures with "fisherman Carl" or trips to Riverside, the town where children could shop for toys.[9]

In the same period, Scott Foresman's Curriculum Series used the rural/small-town model in their Elson-Gray Basic Readers [1930/1936]. Molly "ran to the general store" on a clearly small-town Main Street, whereas Billy attended a large, brick school building in an urban setting. Meanwhile Billy's grandparents continued to live a rural life on the farm, where Billy spent his summers.[10]

In 1947, Scott, Foresman's Curriculum Foundation Series shifted the setting, echoing the new move to the suburban subdivision. The opening story featured a young girl who had "just moved to a house on top of a high hill *near the city*" [emphasis added] and who missed the children "in the city where she had always lived." Her happiness is restored with the construction of another new house on the plot next to hers, in which she finds a friend.[11] Other aspects of the suburban phenomenon were featured in adventures such as "The Big Red Car," in which Mother drives the children to town to shop.[12] The commuting father and the car-driving wife and mother were also increasingly featured in short stories in the womens' house-and-home magazines of the late 1940s. The narratives in this genre frequently included some reference to the homemaker-heroine's driving to the railroad station to pick up or deliver her commuting husband.

By the end of the decade, television and radio families had followed their audiences to the suburbs where the ideal family lived in their very own Cape Cod within commuting distance of the city.[13] The suburban icon also appeared in movies in these years. *Miracle on 34th Street* (1947) ended happily with the promise that the city-dwelling, career-oriented single mother would marry the man in the apartment next door, and that they would move into the home of her child's dream—a single-family house in suburban Manhasset, Long Island.

Implicit in the postwar housing programs was the promise that every veteran would be able to participate in the American dream; the opportunity to own a home had become a part of the reward for wartime service to the country.[14] Yet, at the time of their construction and for several decades thereafter, the suburbs were attacked by a variety of social analysts from journalists to urban planners, from social scientists to architects. Many of the early analyses of these suburbs found the built environment wanting. The houses of the postwar period were frequently presented as the archetypes of Malvina Reynolds' "little boxes" in "rows of ticky-tack"—places that lacked architectural variety and imposed static conformity.[15] Although some of these critics found fault with suburban life in general, many of the most negative assessments were aimed specifically at the houses and subdivisions built under the terms of the postwar housing policies. The houses were condemned as substandard— poorly constructed and badly designed; the subdivisions, as culturally isolating and/or subversive of traditional family values.[16] However, in contrast to the negative conclusions on the part of so many social analysts, the recorded experience of the residents has been generally positive. The residents reacted defensively to the criticism, individually and collectively taking a public stand to show that their homes did not fit the negative stereotype.[17]

The private home would seem to be an unlikely subject over which to wage a battle of public opinion. What was there about the houses that generated such contradictory reactions? If the subdivision suburbs and their houses were as ill-conceived as their critics contended, why were they so well received by their residents? The answers hinge on the meaning of the houses—not only on an individual level, to their owners and producers—but also collectively, in the cultural and political milieu of the period. A study of the postwar suburbs that fails to examine the overwhelming satisfaction expressed by the residents with their homes and their community misses a key factor in the story.

The opportunities for increased equity and political expression implicit in the subdivision suburbs have already been noted. At another level, however, they allowed for a more subtle form of social mobility. During the years in which the government was most active in promoting home ownership, there was a marked expansion of the American middle class, which consisted largely of a redefinition of its parameters.[18] As those from the socioeconomic tier below acquired the most heavily weighted symbol of the middle-class status, homeowning took on a greater relative value in defining class, outweighing the traditional standards of education and occupation, background and wealth as measures of social standing. It is significant that in this process, the symbol was provided as a direct result of government funding policies. In effect, their status descended upon the new homeowners by virtue of a shifting, or redefinition, of the weight of one particular status symbol—the privately owned, single-family dwelling.[19] The FHA/VA subdivisions thereby generated a process of sociopolitical inclusion, as the lower-income homeowners were gradually self-identified with the needs and values of the prewar middle class.[20]

This process is typified by Levittown, a community of some 17,500 houses built on Long Island between 1947 and 1951.[21] Because of the low-cost nature of construction and materials, as well as the economic level of its intended constituency, the project was initially opposed by the residents of the older, surrounding communities as an incipient slum. Yet, within 20 years, the community had shed its worker-housing/incipient-slum image and joined its neighboring communities as an acceptable address for middle-class residents.

Levittown's reputation had essentially completed the metamorphosis from that of housing development for lower-income workers to a middle-class suburb by 1967. Yet statistically, the demographics of the community had not undergone a comparable transition.[22] Rather, the process of transition from lower-income housing to middle-class neighborhood was dialectic: as the residents reshaped their built environment, they raised it to a new socioeconomic level and then, in turn, derived their own status from that of the community and from their membership in the homeowning class.

Starting with the basic four-room houses that were nearly identical in plan and design, the residents customized their homes to meet their individual needs, creating the combination of picturesque variety and community harmony that was the hallmark of the nineteenth-century model suburb. Through a combination of government housing policies, economic inflation, and sweat equity, they altered the socioeconomic level of the subdivision. Indeed, the measure of the success of those postwar emergency housing policies is perhaps most readily apparent in the fact that the communities built under their terms are today routinely classified as middle-class communities, not only by their residents but also by polltakers, the media, and those politicians who seek the middle-class vote.[23]

There was nothing strikingly new about the postwar subdivision suburbs themselves. Individually, each of their elements had existed since long before the war, and the idea of a residential sub-

urb for the middle class dated back to the turn of the nineteenth
century.[24] Nevertheless, the combination of these elements into
large, single-use, suburban tracts of small, low-cost, single-family,
owner-occupied dwellings had merged into a new phenomenon by
the end of the 1940s.[25]

Added to this was the one aspect of the postwar suburbs that
was new—the role of the federal government in underwriting both
the bridge loans which financed the construction of the suburbs and
the mortgages with which they would be purchased. In that capacity, the government had also assumed the role of arbiter in the design of the houses. Since its inception in 1934, the Federal Housing Administration had produced bulletins that promoted a series of
recommended house and subdivision designs. Although presented
as advisory in nature, these bulletins—published by the same
agency that funded the construction—were endowed with an aura
of authority by those who needed such funding.[26] The promotional
bulletins routinely advocated the construction of freestanding, single-family, one-and-a-half-storied houses of the "Cape Cod" or
"bungalow" design with a few simple modifications and architectural embellishments to create individualized façades. With some
minor local variations, these official recommendations were widely
implemented in those postwar subdivisions which were clustered at
the low-cost end of the housing market and funded under the terms
of the FHA and VA housing programs.

Using the houses of Levittown as a laboratory, this study com-
bines an intellectual history of the concept of house and home during the postwar years with a cultural history of the built environment of a subdivision suburb. It examines the forms of the houses as
they evolved over time and focuses on the process by which the
design of those houses interacted with the lives of their residents to
reinforce the cultural consensus of postwar America. It also examines the homeowners' reinterpretation of the builder-delivered environment, measuring the degree to which the houses, as originally
designed, fit the homeowners' self-defined value system.

By focusing on changes in the interpretation of space within
the houses, it attempts to shed further light on the nature of the
domestic environment that was created by the FHA/VA housing
programs, and on the role of that environment in redefining and
expanding the American middle class.

Levittown and its houses are profiled in three stages: the deliverer-designed, rental Levittown of 1947/48 with its basic Cape Cods;
the transitional, market-driven Levittown of 1949 and 1950/51 with

its proprietary ranch models; and finally, the owner-redesigned Levittown of individualized residences that was celebrated by the community in 1957 and 1967. In each stage, the physical and spatial factors within the houses and the community that fostered or reinforced a particular way of life among the residents are considered.

Chapter 1 provides an overview of the building of Levittown, set into an historical context of technology and political culture. It is intended to provide background reading for those who have not read other accounts of the construction and the early settling of the community. Those who are already familiar with Levittown and the suburban development of the 1940s and 1950s may find it repetitive.

Chapter 2 examines Levittown as a time-specific version of the planned community whose design and delivery was the result of an underlying belief in the importance of private property in developing a civic involvement on the part of the American workers.

Chapter 3 analyzes the spatial elements of the houses by comparing the basic, deliverer-designed form with contemporary ideals of American family life. This analysis is based on two phases of the construction of Levittown, the 1947/48 Cape Cods, which were originally intended as rental housing, and the 1949–1951 ranch models, which were built to be sold.

Chapters 4 and 5 examine the general nature of the structural and spatial changes that were made over time by the homeowners of Levittown, measuring these changes against the contemporary standards for middle class residential architecture and family life in the 1950s and 1960s.

Chapter 6 concentrates on the evolution of a number of individual Levittown houses, examining the implications of the remodeling elements imposed on the houses over time in the light of the lifestyle of the homeowners whose needs and desires shaped the renovations.

Chapter 7 examines two contrasting interpretations of the Levittown experience, focusing on the cultural significance of Levittown in the postwar expansion of the American middle class.

Chapter 8 provides the conclusions drawn from the study. In particular, it discusses the redefinition of the role of government in the construction of lower-income housing that took place during the years of Harry Truman's "Fair Deal."

The Postscript brings the Levittown story into the present. Although it is not the "happily ever after" ending that the housing reformers of the nineteenth century might have predicted, it does end on an optimistic note.

1

CONSTRUCTION

In the spring of 1947, Levitt & Sons broke ground for a development of 2000 rental units for veterans and their families. Despite their modest size, the four-room Cape Cod bungalows would eventually offer the fulfillment of the American Dream of property, privacy, and independence. The houses were made possible by a series of amendments to the National Housing Act of 1934 which encouraged the production of low-cost housing. As a result of these changes, the veterans of World War II would return to a warmer welcome than that which had greeted their predecessors from earlier wars.[1]

This is not to say that the veterans were the only, or even the primary, reason for modifying the housing policies. The veterans were the formal beneficiaries of their efforts, but the postwar housing programs would have implications for American society as a whole. Although the rhetoric that promoted many of the reconversion policies may have emphasized the veterans' right to government assistance in reestablishing their peacetime lives as a *quid pro quo* for their service, the methods used to provide that the assistance assured that it would remain squarely within the American sociopolitical traditions.

Washington had drawn heavily on the lessons of the Depression and the solutions of the New Deal in planning for the postwar reconversion. Both the education titles of the GI Bill and the establishment of armies of occupation were designed to prevent a return to the economic difficulties of the 1930s. These policies served to reduce unemployment by restricting the flow of veterans into the labor force without resorting to obvious make-work projects or home-relief, which were evocative of socialism and the welfare state.

Similarly, the housing programs were designed as much to provide incentives to investors as to create housing. The mortgages were insured by the government, but they were issued by and through the private sector.[2] Moneys were funneled through several vital sectors of the economy, rather than through direct government assistance. The preconditions for the housing programs were therefore deeply rooted in pre-New Deal American ideologies and meshed with long-established American beliefs that emphasized the importance of private property, personal initiative, and free enterprise, as well as the traditional nineteenth-century themes of republican virtue and Christian domesticity.

The opposition to government involvement in housing traditionally expressed by the business community was mitigated by the self-interest of banks and real estate investors, and of builders and suppliers, all of whom stood to gain in a revitalized housing market. Moreover, the stimulus to residential construction and related industries in domestic hard goods, which could be expected to generate increased employment, was an added inducement for those concerned about the needs of the American worker and his family.[3]

As a result, the postwar political climate was receptive to the expansion of New Deal housing policies. The returning soldier provided a sympathetic symbol around which to promote the postwar housing programs; he had earned the nation's support in his need for shelter.[4] Government-insured housing projects were cast as not only acceptable but expedient, both as a means of stimulating the reconversion economy and as compensation for the veterans' service to their country. Underlying and reinforcing these factors was the persistent American belief in homeowning as a concomitant of sound republicanism.

By 1947, builder-developers in large numbers were taking advantage of the emergency amendments to the National Housing Act to turn vacant or underutilized land into basic housing as quickly as possible. Few of them were newcomers to building; most had cut their economic teeth in the prewar period and come of age during the vast buildup of housing for defense workers after Pearl Harbor. However, it was the scale of their postwar construction that would catapult them into national prominence.[5]

A number of circumstances fostered the changes in the scale of postwar residential construction. One was the housing crisis, which provided a ready market. Another was the technology developed during the defense buildup. The war had encouraged the builders to streamline the construction process through the development of new materials and methods for the rapid construction of inexpensive worker housing. Available land was still another factor. The rise of agribusiness in the West and the subsequent urban migrations at the turn of the century, coupled with the foreclosures of many family farms during the Depression, had contributed to a widespread

1.1

Model houses from Levitt & Sons' prewar Strathmore development, Manhasset, 1939. (NCM)

(a)

(b)

availability of large tracts of underutilized farmland in formerly rural areas, particularly in the Northeast. This land provided enterprising builders with the acreage needed to implement the new construction techniques on a cost-effective scale. All of these factors—a ready market, efficient technological strategies, and available land—in combination with government assistance and a sympathetic symbol, created an ideal builder's market in 1947.

One of those who would maximize the opportunity provided by the postwar situation was William J. Levitt, the president and general manager of the Manhasset firm of Levitt and Sons. In partnership with his father and brother, Levitt had been building homes on Long Island for over a decade when America entered World War II.[6] Their prewar production was limited to small developments in middle- and upper middle-class suburban communities on Long Island.

During the war, Levitt built emergency housing for defense workers at the naval base at Norfolk, Virginia.[7] The four-room, slab-based units at Norfolk bore little resemblance to any prewar houses built by Levitt and Sons, but their components provided the prototype for many of the innovations that would be incorporated into the firm's postwar construction, especially those at Island Trees.[8]

The housing shortages—for defense workers during the war, and for veterans after it—opened the window to many substantive changes in residential construction. Neither unions nor local governments wanted to risk being charged with obstructing either the war effort or needed solutions to the veterans' housing crisis, and one by one traditional building practices and codes gave way to a variety of factory-like methods implemented at the construction site. These methods produced houses that were rudimentary and standardized, but they were available and affordable.

Although Levitt would greatly expand his fortune by incorporating these new methods in the Island Trees project, the use of the new methods was not enough. He would also need the skills to take advantage of the opportunities that the housing shortage was creating in the form of economic support from the federal government and the subversion of local building and zoning codes.

The Veterans Emergency Housing Program (VEHP), under which the first houses at Levittown were built, had been announced by President Truman in February 1946. The original VEHP goal was the construction of more than two and a half million units of housing by late 1948.[9] Headed by Housing Expeditor Wilson Wyatt, the short-lived VEHP was part of Truman's war reconversion program

1.2

Midwest City, Oklahoma, built in 1942 by William Atkinson as defense
workers' housing for Tinker Air Force Base. (1987 photo, Author's
collection)

and called for such emergency measures as continued rent control,
"strict allocation of scarce materials," and money to encourage their
production, as well as loans under the New Deal's Reconstruction
Finance Corporation to nurture the infant industry in factory-pro-
duced houses. The agency also projected a goal of 750,000 prefabri-
cated dwellings by the end of 1947. The housing bill of 1947 reem-
phasized the government's interest in prefabrication in the housing
industry and offered monetary guarantees to those who would venture into the field.[10]

Although Levitt did not deal directly with prefabrication, his
reorganization of the traditional construction methods was a modified version of the prefabrication process.[11] He, along with other
large-scale builder/developers, incorporated many of the techniques
of his defense-housing projects into his postwar projects. These production methods were referred to in trade publications and news
releases as "on-site fabrication," and the construction sites as "on-
site factories." These terms placed the builders in a semantic posi-

tion to take advantage of a variety of legislative supports that might emerge from the housing debates in Congress. Their "on-site factories" might qualify if pre-fabrication were to be funded, whereas their Cape Cods would fill the bill if more traditional methods were favored.

In addition to government support, the builders needed the cooperation and support of their workers. Traditional construction methods would have to give way to modern techniques; union job descriptions, pay scales, and seniority rankings would have to be renegotiated. Rather than alienate the industry's rank and file by imposing these changes, Levitt enlisted their support. He hired his workers as subcontractors in order to bypass the union leadership and contract terms. By contracting directly with the workers he was able to pay them not by the hour, but by the number of completed production units, thereby evading the union scale restrictions on hours, skills, and seniority. This arrangement had the intended result of inducing the workers to produce more units per day, using the techniques of the on-site factory.[12]

The speed of production was unprecedented. Contemporary commentators compared the process to an automobile assembly line in reverse. Where at General Motors the car would move from worker to worker, on the construction site it was the worker who moved. Workers moved in teams from unit to unit, completing just one stage of the construction before moving on to repeat that stage at the next site. Levitt also redesigned the work week; in order to reduce the loss of work time, the week's rainy or other bad weather days were traded for Saturdays, Sundays, and holidays.[13] Acres upon acres appeared to turn overnight into houses, complete with streets and landscaping.

In retrospect, the construction of Levittown would be treated as something of a cultural turning point in suburban development, but at the time there was little other than the scale and speed of production that attracted public attention.[14] Between April and July of 1948, the production rate in Levittown rose from 60 houses per week to 150.[15] The speed with which his contractors worked was an important factor in the reputation that Levitt was developing as a major solver of the housing shortage.

Levitt also made excellent use of the new materials and techniques, especially standardized components, which were just coming into their own in 1947. His houses were built in multiples of four feet to take the greatest advantage of 4' × 8' sheetrock panels. He arranged to have some 14 carloads of precut or partly assembled materials delivered by the Long Island Railroad to the Island Trees site.[16] He bought supplies—hardware, appliances, and cabinetry—in bulk, directly from the manufacturer. This was done not only to by-pass the profits of the middleman but to guarantee, through sheer volume, the ability to acquire the newly deregulated white goods, which were in short supply. Where that was not feasible, Levitt cre-ated a vertical monopoly on building materials in order to bypass the middleman's profits and eliminate competition from other buyers. He invested in a forest in California with a nearby lumber mill to avert a lumber shortage, and built a nail factory on the prop-erty when nails were hard to get.[17] *Architectural Forum, Better Homes and Gardens, Architectural Record*, and *Time* all covered the story of the construction of Levittown, commenting favorably on the pace and rate, as Levitt industrialized the building trade on Long Island.

Ironically, more than half of the first 2000 houses of Levittown would be built on land belonging to the estate of a man who had attempted to create a community of rental houses nearby, and failed. The land had originally been purchased in the mid-nine-teenth century by the Manhattan merchant/developer A. T. Stewart. Stewart had bought a vast tract of the Long Island plains (seven thousand acres, stretching from Franklin Square to Hicksville). On part of it he created Garden City, his planned community of rental houses. In reporting the sale of the property, *Harper's Weekly* fore-shadowed the hyperbole that would mark Levitt's later announce-ments of his plans for the area:

> This tract cost Mr. Stewart $400,000; and we understand that it is his design to spend from six to ten millions of dollars in the erection upon it of homes for the working-classes of New York and Brooklyn. This design is so gigantic that it throws into the shade every attempt of the kind hitherto made. . . .
>
> With the improvements which Mr. Stewart will carry out; with a township of beautiful and healthful homes; with parks, gardens, and public buildings for educational purposes and for those of amusement, Hempstead Plains, hitherto a desert, will be made to blossom as the rose; it will be the most beautiful suburb in the vicinity of New York. God speed the undertak-ing.[18]

The idea of renting did not appeal to the constituency for whom Stewart had built, and his idea of a working-class suburb was never fully realized.[19] The Merillon Estates properties that Levitt bought were among several undeveloped parcels of land remaining from Stewart's estate.[20] Stewart's Garden City, meanwhile, had become a solidly middle-class community, with large single-family homes set on wide lawns on shady, tree-lined, streets.[21]

Levitt was about to recreate Stewart's dream of a rental community on a more modest scale; he would tailor his twentieth-century version for a lower socioeconomic market than that for which Stewart had planned his suburb.[22] In so doing, Levitt ran the risk of alienating nearby residents, many of whom viewed renting as less socially acceptable than owning. Local residents considered the houses to be substandard, due in part to their size and in part to the replacement of traditional materials with newer, less expensive, and seemingly less substantial ones. Moreover, most were opposed to lower-income rental projects within their middle-class suburban county on economic grounds. The redlining of lower-income housing districts by the FHA had its parallel in the suburban fear of property devaluation due to contiguous "nuisances."

But Levitt did not have to face these objections alone. Among those who provided the necessary support were George Hubbell, who arranged the sale of the land; the fledgling newspaper Newsday, which defended the technological innovations Levitt used to produce the houses; and—by default, if not design—the preeminent urban developer, Robert Moses.

George Hubbell was a senior partner in the real estate firm of Hubbell, Klapper, and Hubbell. Along with his partner, Theodore Klapper, he had been playing an important role in the development of Nassau County for over a quarter of a century when Levitt began buying property in Island Trees in 1946.[23] Hubbell was also the general manager of the Merillon Corporation and Garden City Estates, the holding companies for the remaining land of the A. T. Stewart Estate, all of which had become Levittown by 1948.[24] Moreover, the firm of Hubbell, Klapper, and Hubbell represented those companies when the land was sold to Levitt. There is no indication in the local newspaper coverage of this period that either Hubbell, who represented the land, or Klapper, who was serving as a member of the town planning commission, were opposed to Levitt's plans for the property.[25]

Nor was the Town of Hempstead. Despite some early and perhaps pro forma resistance, the building and zoning board was cooperative, revising the town's prewar building code in order to accommodate the radical new method of slab-based construction that Levitt proposed. At their meeting on May 27, 1947, the town board repealed section 809 of Article 8 of the Hempstead Town building law. The meeting was heavily attended, largely by veterans and their families in need of housing.

In a later interview, Levitt claimed to have drummed up the veteran support himself.[26] He may well have done so, but not without help. *Newsday's* promotion of Levittown was unabashed boosterism, which will be made clearer in later chapters. Just starting its career, the paper would naturally stand to benefit from an increase in the area's population. In an editorial on May 11, 1947, *Newsday* had urged veterans to support Levitt's plan for the basement-less houses by turning out in force at the hearing. Whether generated by Levitt or by *Newsday*, the show of support may not have been necessary.

In a welcoming column in the first issue of the *Island Trees Eagle*, A. Holly Patterson, the presiding supervisor of Hempstead Town, pointed out that the board had "acted as promptly as the law would permit on all requests for the construction of your comfortable little homes" and assured the new residents that the town had not opposed either the houses or the new technology, but had simply followed appropriate procedures for revising the code.[27] Although it may be that the Patterson column, directed at the new residents of Levittown, was in part a face-saving maneuver designed to capture the political loyalty of the new residents, the town had certainly not offered any serious resistance to the code revision.

Robert Moses' role, on the other hand, was more subtle; in the area of planning and development on Long Island, Moses' lack of opposition was tantamount to approval. The earliest parcels of Levittown were located within a triangle described by three of Moses' state parkways. Given the combination of Moses' interest in planning, his power across the state at the time, and the location of Levittown, it is hardly likely that he was unaware, much less disapproving, of the project.[28]

Despite the recorded lack of opposition, there is suggestive evidence that such opposition did exist, and that some of it was extremely potent. Among the construction unions whose traditional power was challenged by Levitt and his new technologies was the sheathers' union. When one of the Levitt experimental models in Albertson exploded on May 1, 1947, *The Nassau Daily Review Star* assured its readers that the explosion appeared to be unrelated to the sheathers' union's picketing of Levitt and Sons construction sites. The need to add such a statement suggests that, to at least one journalist, the involvement of the sheathers was a distinct possi-

bility.[29] Although there is no further indication of organized opposition, the town rejected Levitt's application to replace the code-man-
dated ¾" sheathing with the less labor-intensive, 5/16" plywood
sheets.[30] Thus, the town might well have wanted to ensure a climate
of positive public opinion for their code changes in order to mini-
mize political opposition among local labor groups, as well as among
the more established communities.

It was while his innovations were still in contention, and before ground was broken for the project that Levitt announced the
availability of the first of the rental units at Island Trees.[31] Within
weeks after the initial construction was underway, the Levitt organization had announced plans to add another 4000 units to the Island
Trees/Levittown project. The public response—as recorded in the
local press—was overwhelmingly favorable.[32]

That there were rumors of "there goes the neighborhood" and
considerable public opposition to the development can only be inferred from *Newsday's* ad hominem attacks on nameless "elitists" who
criticized the project. The defensive tone registered about the quality
of their homes by the early residents of Levittown and the residue of
disapproval that persists among some residents of the older, surrounding neighborhoods even today also lend credence to the belief
that the development was not as well received by the existing communities as the media were suggesting. One such criticism, by a
Hempstead Town councilman running for reelection from a neighboring community, was roundly denounced in a *Newsday* editorial.[33]
Levitt's media blitz successfully kept such criticism to a minimum.
His press releases and news conferences pitted the plight of the
homeless veterans against the proposed solution—the Levitt rental
housing project at Island Trees. By implication, this solution was
impeded only by the town and county's obstinacy over details in
building and zoning regulations.

Yet, despite the confident tone expressed in the news coverage, Levitt appears to have been ambivalent about the future direction of the development from the very beginning.[34] While the rental
project was still under construction, he had built 191 of the Cape
Cod models a few miles west of Island Trees to test the sales market.
From May until July 1947, press releases from the Levitt organization, coupled with editorials in *Newsday* and comments from the paper's readership, focused almost exclusively on the rental housing.
Yet, when the availability of the houses was formally announced, it
was in the form of an advertisement for those houses that were being constructed for sale. The rental housing, on the other hand, was

not advertised. There was little need to advertise it; the public had been kept aware of this development through Levitt's press conferences and *Newsday*'s supportive editorial commentary.[35]

In October the first of the rental units were made available at $60 per month with a one-year lease, for veterans only. This corresponded with existing federal law.[36] Meanwhile, the advertised mortgage payment on the other houses, "$52 A MONTH, FOR VETERANS ONLY," was almost ten dollars lower than the monthly rental at Island Trees, and—coupled with full financing of the mortgage—made the proprietary housing by far the better investment for home-seeking veterans.[37]

Levitt had also made clear early in the project that he did not

under ordinary conditions, believe in rentals. However, this is the only way to enable the former serviceman, who is without sufficient funds, or whose life is still somewhat in a state of flux, to secure a home, a pleasant home, at a reasonable cost. We may, in the future, announce the homes of Levittown for sale, although this is not, as yet, definite. If we do offer them for sale, we assure the present tenants, that they will be permitted to re-lease on a rental basis for at least another year.[38]

Levitt's apparent ambivalence about the rental project at Island Trees is, in retrospect, not surprising. Even as the ground was being broken for the first of the houses the political situation regarding lower-income housing had begun to show signs of change; before Levittown was completed, changes in federal housing policies would limit the profit margin in rental housing while encouraging the construction of proprietary housing. Emergency rent controls were extended, and the construction of privately owned single-family dwellings was stimulated through various forms of government-sponsored insurance and incentive programs. In one of its most wide-reaching provisions, section 505 of the Serviceman's Readjustment Act—the GI Bill—underwrote the economic risk inherent in the construction and finance of low-cost houses for veterans by insuring their fully financed mortgages in conjunction with existing FHA policies. This provision would result in the construction of tens of thousands of proprietary housing units for lower-income veterans.[39]

Insiders in the housing field had good reason to expect that government support would be moving away from programs that promoted rental housing toward others which fostered home ownership.[40] Their business decisions would reflect those expectations. William Levitt was no exception. In December 1947, two months after his first tenants had moved in, the substance of Levitt's press releases in the local community papers underwent a subtle change. After several weeks in which his announcements were those of a benevolent landlord, Levitt's weekly news releases began to mention the possibility of home ownership for his Levittown tenants. As noted, these suggestions that the firm "might" make the homes available for purchase, at least to the present tenants, were juxtaposed to the announcement of a pending rent increase.

In addition, Levitt's hints at divestiture coincided with President Truman's efforts to extend existing rent controls. Despite the strong attack on his domestic policies by the conservative 80th Congress, President Truman did manage to salvage the rent control provisions of the Housing and Rent Act of 1947 for at least one additional year. Continued rent control would seriously diminish the return on investments in large-scale rental projects such as Levittown.[41] In addition, the rental projects tied up millions of dollars in capital, which the builders could use to greater advantage. Across the country, operative builders like Levitt began to divest themselves of their rental properties. The war years had taught them much about their profession, and about the need to adapt quickly to new conditions.

Levitt began preparing the tenants for the transition from rental to ownership. "News" articles in the Island Trees newspapers—one of which Levitt had bought—informed the tenants about new developments in Washington, particularly those affecting veterans. A column was introduced that offered the tenants advice for taking advantage of the loan programs being offered by the GI Bill. In a manner consistent with the public image he was creating, Levitt presented the proposed transition as a generous offer to his tenants, rather than a profit-motivated business decision.[42]

The actual transition, by which Levitt would begin to dispose of the rental units, began in the spring of 1948. Truman's extension of the rent control provision—originally scheduled to expire on March 31, 1948—was extended through March 1949.[43] Levitt divested himself of most of the 6000 rental units, along with the real estate company through which he had managed them. Those he could not sell directly to the tenants he transferred, along with the Bethpage Realty Company, to a Philadelphia-based adult education project known as Junto, which continued to rent the houses.[44] His capital regained, Levitt then began work on the second phase of the project through which he would eventually earn his reputation. In less than a decade, Levitt and Sons had matured from a relatively obscure building firm to national prominence as "the nation's biggest house builder"—a reputation for which he and his news releases were largely responsible.[45]

At its completion the development would incorporate 17,447 four-room houses spreading over two towns (including some six hamlets) crossing municipal, postal, school, and fire district lines. In addition to the houses, Levittown had seven "village greens" with shops and services, nine swimming pools, and a community meeting hall, all provided by the builder. The community—residents as well as religious and civic leaders—provided churches, synagogues, schools, and libraries, and local merchants added such recreational activities as bowling alleys, skating rinks, and movies.

2

ThE PlAN iN thE PlANNEd COMMUNiTY

In 1949, when he completed the Hicksville section of the new ranch models, William Levitt installed a sign that identified the development as "Levittown, A Garden Community." The words were not casually chosen; rather, they served to identify Levittown with a long series of planned model communities that had been developed in America since the inception of Ebenezer Howard's Garden Cities program in England.[1] The use of the term *planned* had begun early in the community's history. In interviews, articles, and commentary, the Levitts frequently referred to their development at Levittown as a "planned" or "garden" community. Although they never claimed that Levittown was intended to follow the Garden Cities model, they frequently used the language of that tradition in speaking of Levittown.

The Levitts' linking of the Island Trees development with the concept of a "planned" community thus raises a number of questions. What was the plan? At what target population was it aimed? Who were the planners and what assumptions about the American family shaped the plan? And finally, How did the finished project mesh with the social culture of the period?

The Plan

In the December 12, 1947 issue of the *Island Trees Tribune*, Abraham Levitt wrote a "Welcoming Message from Founder," in which he outlined the company's plan for the new development. The language he used is reminiscent of the writings of the nineteenth-century housing reformers who saw the built environment as a means of structuring a social order.[2]

[The Island Trees development] has been planned to be a place of incomparable beauty. . . . Island Trees is intended to be not just a collection of houses. Our purpose is to make of it a complete, integrated, harmonious community. We aim, among other things, to provide a pleasant and wholesome social life.[3]

An editorial in the same issue related the planning to Americanism:

The entire concept of the Island Trees development—its planning, engineering and construction—is a tribute to our American way of life.[4]

Alfred Levitt, the architect/designer son, was more tentative in his assessment of Levittown. He defined the community less as a "planned" community than as one that had evolved through a series of planning stages into something quite close to a model town. He pointed for example to the village greens, the shops, the restaurants, bowling alleys, and recreation areas—pools and playgrounds—as signs that the community was more than a subdivision. Had he chosen to, he might also have claimed credit for its location adjacent to industrial employment, long a factor in the ideal planned community.[5] Yet he held back; there was something not quite ideal about the evolution of Levittown, and Alfred Levitt acknowledged that fact.[6]

In his 1964 retrospective on Levittown, "A House Is Not Enough" William Levitt called Levittown "the grandfather of the pre-planned community." Yet his ambivalence regarding Levittown's qualifications as a true "planned community" is apparent in the nature of his references to planning. On the one hand, he admitted, "Looking back, the most un-Levitt thing about [it] was that it began without a comprehensive plan." Yet he continued,

Solutions didn't come in flashes of blinding light. They came as the result of planning and thinking. Something evolved.
     It was the combination of planning and a little boldness that made the Levitt approach work.[7]

There is a contradiction in the meaning of the words *planned* and *community* even as Levitt was using them. His use of the phrase *pre-planned community* suggested more than mere preparation for construction, yet he stopped short of claiming to have had a comprehensive plan. Similarly, his substitution of the socially charged term *community* for the more neutral *subdivision* or *development* echoes the promise in his father's "Welcoming Letter" cited previously, even as he suggests that the project simply evolved. No doubt his ambivalence was at least partly due to the number of critical assessments of Levittown that had intervened between the time of the earliest publicity for the development and his own retrospective analysis.

The Levitts' continued references to the Levittown project in their discussions of planned communities are particularly significant since the firm had already incorporated many of the more highly desirable elements of the nineteenth century planned communities in their prewar, upper middle-class developments in Rockville Centre and Manhasset. These included staggered setbacks, fully landscaped plots, and curvilinear roadways to restrict traffic flow. They had also converted the old Vanderbilt mansion into a clubhouse and civic center for the residents in their Strathmore/Vanderbilt development at Manhasset. In addition, they included a process by which the first cohort of homeowners was given the right to interview and reject subsequent applicants for houses offered in the development. Yet, despite all this, the Levitts applied the phrase *planned community* only to their Island Trees development, and not to these earlier developments.[8]

In one of the first—and to date the most comprehensive—studies of Levittown, John Thomas Liell questioned whether Levittown fulfilled the requirements of a planned, model, or garden community by measuring the development against the standards for the prototypical "planned communities" of the late nineteenth century. He found that the characteristics which were fundamental to most of these earlier plans were either lacking or, at best, weakly imitated at Levittown. As a result, he argued, the desired community formation was developing poorly among its residents.[9]

Still, the concept of a planned community remains an important key to understanding the nature of the built environment that took shape at Levittown. One of the problems in applying the term *planned community* to a subdivision lies in the fact that there were two distinct types of community which were advocated by the planners of the nineteenth century. The discrepancy can also be attributed to the two very different stages in the development of the community. Levittown, in its two phases of construction, contained elements of each. The first, which was the standard against which Liell measured Levittown, was primarily a marketing strategy of architects and developers. It was a community aimed at the upper-middle class and reflected the tenets of the Arcadian ideal: large, English-style homesteads, set on lushly landscaped plots in a private community complete with such amenities as country clubs, ponds

2.1

Curvilinear road layouts from three prewar developments on Long Island.
(a) Green Acres, Valley Stream (proposed 1937, built 1940). (b) Strathmore
Homes, Manhasset, c. 1939. (*continued*)

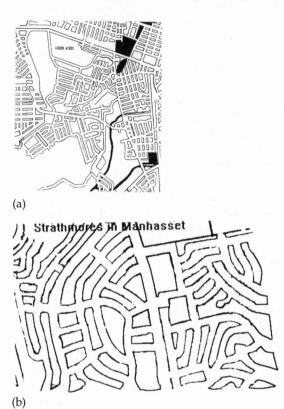

(a)

(b)

2.1 (*continued*)

Curvilinear road layouts from three prewar developments on Long Island.
(c) Gross-Morton Homes, Queens, c. 1940. (d) Levittown, c. 1950.

(c)

(d)

and rambles, and an absence of traffic and commerce. These were the communities built by planners such as Frederick Law Olmsted, Llewelyn Haskell, and J. C. Nichols—and by the Levitts in their more affluent developments.

However, the term was also used by those housing reformers whose ideas were rooted in environmental determinism and whose goals included improved housing for urban dwellers of the lower, working classes.[10] These were the people who could not afford to build for themselves and were more likely to "inherit [the deteriorating] housing abandoned by the classes above them."[11] They were also economically, and in many instances culturally, ill-prepared to purchase a dwelling that would be conducive to what the planners considered an appropriate way of life.[12] To the housing-reform advocates and urban planners of the Progressive period the phrase *planned community* therefore meant an environment that was designed to induce, if not impose, the lifestyle of the American middle class. Their plans attempted to address—through the physical arrangement of space—such issues as easy access to education, recreation and employment centers, and the development of social community while providing dwellings that emphasized and imposed nuclear-family living and middle-class values through their room layout. As a result of this emphasis, the terms *planned* or *model* community were often applied to rental housing projects that were designed to uplift—or reform—the ways of living among the lower-middle and working classes.[13] It is this type of "planned community" that Levittown most resembled in its first two years.

The first phase at Levittown was the Cape Cod rental project. Levitt's original plan was for a relatively modest development of 2000 dwellings.[14] The public response to his announcement of that plan was so positive that Levitt immediately added another 1000 units to the proposed project. When they were finished five months later, an additional 1000 were promised. By the end of 1948, the project had grown to 6000 houses, all of which were Cape Cods in design. Of these, approximately 2000 were still being rented, although the Levitt company was virtually out of the rental business by 1949.[15]

When the Levitts began building these rental houses at Island Trees in 1947, they were building shelter. When they shifted from Cape Cods for rent to ranches for sale, in 1949, they had begun to build their "new town." The difference between the two stages reflects several differences in outlook toward the houses, the residents, and the community. In 1947, the rental houses were deliv-

2.2

Scale model of the 1947 Cape Cod model with floor plan. (Douglas
MacArthur High School, Levittown, NY)

(a)

(b)

(c)

erer-designed, traditional in structure and style, and imposed upon a shelter-hungry population of young workers. In 1949, the housing crisis had eased, and the new Levittown was redesigned to capture the veteran market for modest, proprietary housing.[16]

In 1949 Levitt offered a new model, the ranch. Although similar in mass and size to the Cape Cod, the ranch offered several innovations.[17] The front elevation was more "modern" in design, with an irregular roofline and façade. The floor plan and the added accessories were different and more sophisticated; a significant addition was the wood-burning fireplace. This model and those that followed it were tailored for the buying market; none were built as rental units.[18] It is these post-1949 sections of Levittown that bear most resemblance to the traditional "planned" community.

The 1950 and 1951 ranch models, although essentially the same house, offered even more accessories than the 1949 ranch. The nature of these amenities suggests that marketability had begun to play an important part in their selection and design. In this the three Levitt ranch models are more resonant of the first type of planned community, the Llewellyn Haskell/Frederick Olmsted/J.C. Nichols variety, and it is this generation of houses to which William Levitt first applied the label of a "Garden Community."

By 1951, when Levitt had sold the last of his houses at Levittown, many of the elements of the planned community had been institutionalized by the FHA in its prescriptions for suburban subdivisions. These elements reflected a growing consensus about the nature of the American character and about the role of house and home in its formation. The ideas were not new; an ideology of house and home had been part of the American political culture from the colonial days through the founding of the Republic and into the reform periods that followed it.[19] Expressed from the top in the form of land grants and voting privileges for the landed, and from the bottom in the form of a restless wandering in search of a better piece of land, the consensus was rooted in the theory that the privately owned homestead was the most appropriate form of housing for a republic.[20]

Thomas Jefferson had expressed this belief in his call for a nation of yeomen—landowning farmers whose interest in the land and its governance would assure their commitment to the republican ideal.[21] Later, Andrew Jackson Downing codified the belief in his book, *The Architecture of Country Houses*:

So long as men are forced to dwell in log huts and follow a hunter's life, we must not be surprised at lynch law and the

2.3

Architect's renditions of 1949 and 1951 ranch models. (NCM) (a-e) Five models for the Levitt Ranches 1949–50. (f-h) Three models for the Levitt Ranches 1951.

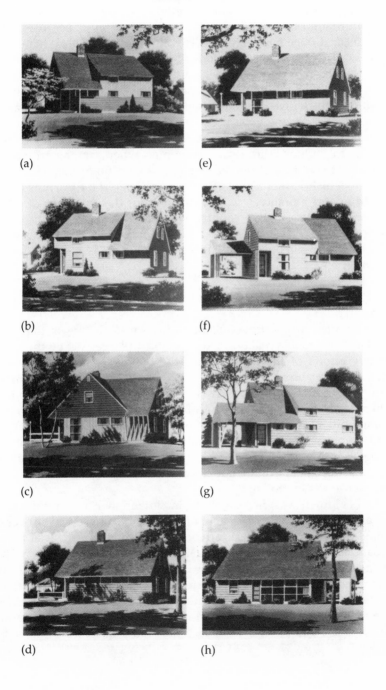

(a)

(e)

(b)

(f)

(c)

(g)

(d)

(h)

use of the bowie knife. But, when smiling lawns and tasteful cottages begin to embellish a country, we know that order and culture are established. . . . The second reason is, because the *individual home* has a great social value for a people. Whatever new systems may be needed for the regeneration of an old and enfeebled nation, we are persuaded that, in America, not only is the distinct family the best social form, but those elementary forces which give rise to the highest genius and the finest character may, for the most part, be traced back to the farm-house and the rural cottage. . . . The third reason is, because there is a moral influence in a country home—when, among an educated, truthful, and refined pople, it is an echo of their character—which is more powerful than any mere oral teachings of virtue and morality. . . . For this reason, the condition of the family home—in this country where every man may have a home—should be raised, till it shall symbolize the best character and pursuits, and the dearest affections and enjoyments of social life.[22]

Levitt's Island Trees development reflected and reinforced that doctrine.

Levittown was the reduction of the American dream to a practical and affordable reality, made possible in large part by the cooperative efforts of the government, the builders, and the banks. It was not a planned community in the sense used by the Utopian reformers of the Jacksonian Era. It did not follow the prescriptions of Ebenezer Howard's garden cities. Nor was it a new town or planned community as the City Housing Corporation, the Russell Sage Foundation, and the Regional Planning Association of America of the Progressive period would have understood the terms. Indeed, architectural designers would not have applied the term "planned" in that sense to Levittown.[23]

Levittown was, nevertheless, an "intentional" community with an agenda of its own. The goal of the second phase was universal home ownership and it was advocated not only as beneficial to the tenant class, but as a panacea against social and political problems. Its advocates ranged from the FHA and VA, who underwrote the experiment, to builder/developers like William Levitt, who conducted it. In this respect the product, if not the process, resembled the agenda of the environmental determinists, from the Fourierites to George Pullman and John H. Patterson—structuring the social order.[24]

Therefore, it is the second type of planned community, the planned environment of publicly sponsored housing projects that had been advocated by the social reformers of the Progressive period, which is the more appropriate model against which to measure Levittown. However, there are important differences. The postwar low-cost housing funded by the federal government succeeded, not by violating the existing social customs of the residents, but rather by reinforcing and expanding the prevailing cultural norms of the middle class. Although no single aspect of the postwar housing programs was new, the combination of government sponsorship of newly constructed single-family villas for the rental and lower-income proprietary markets was a postwar innovation.

The Targets

Levittown was built for a population that was predominantly drawn from the prewar tenant class. As a result, the initial emphasis in both Levitt's and the government's agenda was the construction of rental houses. These houses would not follow the traditional pattern and filter down to the working classes as hand-me-downs to be subdivided and made over into affordable dwellings; rather, they would be designed and built specifically for this socioeconomic tier. Moreover, even those which were built as rental units would be freestanding, single-family dwellings, rather than tenements, apartments, or even two-family structures.[25]

The target population composed what Levitt referred to as the "typical" market: blue-collar workers in the main, but also a number of those in the recently emerged white-collar middle class, wage-earning people whose work was clean, but not well-remunerated, and whose prewar status would not typically have included home ownership.[26] Although it may have been in the statistical middle of the population economically, this group was not the cultural middle class as measured by wealth, education, or social standing.[27]

When he offered the houses for sale, the initial selling price was $7500.[28] The rule of thumb for a standard ratio of mortgage to annual income in the 1940s was generally set at 2:1, not only by economic advisers but by lending institutions as well.[29] The houses of Levittown were therefore geared to families whose incomes ranged up to $3750, depending on the amount of their down payment.[30]

In order to maintain the selling price of $7500, Levitt not only stayed within the VEHP ceiling of $1800 per room, but limited the

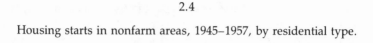

2.4

Housing starts in nonfarm areas, 1945–1957, by residential type.

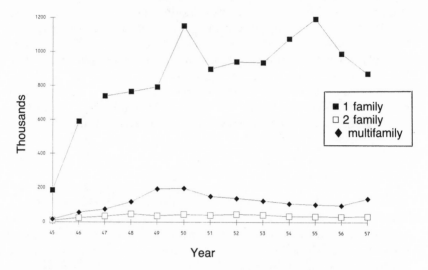

(Based on figures in N 106–124, "Permanent Dwelling Units . . . 1889–1957" in *Historical Statistics of the United States, Colonial Times to 1957,* p. 393.

total number of rooms to four.[31] The addition of a fifth room at $1800, which would have raised the cost of the Levitt houses to $9000, would have remained within the guidelines and could have provided another bedroom, a family room, or, for those with a more more formal family life, a dining room.[32] But it would have required an income of $4650.[33]

Although the housing shortage may have led some families from the prewar middle class to take advantage of the housing Levitt provided at Island Trees, they were not his primary market.[34] Levitt had built the community at Island Trees for a particular economic market, and the houses he built incorporated certain assumptions about the social needs of that constituency.

The Planners

The two construction phases of Levittown represent more than aesthetic change; there were political implications as well. In the spring of 1947, the primary decision-making control on the design of both the houses and community was in the hands of several agencies, both civic and economic. Local town boards set limits on both the nature and the style of the housing, as well as on the materials and methods of construction, through traditional building and zoning codes. At the federal level, the FHA set minimum standards for cost, structure, and style, and then insured the economic risk for those lenders who underwrote the construction of the development. The lenders, in turn, working under federal guidelines, established the terms of the economic investment. Finally, the builder/developers, working within the constraints established by these agencies, selected materials, colors, design, and location. Collectively, the decisions of these providers housed the veterans in the basic Cape Cod, the reductionist rental version of the American Dream in 1947 and 1948.

The houses constructed at Levittown thus constitute a form of "capitalist realism."[35] As officially approved residential architecture, their environment reinforced and conveyed the dominant American social values of the period. Their design was approved by the Federal Housing Administration, the Veterans Administration, the Bank of Manhattan Company (which funded the construction), the Bank of Buffalo (which held the mortgages on the first resales), and the Building and Zoning departments of the Town of Hempstead.

Although officially the Levitts attributed the designs of the houses to Alfred, the Cape Cods were little different from the other FHA-sponsored houses constructed in the Northeast throughout the late 1930s and early 1940s.[36] In the abstract, Levittown was virtually a replica of the officially recommended subdivision styles of the FHA; indeed, the design elements of Levittown so resemble those the FHA was advocating that it is questionable whether Alfred Levitt 'designed' the houses so much as assembled their design from an FHA-approved list of acceptable elements. The Levitt house may have been called "rudimentary and inflexible"[37] by social and architectural critics, but the architectural plan of that first generation of Levittown houses, the Cape Cods, satisfied the requirements of the deliverers.

By the middle of 1947, however, the easing of the housing shortage began to alter the balance of power from the providers to the consumers. The Cape Cod model—offered for sale—proved not to be as readily marketable to the veterans as it had been as rental property, and as the housing shortage had indicated it would be.[38] By the time the first 1000 houses at Island Trees were occupied, therefore, Levitt had initiated his public retreat from the rental housing market.[39] As early as February 1948, when introducing his rent increases, Levitt pointed out that he had always seen rental housing as simply a temporary measure, and that "a 'home ownership' program was the ultimate in his organization's planning."[40] With that statement he unofficially inaugurated the second phase of the construction of Levittown.

Speaking in a newsreel in 1949, Levitt stated his belief that "every family in the United States was entitled to decent shelter," and that "private enterprise should provide that shelter insofar as it can."[41] Unstated was the Levitt corollary that the shelter in question was (or ought to be) the privately owned, single-family house in a suburban or rural setting—like those at Levittown. When private enterprise proved insufficient, government's role was to provide the necessary assistance, not to usurp the private sector's role. The housing of 1949 reflected this belief as the FHA and VA cooperated with the financial industry and the builder/developers to actualize its tenets.[42]

The ownership aspect of this agenda had been advocated consistently by housing reformers thoughout the early part of the twentieth century. In the mid-1920s, Herbert Hoover added his voice to the home ownership discussion:

> Maintaining a high percentage of individual home owners is one of the searching tests that now challenge the people of the United States. The present large proportion of families that own their own homes is both the foundation of a sound economic and social system and a guarantee that our society will continue to develop rationally as changing conditions demand.[43]

As John Dean has shown, the idea took on greater force in the 1930s as the deepening depression increased worker dissatisfaction with the economy. A number of housing advocates in that period argued the position that home ownership—as opposed to good housing—was also a protection against various forms of socialistic activities. Their opinions appeared in scholarly journals,

> Ownership of homes is the best guarantee against communism and socialism and the various bad "isms" of life. I do not say that it is an infallible guarantee, but I do say that owners of homes usually are more interested in the safeguarding of our national history than are renters and tenants.[44]

and in lectures and speeches,

Socialism and communism do not take root in the ranks of those who have their feet firmly embedded in the soil of America through home ownership.[45]

Franklin Roosevelt rephrased the sentiment in the middle of World War II when he spoke before the United States Savings and Loan League in 1942 and declared that

a nation of homeowners, of people who own a real share in their own land, is unconquerable.[46]

William Levitt, speaking in 1948, continued the tradition:

No man who owns his house and lot can be a Communist; [because] he has too much to do.[47]

The relationship between homeowning and good citizenship was expressed in popular culture as well. In Frank Capra's 1946 film *It's a Wonderful Life*, George Bailey's father assured America, as well as the villainous Mr. Potter, that homeowning was an essential part of the American way of life, and that the denial of that basic right to the workers of Bedford Falls would lead to political as well as social tragedy.[48]

The postwar expansion of the American Dream of home ownership was thus seen as a form of insurance against the political subversion of those who were less likely to be committed to the republican ideology and, by extension, more susceptible to subversive rhetoric—young men who owned no property. The differences between the nature of the postwar and the Progressive Era "planned" communities are thus not so much indicative of a distinction between planned and unplanned as they are of the differences between the social and political needs of American society in the two periods.[49]

The Assumptions

As a result of the involvement of the FHA in their design, the patterns of the houses built under the terms of the FHA/GI Bill reveal the official code for what the life of that "typical" buyer was, or was supposed to be, in the 1940s. Yet, the degree to which both the FHA and the builder instituted social and behavioral regulations for the residents suggests a perceived need to pressure the new residents to conform to these standards. For example, throughout the first year, when he was still the landlord, Levitt or his spokesmen inserted notices in both the local Levittown papers on a regular basis to remind residents of a variety of community regulations.[50]

In 1947 two newspapers were established in Island Trees. The first, *The Island Trees Eagle*, published its pilot issue on November 20, just six weeks after the first residents moved into a Levitt house. The second, *The Island Trees Tribune*, began publishing in December.

The Tribune, which originally operated as an independent organ, was purchased by Levitt in April 1948 "in order to 'eliminate distortion of facts which have from time to time enabled a small group of individuals to provoke antagonism and misunderstanding.'" The timing of this purchase coincided with that paper's opposition to several Levitt initiatives.[51] These included the change in name from Island Trees to Levittown in honor of the Levitts;[52] the gradual movement toward divestiture of the rental units, and finally, a proposed rent increase.[53]

Using both papers, Levitt published instructions regarding such activities as emergency parking of cars on the lawns of Levittown to facilitate snow removal by the town. His press release defined the permitted lawn as those areas which extend from the curbside driveway aprons to the side yard. Residents were warned to keep the cars within the parallel lines delineated by those aprons, and reminded that such parking was only permitted during snow emergencies.[54]

In another press release, tenants were advised on the proper care of the floors and attics:

Must Take Care of Floors
New families of Island Trees with job numbers higher than 800 are now receiving booklets with their lease on the proper care of "Kentile" floors.[55]

Another release admonished against hanging wash on weekends:

The Levitt office has asked us to remind tenants to remember the lease clause that forbids hanging of wash outside on weekends. The clause has not been enforced since the landlord recognizes some of the resultant difficulty. At this holiday season, however, please keep to essential washing.[56]

Levitt's purchase of the *Tribune* when tenant opposition to his policies became too strident is also indicative of his position vis-a-vis his tenants. It guaranteed him a means for promoting official company policy to those who might need reminding. This approach was similar to that of many of the more paternalistic industrialists who included a combination of employment, housing, and education in their relationships with their workers.[57] The pattern persisted into the twentieth century with such leaders as Henry Ford, George Pullman, and William Atkinson, among others, who produced periodicals that conveyed the house policies to those who were required to abide by them. Levitt's control of the local papers also protected his interest in the reputation of the housing project by controlling the visibility of any tenant-generated opposition.

When he sold the houses, Levitt included covenants that institutionalized his restrictions in the deeds. These covenants forbade the construction of fences and specified permissible renovations—including colors and materials—and other conditions of residence for the next 25 years.[58] Although Levitt had revealed a similar preference for harmonious behaviors among the populations in his middle-class communities, there was a qualitative difference in the way in which he expressed that preference. In part this was due to the fact that he was a landlord only in Levittown, but that does not explain the inclusion of his covenants in the Levittown deeds when he sold the houses. Restrictive covenants were included in his other, more expensive developments, but the limitations were neither created solely by Levitt nor imposed on the residents. Rather, they were developed in concert with the homeowners' associations that were established on completion of a stated percentage of the construction.[59] Although a "community association" was formed in Levittown, it was not given the authority that was vested in the homeowners' associations in the other Levitt communities.[60] The Levittown group was not even consulted when Levitt changed the name from Island Trees to Levittown, a move that offended many of the members.[61] And the operation of the Levittown pools and recreation areas was turned over to the control of the Town of Hempstead rather than the association as Levitt began the last phase of construction in 1950, although at Strathmore Vanderbilt the operation of the country club, as well as the right of first refusal of sale to new residents, had been vested in the homeowners' association.[62] Clearly, Levitt's plan did not include the same autonomy for the residents of Levittown. The nature of the restrictions and the fact that he imposed them is more reflective of the paternalistic type of "planned community" that was designed to shape as well as house its residents. Unlike the paternalistic landlords, however, Levitt did not remain to guide the community's development.

The Mesh

Although Levittown was generally well received by its tenants, by the local media, and by those who had advocated housing for the veterans, it was less well received by its neighbors. The criticism of the subdivision had some validity. The scale of construction on which Levittown was built created a new form of instant "town" that lacked the visual amenities which marked older, more gradually evolved communities. The 17,500 houses of Levittown looked more like a dusty Midwestern railroad boom town of the late nineteenth century than a middle-class suburb thirty minutes from Manhattan. Despite Abraham Levitt's efforts at landscaping, the houses dwarfed the sapling fruit trees and evergreens, creating a barren, unfinished look to the rows of house lots.

Added to the criticism of the existing environment, there were also economic aspects to the local objections. The objection to the continued expansion of Levittown was based on the fear that nearby property values would be lowered as the communities in which the average houses were selling for $12,000 to $15,000[63] found themselves surrounded by several thousand houses selling at the $7000 level. Indeed,

> [t]he inhabitants of one community, when they discovered that Levitt was intending to build, put through a special code with deliberately ridiculous provisions. . . . A building code is one of the few defenses against Levitt that they have.[64]

Less overt, but no less real was the concern with the socioeconomic level of the residents. The Levittown newspapers continued to refer to that opposition in much of their editorial comment, if only to dispute it.

> It seems that the people of the surrounding areas were a bit afraid of what sort of people would move into Island Trees. . . . When we do our shopping we have a wonderful opportunity to build good will for Island Trees.[65]

The surrounding communities also found the newcomers to be an inconvenience. Earlier developers had added their houses to existing towns and the new development was quickly subsumed by the preexisting community, albeit with some straining of local services. In Levittown, however, there was virtually no pre-existing community. The few families who were living in the hamlet of Island Trees used surrounding communities for the normal services such as stores, hospitals, and churches. Thus, the addition of 17,500 families placed heavy demands on the existing services.

It would take the first decade of its existence for the necessary refining that would allow Levittown to take its place among the more established communities that surrounded it. During that decade the new subdivision suburbs were monitored closely at many levels.[66] Observers were particularly interested in the social effects engendered by the built environment. To a large degree their assessments were negative. By the mid-1950s, the suburbs had become the focus of a number of popular articles and sociological studies that suggested that this new postwar phenomenon was responsible for the apparent increase of a number of disturbing social and psychological phenomena among a large number of its residents.[67] In much of this literature, "Levittown" was used to encode the pejorative characteristics attributed to life among suburbanites.

In the four years between the occupation of the first house in 1947 and the completion of the final unit in 1951, Levittown assumed a national identity as the quintessential postwar American suburb.[68] Levittown and its residents were frequently cited as examples of these problems and "Levittown" became a synonym for suburban sprawl.[69] Urban planners spoke disparagingly of the replication of other "Levittowns."[70] Humorists employed stereotypes of Levittowners, referring to pregnancy as "the Levittown look," or portraying harried commuters unable to find their own home in the mass of replicated Cape Cods.

Even in fiction the offending examples bore striking resemblance to the houses at Levittown. For example, in novelist Sloan Wilson's *The Man in The Gray Flannel Suit*, the hero Tom Rath and his wife find their lives drab and meaningless in their little suburban tract house. They find happiness, however, when they move to the traditional home they inherit in an exclusive but still suburban area of Connecticut.[71] Other fictionalized accounts made similar distinctions between the more affluent suburban communities and the subdivision suburbs of the GI Bill.

As early as January 1948, the local newspapers had recognized this interest in Levittown and were advising the residents of their importance as models of American democratic behavior, particularly since they were so clearly in the public eye.[72] After the first meeting of the newly established civic association, *The Eagle* published this comment:

We are a young town, yet a famous one. The whole country is looking at us to see what we will make of ourselves. An interested, active citizenry, working through a Community Association, can make of our community a model town—a model of democracy, community standing, and community spirit.[73]

In part, the objections were sparked by the sheer size and scale of the new subdivisions, and in this Levittown was indeed typical. Before the war, the nature of the construction industry had ensured a *de facto* control on the scope of development. The houses built would be no more numerous than what a builder could expect to sell quickly and profitably. Similarly, the reduction of the size of each house was limited by the reality of the market. The economic level of those clients who could afford to buy determined the acceptable minimums of space and quality. After the war the combination of the housing shortage, new building technologies, government regulations, and new financing strategies changed the nature of these limitations. The erection of basic economy-level housing in volume became more profitable than custom building for those developers, like Levitt, who were able to produce large-scale subdivisions. To their critics, these new suburban "wastelands" were simply poorly planned communities of cheaply constructed, badly conceived, cookie-cutter-styled "dream houses."

The attack was not so much on the suburban location as it was on the nature of the domestic environment created by the FHA-approved houses that were being built there and on the concomitant effect on the lives of the people who would live in them. The prewar suburbs were a pastiche of spot-built custom houses and small development tracts at different economic levels, interspersed with small businesses and an occasional factory. In contrast, the postwar scale of production resulted in suburbs that were composed of acres upon acres of mass-produced houses relieved only by small stores and an occasional recreation facility. When not singled out specifically, Levittown was included generically in such studies, as the target of the social critics became the small, postwar house in a dormitory suburb.[74] The houses, like the suburbs, were denounced for their social and physical homogeneity, which in turn were blamed for contributing to the decline of the extended family by excluding all but the typical nuclear family of two parents, two children, and one dog.

The quality of the new construction also came under attack. Many of the tract houses constructed under FHA/VA funding were found to be not only substandard in materials, design, and spatial organization, but poorly constructed as well. In 1952 a government study was appointed to discover why the new houses were leaking, cracking, settling, and in many cases, structurally incomplete. The study concluded that in far too many cases, builders rather than veterans were the primary benefactors of the housing programs.[75] This was not the case in Levittown. Although there had been much local concern about the materials and construction quality during the construction of the Levitt development, these fears never materialized. The houses were small and uninspired, but they were well built. When the postwar critics attacked Levittown, they found little to fault in the quality of the construction; the houses at Levittown were—and are—generally considered sound.[76] When Levittown was denounced it was not for the quality of its construction, but for the environment it produced—the size and sameness of the houses and the ghetto of domesticity that they engendered.[77]

A concomitant criticism was that voiced by Lewis Mumford, who contended that the suburbs had become stratified not only by class and age, but also by state in life. The subdivision suburbs were also stratified socioeconomically by virtue of the sheer numbers of dwellings replicated at the same cost and selling price. This resulted in what Mumford called "a low-grade uniform environment from which escape is impossible."[78] The unrelieved residential character of these suburbs, such critics held, created a stultifying environment in which all disharmony was either removed or denied. The houses were architecturally bland, uninspiring, and repetitive; the children, "homogenized."[79]

The unrelieved dormitory aspect of the subdivision suburbs and their cultural inadequacies were causally linked to the disorders attributed to the suburban lifestyle. In general, the assessment was that the new suburbs had failed, if not structurally, then socially and aesthetically. The attack on the postwar houses culminated in John Keats' 1956 satire, *The Crack in the Picture Window*. Keats' critique was loosely disguised as a novel, which savaged both the houses and the suburbs of the postwar building boom as inferior in construction and design, as well as stifling to their residents, particularly the women.[80] To Keats, the FHA/VA program had inadvertently produced housing that combined the worst aspects of apartment living with the worst of homeowning.[81] Where apartments had provided common spaces—laundry rooms, lobbies, and playgrounds—the new houses substituted the loneliness of the privatized lifestyle. Yet, where prewar private houses had offered extra space for a variety of these activities in basement, garage, porch, and garden, their four-room postwar counterparts did not. Moreover, they provided no place for solitude.

Although the new suburbs had their champions, many had begun to question the wisdom of the postwar housing policies. Critics renewed the argument that had surfaced during the housing policy debates of the 1940s. This theory held that below a certain socioeconomic level, homeowning was not only unwise, but counterproductive. Below that level, homeowning was not an investment but a burden; people were more likely to purchase a home during sound economic periods when both incomes and prices were high. Then, when the economy faltered and incomes were reduced, those of low earning power were likely to default on their mortgages, thereby losing not only their homes, but their equity. Although rental housing would to some degree have to respond to the fluctuations in the economy, a landlord would be more likely to ride out the recession without losing his properties. Tenancy was therefore recommended for those of low to moderate income. To these analysts, the pressure on the veteran to buy, rather than rent, was considered unfair and impractical, particularly for those at the economic margin.[82]

It was becoming apparent, at least to the critics, that a good workingman's house had to be something other than a miniaturized rich man's house; that space had to be differently interpreted if it were to function effectively at different socioeconomic levels. Moreover, it was seen that there is a minimum ratio of humans-to-space, below which an acceptable dwelling cannot go.[83]

Regardless of the outcome of the debate on the merits of the new suburbia, however, the use of "Levittown" as a synonym for the quintessential postwar suburban environment in such discussions is in itself misleading. The suburban critique, whether positive or negative, is almost always a critique of a static environment. It presumes a single, unchanging entity; in the case of Levittown, the finished housing development of 17,500 units as it stood in 1951. A reflective analysis of Levittown must take into account the fact that the development was not created as a whole; rather, it evolved. This evolution involves more than the sequential acquisition of large parcels of property on which to build an ever-increasing number of identical houses.

In the construction of Levittown, there were three separate architectural phases of development—the rental project of 1947–48 Cape Cods, the sales development of 1949–51 ranches, and finally

the owner-generated, redesigned, residential suburb that followed
the withdrawal of Levitt and Sons. Each had its own distinct nature
with varying implications in the interaction of layout and design. It
is this three-phased aspect that is critical to a clear understanding of
the role played by the built environment of the postwar development suburbs and which forms the substance of the balance of this
study.

3

HOUSES FIT FOR HEROES

The years after the war were necessarily years of change. Soldiers who had given up the security of guaranteed military employment were seeking civilian jobs; veterans and workers shuffled for rank in employment. Women who had held well-paying nontraditional positions in all phases of the war effort were both pushed and pulled back into the home.[1] Men who had postponed marriage "for the duration" were encouraged to begin a family. It was the time for a return to traditional values.

A close examination of the characteristics of the Levittown Cape Cod reveals the dominant values of the postwar period: conformity and privatization, as well as the revival of several nineteenth-century themes: the cult of domesticity, the doctrine of separate spheres, and the agrarian myth. Each of these themes was also related to another value of American life, the right to private property. In the America of 1947, these themes had wide appeal.

The design of the domestic space at Levittown logically follows from this preexisting set of social assumptions. Through their physical layout, the houses supported these values, and, by extension, a traditional family life. Conversely, they failed to support lifestyles that were at odds with the prevailing culture.[2] There was little need to do so: the postwar period was marked by a strong consensus on family values, particularly among the aspiring middle class.[3]

Moreover, the population of Levittown was unusually homogeneous in many of their most important characteristics: they were similar in age, stage in the life cycle, socioeconomic level, and race. Not only had the residents shared the war experience—as soldiers or as waiting wives and sweethearts—but most were also recently-married couples, many with small children. The similarity in age was the result of the VEHP restriction that the houses be made available only to veterans of World War II, most of whom ranged in age from 21 to about 32.

The homogeneity in Levittown was also economic. The houses,

all built to rent or sell for about $60 a month, were eagerly sought by people whose income level was about $3500 a year. Although there was no *de jure* income ceiling, the houses' lack of amenities limited the community's appeal for the more affluent, especially as proprietary housing. As a result, most of those who remained in Levittown when it was made available for sale were those whose purchase of a house was facilitated by the GI Bill's "no down payment" clause.[4]

Finally, Levittown was homogeneous in race; the property came with restrictions on the racial mix of the community. Initially, some black veterans were allowed to rent, but the deeds restricted the sale of the houses to Caucasians. In this, Levitt was essentially following standard FHA practice. The FHA strongly recommended in its technical bulletin, *Planning Profitable Neighborhoods*, that builders aim at a particular market, based on similarities of age, race, and economic level.[5]

Although the population of Levittown included members of many different national and religious groups, these variations were largely offset by the similarities in age, stage of the life cycle, economic level, and recent war experience. Social conformity was therefore predetermined to some degree by the composition of the Levittown population. It was also reinforced by the temper of American society at the time.

Function Follows Form[6]

Comfort and Conformity: The Cape Cod

The assumptions about family life that were built into the houses of Levittown in 1947 and 1948 imposed a high degree of conformity upon Levittown and its residents. This conformity was not an uncomfortable fit for most of the families who lived there, however.[7] After years in uniform, the American veteran was inured to uniformity in his dress and environment. Despite the popularity of the rhetoric of rugged individualism, the values of the period stressed moderation and conformity. There was a growing consensus that American workers should be encouraged neither to be overly individualistic nor to develop the collective solidarity of labor under socialism. Seeking security, many Americans had become suspicious of collective activity. Seeking stability, they had become equally suspicious of differences.

This was particularly true in late April and early May, when the annual celebrations of May Day (May 1st) brought forth a spate of speeches and anecdotes intended to counter socialist or communist infiltration of the labor movement.[8] "Deviance," whether social or political, became the professional code word for such differences—in magazine articles, editorials, advice columns, and political analyses.

The popular literature of the period was filled with assertions of loyalty, reminders of traditional American values, and warnings against the threat implicit in those who were deviant.[9] These were offered in many guises. One was the "self-help" article in the popular magazines in which the author, writing in a pseudopsychological tone, offered 'guides' to better living. Invariably, these guides included a test to help the reader gauge his or her own status. For example, Jean Griffith Benge, writing in *Household* magazine, advised her readers,

> If you suspect that you are not adaptable and the test on page 80 confirms your suspicions, cultivate some of the desired traits of adjustment to situations and to people. Establish these new traits until they become habits.

After broadly defining the extremes of behavior, the introduction concluded, "The comfortable person strives for a middle-of-the-road course between these two extremes."

The test scored the respondents in five categories: excellently adjusted; good adjustment; about average; poor adjustment; apparently greatly maladjusted. Included as negative responses were such "unadaptable" traits as

> I rebel against customs.
> I'm an individualist.
> I crave many things I don't have.
> My only friends are of my sex.
> I am afraid of mice.
> Life has handed me a dirty deal.
> I lack persistence.
> I get excited, or swear, readily.

Offered as "desired" traits were

> I rarely get excited.
> I obey laws and rules.
> I respect authority.

I conform to most customs.
I am consistent in my actions.
I'm just an average person.[10]

Social nonconformity was viewed as tantamount to political subversion; in 1947, to be a nonconformist was to take sides against "us." Conformity was a value shared by many of the more outspoken early residents of Levittown. In this, the Levittowners were not unusual.

Yet it was not merely political deviance to which many of the Levittown residents objected. They frequently found fault with neighbors whose lifestyles failed to conform to the community norms. Diffidence or introversion were viewed as anti-social.[11] Their accusations against nonconforming neighbors, revealed in letters to the editors of local papers, invariably included some reference to the nonconformist as "commie," "Russkie," "Comrade," or some similar epithet. An episode in December 1947 provides an example of the group mentality that was developing. In the episode concerning the community's name change, the follow-up letters to the editor were strongly supportive of the Levitt organization and its position that the Levitts had the right to name their community as they chose.

The letters were also extremely critical of the *Tribune's* Lieutenant Rakita for opposing the name change.[12] One such letter that attacked Rakita referred to the lieutenant as "Mr. Vishinsky."[13] Red-baiting letters of this type applied equally to those who failed to conform, whether for the offense of tying one's dog on too long a rope, objecting to a rent increase, distributing political leaflets, or organizing a Communist Party cell.[14]

Despite the paternalistic, authoritarian tone of the mandates from the firm that were announced periodically in the Levittown papers, the residents supported the efforts of Levitt and Sons to police the community. Authoritarianism was a value that was strongly shared among the more vocal residents whose views were published in the two local Levittown papers in the early years. There were several attempts to oppose or expose these mandates as autocratic and antidemocratic. Councilman John O'Connell of N. Bellmore, for example, attacked the restrictive covenants in the Levitt agreement at a Republican meeting in October 1949. In particular, he singled out the restriction against weekend and holiday washing as placing a burden on the young families whose children produced laundry as readily on weekends as on other days. O'Connell was attacked for his criticisms in letters to the editor of *Newsday*. The thrust of this counterattack contained the elements of the Levitt mystique, which has persisted among Levittowners to this day: Mr. Levitt solved the housing shortage, he provided a good house, the area did not become a slum, and any criticism of Mr. Levitt or his ways is therefore tantamount to an attack on the American way of life.[15]

Public positions taken against the Levitts or letters to the editor questioning their decisions would invariably be followed by a series of attacks on the Americanism of the critic, coupled with extravagant praise for Levitt and his houses as well as blanket approval of his official position. The letters to the editor supporting the Levitt edicts bordered on the idolatrous, leading at least one contemporary critic to believe that they were being "planted" in the paper by the organization. However, long after William J. Levitt had moved on, the Levittown Property Owners Association retained many of his mandates, restating them in the introductory brochure that they produced to initiate newcomers into the community.[16]

In a world threatened by political subversion and atomic annihilation, nonconformity was interpreted as a danger signal.[17] The Levittown Cape Cods fit this mood quite well. The single-family houses on separate plots reinforced the American myth of rugged individualism without encouraging nonconformity. Their design, plan, and setting were neither individualistic nor identical; although the interiors of the houses were identical their exteriors varied somewhat in appearance. Despite the contemporary rhetoric praising their "individuality" of design—subtle differences in color and window arrangements, along with staggered setbacks—the 6000 houses built in 1947 and 1948 were essentially undistinguishable. Their replication suited both the economic need for standardization and the political need for conformity.

Tradition

The topography chosen to ornament the Levitt houses further reveals the value system of the period.[18] The use of what Robert Stern has called "architecture with Memory"[19]—that is, encoding into the design of the buildings symbols evocative of the American past—imposed a type of sociopolitical imprimatur on the very nature of family life that the geography of the houses supported and enhanced. The application of the term "pioneers" to their postwar experience; the adornment of the houses with picket railings, cross-and-bible doors, and other nostalgic ornamentation—even the use

3.1

Levitt & Sons' drawings of five Cape Cod models, 1947. (NCM)

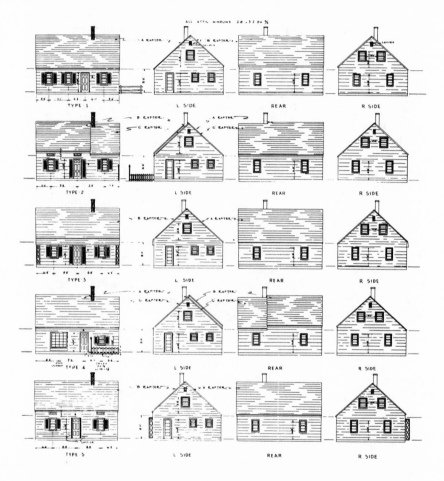

of the label "Cape Cod" for what was essentially a square box—all evoked a nostalgic image of an earlier, apparently more controllable past.[20]

The topographical variations among the five models drew heavily on nostalgia for America's past. Each house was trimmed with decorative elements evocative of myths that have been part of the American canon since the founding of the nation. The houses were all variations on the neocolonial Cape Cod cottage.[21] The colonial period was also evoked by three reliefs of a single candle that were punched out of the pine-paneled wainscoting which served as a bannister on the stairway. These candle motifs were applied in reverse to the soffit above the kitchen. Vestigial shutters on the front windows, or knee windows under the front eaves, further carried out the colonial theme.[22] The three exposed artificial beams that "supported" the living-room ceiling suggested rugged frontier construction, whereas the short sections of pickets, split rails, or latticework "fencing" that adorned each entrance suggested the small-town America of the nineteenth century.[23]

Thus, the first Levitt model, the Cape Cod, was both radically new and comfortably old. The elimination of the basement, and the reduction of the overall plan to four rooms was a departure from the traditional forms of suburban residential architecture. But the finished product was more than a 'reduction.' What Alfred Levitt produced was a minimalist version of the prewar suburban home. In effect, Levitt had disassembled the standard package of living room, dining room, kitchen, pantry, bath-and-a-half, three bedrooms and a garage, which the firm had been building prior to the war. He then reassembled a house using only those elements that were deemed essential to modern suburban life: kitchen, living room, bath, and two bedrooms. What he retained was the spatial relationship common to that of prewar architecture: the larger space was devoted to the living room and master bedroom; the smaller, the kitchen and nursery. Except for the bathroom, everything else was considered dispensible, at least for the time being.

Privatization

The house provided each family with the minimum space and accoutrements necessary for privatized domesticity. Indeed, there were no collective domestic facilities built into Levittown.[24] Each house was equipped with the requisite space and appliances to serve one family's basic needs, as the designer envisioned them. Here too, the equipment served not only to reflect but to reinforce the conformity of family life that would become so much a part of the suburban scene.

Life in the Levittown Cape Cod was the focus of the eighth article in the *McCall's* series, "This Is How I Keep House," which featured the home of Mr. and Mrs. Robert Eckhoff.[25] Earlier articles in the series had focused on such prominent housekeepers as Mrs. Alben Barkley, the wife of the Vice-President, as well as on the wife of a rural doctor and the wife of an itinerant preacher. The articles related the housekeeping to three aspects of the subjects' lives: the nature of their husbands' careers; the demands of their social standing; and the spatial arrangement of their homes.

In addition to conveying housekeeping suggestions and product advice to the reader, the articles served also to provide an insider's view of approved American family life. In April, the focus was on the new suburbia, typified by Helen Eckhoff and her Levittown Cape Cod.

At the time of the article, the Eckhoffs' Cape Cod was less than eighteen months old. The illustrations reveal the newness of the house and its setting. A lawn has taken hold. The cement path winds—"bends" is perhaps the better word for its 20-foot length—toward the cross-and-bible front door, which is just off-center in the façade of the house.[26] Several small shrubs flank the entrance. Inside the door, the viewer stands at the foot of the staircase; an archway to the right leads into the kitchen. There is no wall to the left; the living room's fourth wall is that which divides the stairway from the kitchen. Two bedrooms and a bath are approached through a small hallway just behind the stairs. The stairs themselves lead only to an unfinished attic.

The Eckhoffs have used a lot of white in their color scheme to create the impression of space. Black asphalt tile covers the floors throughout the house; the walls are painted white. The standard-equipment, white-enamelled metal cabinets and appliances reflect light and help to make the room appear ample. A wooden bowl of fruit rests in the center of a small, white-painted, drop-leaf table, which is flanked by two white chairs.[27] In the background, through the arch, one can see another table and chairs under the window in the living room; the living room serves as dining room for more formal meals. The living room, or parlor, was a small (12' x 16') room made even smaller by the inclusion of the only passageway to the private space: the two bedrooms and the bath.

In addition to discussing her interior decor, the article comments favorably on Mrs. Eckhoff's efficient use of space. The size of the house is only obliquely referred to in the magazine caption when it speaks of "this convenient kitchen-laundry-dining room." But the house controlled the nature of Mrs. Eckhoff's housekeeping far more than was apparent in *McCall's* analysis of her home. The designer of the Levitt house had assumed (correctly, in all but the most exceptional situations) that there would be no servants in this house. Moreover, it would be the wife of the household who would

3.2

(a) Architect's rendering of basic 1947 Cape Cod. (NCM) (b) Floor plan
CAD Sketch. (Author)

(a)

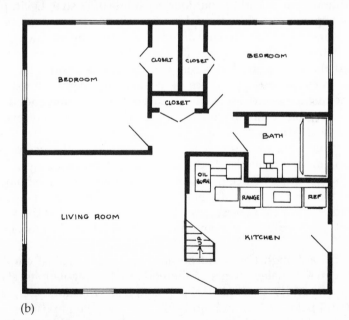

(b)

do the work in this kitchen, and the arrangement of space reinforced her return to domesticity.

The lack of a basement affected her housekeeping in several ways. Storage was either in the attic or within the living space on the main floor. The Eckhoffs had already added a free-standing metal cabinet to the builder-provided storage in the room. The Bendix washer remains in its builder-provided niche under the stairs, facing into the kitchen.

The relationship of public to private space provided in the Levitt house reinforced the domestic role of the homemaker-mother in the nuclear family. The kitchen, a room that had previously been treated as not only private, but somewhat declassé, in most homes now shared the front of the house with the living room.

The washing machine opened into a small space facing the side of the kitchen stove. As a result, doing the family's wash had become a kitchen, or semipublic, activity. Yet, Levitt apparently viewed the public use of outdoor wash-lines as a marginally unacceptable practice. The wash-line was an urban icon; laundry in the suburbs was a private matter.[28]

Although he found the outdoor wash-line offensive, Levitt provided no space within the floorplan in which to place an automatic dryer, even had the residents wanted to purchase one.[29] Though he expected the Levittown housewife to do her own laundry, Levitt enjoined the use of any but a company-approved drying device in order to prevent the appearance of a tenement neighborhood. No permanent lines could be installed; instead, he recommended the use of a portable, umbrella-like collection of lines that his directives referred to as "dryers."

Not only did the residents have to conform to the use of this particular model, they also had to dismantle it on Saturdays, Sundays, and holidays.[30] Since these are the days on which an employed mother would normally do her laundry, the injunction against weekend wash-lines underscores the tacit assumption that the wives of Levittown would be at home during the week to do their laundry.[31]

Thus, although Levitt did not take a position against employment for his female tenants, adherence to his regulations about laundry effectively precluded a population of working—i.e., employed and paid—wives and mothers.[32] Through the imposition of a certain degree of inconvenience, it also ensured that that would be the case.

But there was little opposition to the laundry rules among the women. The postwar tendency toward conformity had already labeled women who worked outside the home as "deviant," thus further discouraging those women who might have attempted it, so that most of the women who moved to Levittown were already anticipating a domestic career.[33]

To either side of the Eckhoff house there are other houses just like it. In keeping with the Levitt covenant against fencing—natural or constructed—there is no division between the plots. The highly acclaimed fruit trees that Abraham Levitt had provided are still spindly, barely taller than the small shrubs which flank the door.[34] Behind the house the lawn stretches past the utility company's right-of-way and on up to the rear of the house beyond.

The openness of the lawn area suggests a lack of privacy. Yet, despite the presence of what sociologist William M. Dobriner has referred to as "the Visibility Principle" of postwar suburbia, the houses of Levittown were designed to be very private.[35] Each was centered on its own plot of 6000 square feet. The side door—the entrance into the kitchen—is on the right wall of the exterior of the house. (The kitchen entry was placed on the right of every house, where it faced the wall of the house next door.) A vestigial eight-foot length of split-rail fence separates this "service" area from the more formal front lawn. Trash was picked up at the street end of the service path in front of each house. There was no communal path, no common service area.

Each wife did her own laundry in her own washing machine in her own kitchen; each husband cared for his own patch of ground. Each nuclear family watched its own television in its own living room.

The privatization of the nuclear family unit did not extend to its individual members, however. Although privatized as households, the houses provided little or no internal privacy for the family members. Rather, the size, selection, and limit of four rooms combined to reinforce the values of family life that were being advocated at all levels in 1947—among them the return to the 'cult of domesticity'.

Domesticity

The social pressure toward homemaking for young women in the 1940s and 1950s has been explored rather thoroughly in the recent surge of interest in the history of women and the family.[36] Less well-developed has been the concomitant pressure on the young men of the period to marry and "settle down."[37]

The houses of the GI Bill imposed a subtle form of domesticity upon the young husbands, and by extension, the family unit, through the distribution of space. The privatization of the family through the individualization of their dwelling served to keep the nuclear unit intact, while limiting the opportunity for the rise of collective activity among the young men. There were few of the traditional male meeting places in early Levittown, and the weekend activities of home maintenance limited the free time of the young residents—particularly during the rental years, when Levitt could dictate the tasks.[38] The community facilities provided by the builder were focused on the assumed needs of women and children; "village greens" provided shopping areas with playgrounds, pools, and—later—schools. Levitt had also included a community meeting house at one of the village greens.[39] By shaping the available recreation, these sites served to limit large-group activities in Levittown to those which were essentially domestic, that is, child- and family-centered. These institutions, predicated by the recommendations of the FHA, were oriented toward the needs of a nuclear family.[40]

This emphasis on family closeness was atypical among young families of both the lower-middle and working classes in the period.[41] It was more common for the men to gather in male-oriented locations such as bars, firehouses, gas stations, or ball fields.[42] Levittown in the early days lacked these staples of male bonding.

Instead, it imposed a form of domesticity that was gaining popularity among the social reformers of the popular press as "togetherness."[43] Variously defined by such slogans as "the family that prays together, stays together," or "the family that plays together stays together," the emphasis in the 1940s and '50s was on the family, domesticity, and the single-family dwelling, a renewal of the "haven in a heartless world" of the late nineteenth century.[44]

In early Levittown, it might well have been said that the family that *stays* together, stays together. For Levittowners in the early years, togetherness was inherent in their houses. Like their apartment-dwelling urban cousins, the Levittown family gathered around the same table in the kitchen, watched the same television in the living room, and retired to the same sleeping quarters (adults to the larger bedroom, children to the smaller).

Combined with the lack of external gathering places for the men, the size of the house all but forced the young couple to spend most of their recreational time together. The design of the house contained all that was necessary for suburban living, but it was not sufficient. The houses lacked the standard equipment like garages, basements, dining rooms, or pantries, as well as the accessory spaces like dens, family rooms, libraries, solariums, or porches associated with upper middle-class suburban homes.

The lack of separate male space in both the houses and the community (den, garage, or game room in the houses; bars, pool halls, or clubs in the community) reinforced the emphasis on togetherness. There was simply no place else to go—at least in the beginning. Within months, the front lawn would begin to pinch-hit as the suburban equivalent of the corner bar.

The Agrarian Myth

The lawn itself represents another form of male domesticity, rooted in the nineteenth-century myth of the yeoman farmer, which perpetuated the vision of an agrarian America long after industrialization had taken hold. Despite the reduction in its interior space, each house was set on a minimum of 6000 square feet of land—50 percent more than the minimum 4000 square feet of property required by the building code of Hempstead.[45] Levittown's 6000-foot lot minimum is clearly a postwar innovation in Long Island housing developments. The apparent contradiction in including an extra 2000 square feet of land while reducing nonessential elements in the house also underscores the intrinsic value of the Arcadian setting to the fulfillment of the American Dream.[46]

The Levitts reinforced this aspect of the myth by landscaping the plots and including four fruit trees as part of the landscape for each house and then including in the tenants' agreement the obligation of maintaining the landscape.[47] Unlike the apartment-dwelling Ralph Kramden, who was free to spend his evenings at the lodge with his brothers, the young men of Levittown had lawns to mow, bushes to trim, and furniture to refinish.[48]

The houses encouraged a second form of male domesticity. This was the promotion of do-it-yourself home production. Due in part to the shortage of labor induced by the postwar building boom, manufacturers instituted a marketing strategy to move such materials as paint, flooring, plumbing fixtures, and the like that encouraged the homeowner to "do it Yourself!"[49]

The postwar technology introduced, among other advances, Dow Chemical's new latex-based paints, which were water soluble and dried to the touch in less than an hour. Ads for Kem-Tone Paints promised that the homeowner could turn "this drab room" into "this," a completely redecorated room, in only an hour.[50]

Some of the projects suggested were more extensive. For example, Bird Armorlite and Linoleum ran an advertisement that showed a young couple making plywood dadoes, refinishing old furniture, and painting walls and floors—"together."[51] The magazines supported their advertisers with articles telling "how to" and suggesting further projects for the couple to do, "together." In 1948 and 1949, *Household* ran articles telling young husbands how to build bedroom furniture using "the new resin plastic type of glue" developed during the war.[52]

The original size of the Levittown houses virtually demanded that they be enlarged in order to correspond to the customary middle-class homes of the period. Although the earliest residents were not expected to have adolescent children when they moved in, the probability that they would still be in Levittown when their children reached that stage demanded at least the opportunity for separate gender-ordered bedrooms. American children, when of different gender, were (and are) expected to have separate sleeping quarters before puberty.[53] The expansion attic was therefore included—to be finished by the residents at such time as it became necessary or affordable.[54] In December, Levitt's press release "suggested" that the tenants might be allowed to turn the attic into bedrooms.[55] Indeed, Levitt expected the residents, whether homeowners or tenants, to do some form of remodeling. His press releases, allowing the tenants to build garages and finish the attics, were clear invitations to enlarge the houses.

In addition, the combination of larger plots and smaller houses served as a spur to the construction of ells and outbuildings as the young families outgrew the basic house.[56] Moreover, the standardized products that had enabled Levitt to mass-produce the houses at Levittown also enabled a handy young man to take on the job of remodeling the house without too much training.

Although the basic Levitt Cape Cod was a clear invitation to home remodeling through addition, no practical space was provided in which to do the work. There was no ancillary space—no garage, no basement, no shed—to provide the workshop for the household. The unfinished attic, which could have served—and indeed, in many cases *did* serve—in this capacity, was not fit for such use in its original state, having no flooring other than a service catwalk.[57] In practice, however, since the wife was obliged to hang her weekend wash indoors to dry, rather than offend the sensibilities of her neighbors, the attic was often used as an alternative.[58] Thus, there was little opportunity for it to become a male workshop or refuge.

Rather than just supporting "do-it-yourself" as a form of recreation, the Levittown Cape Cod, through its lack of amenities, virtually demanded it. There is reason to suspect that this may not have been an accidental aspect of the housing programs. It might well have been as much a political as an economic decision to provide the residents with so much to do. Levitt's statement, quoted in Larrabee, that a homeowner cannot be a Communist "because he has too much to do" suggests that the housing programs that funded Levittown were intended as much to defuse the potential for political subversion as to house the veterans.

By December, when Levitt was urging even the tenants to renovate, he seems to have had a second agenda. By this time he had begun the move, outlined earlier, to divest his company of all rental housing. The tenants' investment of money and effort into finishing the attics and building garages would be an economic advantage only to the owner of the house, since lease agreements uniformly held that materials attached to a dwelling became the property of the landlord. By permitting his tenants to make such an investment, Levitt increased the likelihood that they would want to purchase the house rather than move from it when he was ready to sell.[59]

Private Property: Own Your Own Home

By early 1948, there was a concerted effort to encourage all of Levitt's tenants to buy their own house. This effort, like most of Levitt's activities with his tenants, was announced first in the local papers. Although the *Eagle* headline focused on the possibility of selling the houses, the text of the story was reassuring to those who still preferred to rent.

> If, and a big "if," our homes are offered for sale at the end of our first-year leases, they will only be offered to the veterans who now occupy those homes. In any case we are protected by the Levitt policy of "doing what we can for our former buddies." Mr. Levitt . . . informed an Eagle reporter that, even if the homes are for sale, the present occupants need not buy. "All those who wish to renew their leases for another year will be permitted to do so."[60]

Nevertheless, the rules of the game were changing; the persuasion to purchase had begun.[61] In the December 18 issue, the *Eagle's* Veterans Advisor column explored the general implications of the GI

Bill loan guarantees; the mortgage sections of the bill were not stressed. In the following weeks, the Veterans Advisor initiated a series of columns explaining those terms and conditions of the loan guarantees of the bill which would facilitate the purchase of "a home."[62] Although this was presented as purely informational, the move to turn Levitt's tenants into homeowners had begun in earnest.

If the lure of homeowning did not succeed in convincing the tenants to buy the houses, a second strategy might. Under the headline "Will Raise Rents to $65 at End of Lease," the Levitt press release presented a lengthy discussion of the need for the corporation to break even[63] and a reminder that the rental program had only been a temporary solution to a crisis situation.[64]

Despite the optimistic attitude toward the opportunity to purchase the houses that was expressed in the *Eagle's* editorials and columns, homeowning was not universally desired by the residents. The *Levittown Tribune* carried several letters to the editor and a column deploring Levitt's efforts to "force home ownership on 'unsuspecting' veterans."[65] These public expressions of dissent remained a minority, however.

Within a year the rental arm of Levitt's organization, Bethpage Realty, had sold the 6000 Cape Cods—either to the tenants, or as part of the divestment of the rental units in a major sale to Junto Realty.

From October 1947 until the spring of 1949, the Cape Cod was the only house Levittown offered.[66] It was a rental unit, modeled after the suggested patterns of the FHA. When the Levitts shifted from Cape Cods for rent to ranches for sale, in 1949, they had begun to build their "new town." The difference between the two stages reflects several differences in outlook toward the houses, the residents, and the community. In 1947, the houses were deliverer-designed, traditional in structure and style, and imposed upon a shelter-hungry population of young workers in need of rental housing. And they were primarily aimed at men.

There were five models from which to choose. This distinction between identical interiors and variations in exterior design reflects an important difference between the social orientations of men and women toward their houses in the 1940s. For men the house was primarily a place to which to come, whereas for women it was a place in which to be.[67] This difference is directly related to the cultural gender roles vis-a-vis the home; men left it to go to work, women worked within it. Men returned to the house from their work, women left the house to "get away" from theirs. Men were the house-providers; how well they provided was largely determined by the size, construction, and aesthetic ornamentation of the dwelling. Moreover, men's standing in the community was assessed by the public aspects of their home—the economic value of the house—the house as possession. Hence, the focal point of male interest in their houses tended to be on the exterior. Magazines directed at men stressed this difference in perspective with articles related to lawn care, garden furniture construction, and garage maintenance.[68]

This distinction between gender-related design perspectives is readily apparent in contemporary architectural commentary on the Levittown construction. In the trade journals, there were repeated references to Levitt's five models and to the variety of colors on the façades, etc. Little notice was taken in either the Levitt-generated articles or those written by architectural and housing critics of the fact that the interiors, as delivered, were literally interchangeable: the floor tile in every house through 1951 was black asphalt "Kentile"; the cabinets and appliances, white-enameled steel. Even the candle motif in the stairrail and over the kitchen cabinets in the Cape Cod models was unvaried from one house to another. Yet, even within the mass-produced organization of Levittown, some variation in interior scheme could have been achieved, at less cost than the exterior variations the firm provided. The mere rotation of the house plan on its axis would have offered some variation in interior space. None was provided; the emphasis was on the external appearances.

Men judged houses by these external standards, the public image of the house. Women, on the other hand, were the homemakers. They were judged by the interior aspects of their house: its cleanliness and its decorative appeal. Magazines directed at women focused on such activities as furniture arrangement, decorative detail, sanitized kitchen and bath areas, and products designed to facilitate their housekeeping.[69]

More attention was given to the placement of windows to achieve balance or mass in the exterior elevations than to the eventual placement of furniture, organization of window dressing, or interior lighting that would be affected by such placement. Similarly, doors were treated as visual elements in the organization of exterior design. Little or no consideration was given to the traffic pattern they would engender.[70]

The Levitts' design variations were far more concerned with

3.3

Architect's renderings of five versions of the 1947 Cape Cod model. (NCM)

(a)

(d)

(b)

(e)

(c)

differences in site-orientation, façade design, and landscaping as marketing strategies than with differences in room design, floor-plan, and the articulation of interior space. These houses, after all, were built for "*Mr*. Kilroy."[71]

Market and Design: The Ranch

In the fall of 1948, the housing market was changing. With 6000 Cape Cods already built and more projected, the Levitt Corporation faced a new challenge. The FHA had been sending signals of concern about "market saturation" for several months. Its officials believed that the market was becoming glutted with mass-produced, small-scale houses that were no longer satisfying the needs of the target population. They began to question the advisibility of funding any further projects of the nature of Levittown. Such signals indicated changes to come, both in policy and in funding. Whether or not the housing crisis had been solved, the market for Levitt-type rental housing appeared to be softening, and the government was rethinking its role in the housing market.

Meanwhile the Levitts had acquired considerable additional property in the Levittown area on which they had planned to continue building. Rather than lose on this investment, they began a market-oriented study of their product.[72] While it was underway, the Levitts responded to the changes in housing legislation coming out of Washington by divesting the firm of all rental properties. They then began construction of the 1949 ranch models and the balance of Levittown, solely for the sales market.

Two factors in housing legislation in 1949 made it not only practical but profitable for Levitt to move out of the rental business. First, the Housing Act of 1949 extended the rent controls of the 1947 bill until June 1950. Even more important, the new public housing strand of the Housing Act threatened to place both federal and local governments in competition with any private-sector landlord whose houses rented for $65 a month.[73]

At the same time, the act so liberalized the purchase terms on low-cost houses with Government-guaranteed mortgages

that in many cases buying a house [was] now as easy as renting it. The new terms: 5% down (nothing down for veterans) and 30 years to pay. Thus an ex-G.I. could buy a Levitt house with no down payment and installments of only $60 a month.[74]

In order to continue building and selling, Levitt designed the next generation of houses—the 1949 through 1951 ranch models—for the buying market, modifying both the exterior styling and the floor plan. The firm spent "upwards of $50,000" in research and redesign before they brought out their 1949 models of the Levittown house.[75]

The physical geography of the new Levittown reflected their response to the emerging buyers' market. Whereas the 1947/48 Levittown had responded to the housing shortage with basic housing in an approved variety, the easing of the shortage demanded more marketability in the 1949 section of the development. As a result, more subtle lures were built into the post-1948 sections of Levittown.

The redesign began with the layout of the house lots and roadways. The 1947 street pattern of mildly curved streets ending in T-intersections had been called for by the FHA as a means of reducing the flow and speed of traffic. In 1949 this pattern was replaced by one with much more strongly curved streets and cul-de-sacs. The new street layout resulted in irregular plot shapes and sizes, a more expensive but more marketable use of available land.[76] On Long Island's north shore, where the terminal moraine produced rolling hills with venerable oak trees, the use of a curvilinear street pattern is an economic necessity as well as a more natural adaptation to the landscape. On the vast flat expanses of the Hempstead Plain, the curvilinear street is an artifice. As Robert Stern put it, the grid, curved gently, "adapts the reality of real estate to the illusion of country living."[77] By mimicking the street pattern of his more affluent North Shore communities, Levitt added an upscale illusion to a low-cost development. The new pattern did not actually produce an increase in pedestrian safety. Instead, the safety factor was exaggerated to enhance product appeal.

Levitt adapted other elements of affluent suburbs to the 1949 version of Levittown. In the exclusive nineteenth-century suburban development, Llewelyn Park, the developer Llewelyn Haskell had created "natural" water bodies, creeks, and ponds to produce an idyllic setting for the upper middle-class homes he built there. Less expensive, but equally marketable, are the total of nine swimming pools that Levitt built for Levittown.

At the heart of Llewelyn Park is a 50-acre "ramble." This highly manicured garden area is modeled after Alexander Jackson Davis's concept of enhanced natural beauty; Levittown provided seven "village greens" with playgrounds and lawns as well as shopping and

(a) Basic 1949 ranch at Levittown ($7,990). (b) Ranch model at Country Club Estates, Roslyn, 1949. (NCM)

(a)

(b)

The recoup of the investment in redesign was not limited to the Levittown houses. Levitt & Sons built a more expensive development, Country Club Estates, at Roslyn, which incorporated many of the new concepts in houses selling for at least a third more than the Levittown ranches.

pools. The new attention to the visual and cultural enhancement of Levittown coincided with the transition from rental to proprietary housing, as well as with the weakening of the housing market.[78] If Levitt were to continue to produce low-cost housing under the favorable financing afforded by the FHA and VA housing programs, he would have to make the development salesworthy, too.

Levitt understood his market; the young lower-income white- and blue-collar workers who would perceive Levittown as their permanent home.[79] It was to these people that Levitt addressed his weekly press conferences, filled with advice, admonitions, and suggestions for better living in Levittown—young people who worked in the service sector as clerks or teachers, or in factories on the assembly lines of Long Island's aircraft industry.

In his discussions of Levittown, Levitt stressed the firm's total "redesign" of their 1949 models. Although they remained, like the Cape Cods, one-and-a-half story cottages, there are significant differences between the 1947 Cape Cod and the model he called "the forty-niner."[80] Levitt's research was successful in identifying the housing elements necessary to sell in what was rapidly becoming a buyers' market; the ranch houses sold as briskly as the Capes had rented—often to the same people.[81]

The forty-niner is thus a better indicator of the residents' values than is the Cape Cod. The Cape was deliverer-designed, officially approved, and aimed at a sellers' market of crisis proportions.[82] The forty-niner, on the other hand, was tailored by the builder to the preferences of a softened market before it was approved by the official chain of bankers, insurers, and government. A contrast of the elements that were changed with those which were retained suggests the slight shifting in power between deliverer and consumer which continued throughout the building of the 1950/1951 ranch models, as well.

In October 1949, *Newsday* visited Al and Anita Utt and their two children in the family's "type-four 1949 ranch" model house in Levittown.[83] The Utts had moved into their new home in July, just a few weeks after the new models were advertised for sale.[84] At the time of the *Newsday* article, Al Utt had recently given up commuting to Manhattan for a more convenient job working on the tail assembly of planes at Republic Aircraft in nearby Farmingdale. The Utts represent the second wave of Levittown residents—those who came to buy, rather than to rent.[85]

None of the ranches, the last 11,500 of the 17,500 houses built in Levittown, were built as rental units, and they differed from the

(a) Architect's rendering of basic 1949 ranch model. (NCM) (b) Floor plan CAD sketch. (Author)

(a)

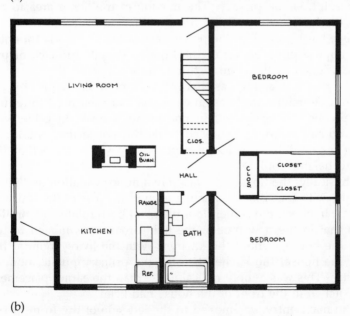

(b)

Capes in several key aspects. The house itself was 50 square feet larger than the Cape. The additional footage provided for larger bedrooms. The remaining changes primarily involved the public/semi-public areas of the house: the exterior elevation, the kitchen, and the living room.

The concept of a ranch house—traditionally, a long, low building—was reflected in the exterior design and trim, rather than in the substance of the house plan. The balanced symmetry of the Cape Cod, with its centered door and vertical double-hung windows, was replaced by an asymmetrical arrangement of the front wall. Asbestos shingles ran across the lower half of the front wall, creating an illusion of the horizontal lines found in a true ranch house. This horizontality was reinforced visually by the wide, sliding windows that were set into the upper half of the façade.

Several basic elements of the Cape Cod model were retained in the new ranches. These include the position of the kitchen in the front of the house, the two first-floor bedrooms with room to expand in the attic, and the use of enamelled-steel kitchen cabinetry.

Other elements were added or modified that contributed to a greater emphasis on privacy. The moving of the living area to the rear of the house while raising the street-facing bedroom windows above eye level, as well as the persistence of the single site for entry doors, impose privatization of the houses, despite the lack of privacy occasioned by the large picture windows.

The roof was as high as that of the Cape to allow for attic expansion, but architectural design elements had been used to reduce the impression of verticality. In one model a reversed gable with board-and-batten siding was used to tie the eye to the ground. In another a raised half-shed roof reduced the visual impact of the standard height roof line.

Physically, the floor plan was only a minor variation on that of the Cape, with four rooms radiating around the axis of the stairway and bath. In effect, the earlier floor plan had been rotated 90° on this axis so that in the new model, the living room was moved to the rear of the house, behind the kitchen. With the living room at the rear of the house, the kitchen became the primary public room of the house. This was a more radical move than the earlier placement of the kitchen in the front of the house had been.

The main entry was moved to the left side of the front of the house, where a three-foot square cut out of the corner of the room permitted the addition of a small exterior foyer before entering the kitchen. Thus, the kitchen, which remained in the front, became the

Comparison of basic floor plans. The 1947 Cape Cod is shown here with its floor plan rotated 90°. In that rotation, it duplicates the room arrangement of the 1949 ranch. (a) 1947 Cape Cod. (b) 1949 Ranch. (c) 1947 Cape Cod rotated 90°.

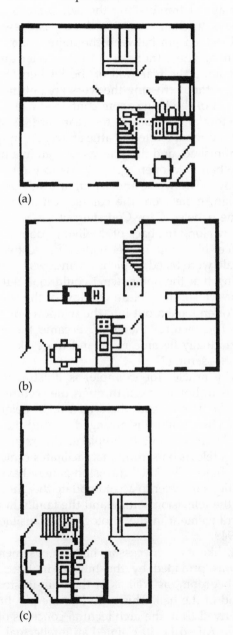

(a)

(b)

(c)

public entryway.[86] The resulting arrangement of traffic patterns in the kitchen was a considerable improvement over that of the Cape. The entry door aimed traffic along the side wall toward the living room at the rear of the house or toward the passageway to the bedrooms and hall, which ran between the living room and the work area of the kitchen. Thus, traffic could flow either directly into the living room, or along the rear wall of the kitchen toward the bedrooms and bath without crossing the work area of the kitchen.

The rear wall of the living room contained a large floor-to-ceiling picture window and a door to the rear yard. A stairway along the side wall of the room led to the attic above. As in the Cape Cod, the attic was unfinished, and the staircase ended in a trapdoor in the ceiling which, when held open, gave access to the unheated, uninsulated area above. The wood and wrought-iron stairrail was more modern in design; gone were the colonial candle motifs that had adorned the pine-paneled Cape Cod stairrail.

The window along the back of the living room was commercial in scale: eight feet high and 16 feet wide. The postwar windows of this size and scale were billed as picture windows by most manufacturers, suggesting that the homeowner could look out at the sylvan view beyond the walls. The picture window of the suburban house, however, most often looked out into the windows of another house just like itself. The picture, therefore, became the interior of the house, which gradually became more and more like a stage—or in 1949, a television—setting.[87]

The *Newsday* article, for example, is illustrated with a large photo of the Utts at home, taken through the picture window. The picture shows the family and their next-door neighbors visiting around the fire. The furniture is arranged around the room to clear the view from picture window to fireplace. Chairs are standing free of the wall, like a television setting that facilitates camera—or in this case, window—angle. The Utts' furnishings may have been moved from other positions in order to accommodate the photographer, but the merging of the television setting and the family home had made the resulting arrangement in the photograph plausible to *Newsday's* readership in 1949.

The ranch, like its predecessor, had no basement and no garage. Storage was provided by the builder in the floor-to-ceiling closets in each bedroom, as well as in the built-in storage center at the bedroom end of the hall. This unit, like the pivoting unit in the kitchen, was derived from the architectural concepts of Frank Lloyd Wright, to whom Alfred Levitt claimed an intellectual debt.[88]

Wright is also credited with the concept of the kitchen hearth as center of the home, recreating the colonial hearth, but introducing the idea of the open kitchen that permitted the mother/housekeeper to remain within the public areas of the home.[89] This concept gained considerable popularity in the home and garden magazines of the 1950s, but Levitt was the first to introduce it in the setting of a basic four-room house. This combination of the kitchen fireplace and the kitchen entry marked the kitchen as primary public space, like the great hall of the medieval period. In so doing, it paralleled the transition of housework from backstairs to public space, and the concomitant acknowledgment of the housewife as an important actor in America's new commercial villages.[90] This recognition led to a series of products and advertisements directed at the middle-class consumer. In the postwar period this realization was augmented by the recognition that the lower-income housewife and her family represented a new economic tier of consumption.[91]

As with other products, the 1949 Levittown ranch houses reflected the producer's concern with marketing to this new tier. The deliverer-designed house was no longer sufficient, even at the most basic economic levels of the market. Care must be taken to tailor the product to the consumer's needs and desires.[92] Levittown's market-driven redesign evolved over the final three years of construction as the basic ranch of 1949 became the core of the newer models. An important aspect of this evolution was the inclusion of luxury accessories in a moderately-priced house. The fireplace, for example, was rarely included in the houses of surbuban Long Island, even those aimed at residents of a significantly higher income level than that of Levittown.

In the 1950 and 1951 models, the persistence of the market-driven redesigning can be seen in the addition of carports, built-in televisions, and a third bedroom to the design of the 1949 ranch model.[93] Although in marketing terms, the 1950/1951 ranches were different, offering as a standard package far more in the way of amenities such as carports,[94] built-in television[95] and a finished attic room, in addition to the fireplace (introduced in the 1949 model) and the appliances (standard since the 1947 Cape Cod), the floor plan remained that of the 1949 ranch. Although the carports were a structural addition, there was no major distinction among the yearly models of the ranch in the arrangement of the interior space or the treatment of the façade.

Therefore, although the nature of their differences clearly underscores the strength of the emerging buyer's market, the ranches represent a single phase of the evolution of Levittown. Although the Cape Cod was acceptable as rental housing when shelter was desperately needed, the ranch offered its buyers more of the elements that reinforced and reflected their concept of domestic life.[96]

The biggest change in the design was the addition, in the 1950 ranch, of the carport. There were important practical reasons for including it. The Korean War, looming on the 1950 horizon, restored the military-industrial complex to its wartime importance. Aircraft and armament manufacturers such as Sperry, Grumman, Republic, Fairchild-Hiller, and their subcontractors would be needing workers once again, many of whom would become the third wave of Levittowners. For these workers, there would be no commutation by train to Manhattan; they would have to drive to work. The men of Levittown needed cars; moreover, they could afford them. Thus, the car and its shelter, emblematic of middle-class suburbia, moved to Levittown.

The carport became an incipient garage, a male place in the otherwise female world of suburbia. Many of the memories shared by the Levittown informants included comments about the pioneer days when the men would assist each other in do-it-yourself home or auto repair.[97]

The carport had economic as well as social implications. By 1950 both Levitt and the Levittowners had become much more sensitive to criticism of the development, its houses, and its residents. If Levittown were to overcome the stigma of its low-cost origins, it would have to avoid the devaluing aspect of young men doing auto repairs or cars parked haphazardly on the lawns. The carport, and later the garage, provided an acceptable location for such work. Suburban communities, conscious of the subtleties of property values, discourage residents from doing repair work in the open. The carport served to combine practicality with marketability.

By 1950 the nature of life in Levittown was such that despite the existence of the stores at the village greens, most of the Levittown housewives needed to drive to get to the larger shopping areas. Even shopping at the greens would be more efficient for the car-driving shopper. The urban concept of picking up the daily needs while walking the baby in its buggy was not applicable to Levittown. Distances were greater, and the babies had become children, with practical and social needs of their own. Moreover, the daily life of the women of Levittown differed markedly from the putative life of their urban sisters. These women were actively engaged in a variety of activities, from establishing a nursery school to running the PTA. Their time was too valuable—not only to themselves and their families, but also to the community—for them to spend it in a daily stroll to the market. Shopping was simply a chore, and like all chores, it was best handled through the use of a machine. The two-car family became part of Levittown's scene.

Meanwhile, the built-in television can only be viewed as a marketing device, an expensive one at that. The cost of the television, added into the price of the house, was therefore amortized over the length of the mortgage, so that the homeowner would still be paying for the set long after it had become obsolete or broken.

Although many of the innovations that Levitt included in the ranch models contained elements which addressed some of the needs of the women of Levittown, the house was still primarily designed for those women who played the traditional role as homemaker/wife. Moreover, they were consistently marketed to her husband.[98] The redesign included no accommodations for working mothers; the pools and playgrounds were not set up to provide day care. Similarly, the houses were not receptive to single mothers; the house-and-grounds maintenance all but demanded the heavy labor of a husband.[99]

The restrictions on wash-lines, fences, and shrubbery imposed by the Levitts in the lease agreements, and later covenanted into the deeds, as well as the introduction of the family hearth, reinforced Levittown as a document for what most Americans believed a home and community should be. The young, nuclear families, in their similar (but distinct), privatized (but conforming) houses, living in their do-it-yourself domesticity, were the ideal model for the young, American family of modest means in the postwar period.

The greatest boom in domestic building in America took place in the ten years following the construction of Levittown. This period was one in which the cult of domesticity—Betty Friedan's "feminine mystique"—was resurrected at many levels, official and popular. Yet, throughout the period, both government and industry had overlooked the insights of women—particularly homemaking women—into the design of the working environment in which they would be making that home.

It was not until 1956 that the advice and counsel of home-making women were taken seriously as a basis for future home design. The Housing and Home Finance Agency's Women's Congress on Housing, held in the spring of that year, addressed the question of what the nature of residential housing should be.

4

THE HOUSE BECOMES A HOME

In 1956 the Housing and Home Finance Agency, under the direction of Albert M. Cole, convened the first Women's Congress on Housing in Washington. The congress was charged with a retrospective evaluation of housing in America, the purpose of which was to discover what American families—and in particular their homemakers—needed and wanted in their houses.

There were several ironies inherent in the organization of this congress that reveal the hold that the nuclear family in a single-family house had on the American psyche in the period. The assumptions that shaped the congress, and the underlying question on which it was convened, limited the discussion to those elements which women—as housewives and mothers—wanted or needed in the design of the single-family house. No alternatives to this particular family model and form of shelter were under consideration. Taken for granted was the wife as the domestic worker, the husband as breadwinner, and children in the earlier years of childhood.[1] Neither apartment houses nor two-family houses were considered. Indeed, a careful reading of the agenda shows that its structure was geared only to a reappraisal and redesign of those postwar suburban houses and families typified by Levittown.[2]

It is also ironic that the women were not consulted until after the peak years of the postwar building boom;[3] their responses came too late to alter the design of the majority of the houses built and financed under the terms and restrictions of the FHA, VEHP, and VA. The congress was, however, well timed to permit better marketing strategies for the builders and designers of the second generation of FHA/VA-financed housing: the houses being built for those about to make the first move up in housing.[4]

The HHFA never convened a comparable congress of men as homeowners. No doubt a masculine viewpoint was taken as a given in the design process, since men had been part of it from the beginning—as builders, bankers, and real estate developers, as well as members of the Congressional finance committees.[5] What this assumption overlooked is the fact that those men who were originally involved in the design process had acted as providers rather than consumers of housing when they contributed their insights to the postwar housing policies and designs. Moreover, as a group these men could well afford to have their home customized to their needs when they decided to purchase one. As a result, there was no vehicle for the expression of the needs of the man of average means; the carpenter or mechanic-turned-home-owner often found himself in what amounted to a freestanding four-room apartment with neither garage nor basement in which to pursue his interests.

Although the women did not, perhaps could not, address the housing needs of their husbands, they did formulate an important agenda for housing in the future. And with it, they expressed a general consensus with both the criticisms being leveled at the design of the rudimentary FHA/VA four-room house and the underlying assumptions of the congress. Although they redesigned many structural aspects of the houses, they accepted the program of government-guaranteed housing in the form of the single-family dwelling as a given.

The 103 members of the congress were divided into ten groups. Nine groups were representative of various regions across the country; the tenth was a composite group that was used to gauge the importance of regional influence in the decision making of the other nine. The groups were asked to discuss the questions from three perspectives—minimum needs, regional adaptations, and general desires—in analyzing what they considered to be appropriate in the arrangement of domestic space for a single-family house. The economy house—based on minimum needs—was allotted a working budget of $10,000, "exclusive of improved lot" with a ceiling of $20,000.[6] At the time, a basic Levittown Cape Cod, with improved lot, was selling for about $11,000.[7]

There were distinctions made between elements the congress determined as essential to the economy house and those which would be added if money permitted; "needs" at the low end and "desires" at the high end. Even at the low end, however, the "needs" of the congress participants were more elaborate than those provided in the basic houses at Levittown.

The design of the Levitts' postwar houses had resulted in two major changes from their prewar middle-class houses. First the house had been divested of all that was deemed unessential. Then,

what remained—living room, kitchen, two bedrooms, and bath—
had been reduced to affordable dimensions.

Although reduced in volume, the spatial distribution among
the rooms remained substantially the same; the Levitt living room is
192 square feet, and the kitchen is 100 square feet. The two-to-one
ratio of space allotted to these two rooms was consistent with the
roles played by these rooms in the prewar middle class home. It
reflects the division between 'frontstairs' and 'backstairs'—formal
and informal, public and semiprivate space that had been typical of
middle-class American suburbs since the Civil War. The parlor, in
which the family gathered and entertained, was large, to reflect their
social standing, whereas the smaller kitchen and/or servants' quarters were intended for production and were rarely seen by guests.[8]
However, in such houses, both rooms would have been considerably larger than those found in the postwar houses. The spatial ratio
of these two rooms in smaller, prewar "workingman's houses"
might appear to have been similar to the Levitt houses, but that
similarity is deceptive. In such houses, the kitchens were generally
augmented with auxiliary space such as pantries, breakfast nooks,
back porches, etc. Similarly, the available public space would also
have included a dining room and a foyer or enclosed front porch.
Although formal activities were options that could be scaled down
to suit the size of the space allocated to them, the production and
storage requirements of the kitchen remained constant—indeed, in
many cases increased, as the size of the house itself was decreased.
Maintaining the prewar ratio between kitchen and parlor was therefore counterproductive in the greatly reduced layout and dimensions of the postwar houses. This was especially so if the houses
were to remain as delivered. In reality, the need for these spatial
distributions even in middle class homes had become more illusory
than real by the end of the Depression. Alison Ravitz points out that

> For the relations of women to their house, 1950 marked the
> close of one era and the opening of another. The date, one of
> historical convenience, is chosen because by then two things of
> fundamental significance had occurred: the middle-class wife
> had finally and irrevocably lost her servants, and the working-
> class wife had acquired, or was in the process of acquiring, a
> house to look after.[9]

Indeed, by 1950 only one house in 42 still employed domestic servants; middle-class women were doing almost all of their domestic
work alone.[10]

Shaping the Middle Class Lifestyle

The spatial distribution in the Levittown house reflects other aspects of the cultural assumptions of the postwar period. The large living room at the expense of needed work space in the kitchen exemplifies the new mentality toward the nature of housework that found its voice in magazines and advice columns devoted to girls and women in the 1940s and 1950s. Gone was the homemaker-as-domestic-engineer that had dominated the women's magazines in the 1920s and 1930s.[11] Gone, too, was the wage-earning Rosie the Riveter. Cary Grant's movie for 1947 was *Every Girl Should Be Married*, and "married" indicated a well-defined social and economic role—at home.

From *Seventeen* to *Woman's Day*, the new advice stressed the female's role as the soft, romantic partner.[12] Girls were urged to become interested in their boyfriends' activities. Hairstyles, makeup, and clothing dominated the advertising in these journals, and the text of the articles reinforced the need for such products. The columns were filled with ways to lure men and boys away from purely male pursuits. Wives were urged to keep the charm in their marriages, to listen with interest to their husbands' conversation, and to remain physically attractive—all the while raising children and keeping house as if they had a staff of servants.

The popular music of the period reinforced the passive role for women in its romantic imagery. The subject of Irving Berlin's "The Girl that I Marry" was loved for such characteristics as being as soft and sweet and kittenlike.[13]

The lyrics to Oscar Hammerstein II's hit song of 1947, "A Fellow Needs a Girl," encapsulated the woman-as-audience view of marriage: advising her to sit and listen when he talks agreeing with what he has to say.[14] Those suburban women who strove to follow this advice were dressed and pretty, finished with their work, and ready to listen by suppertime when their men arrived home from work.

And for those young girls who dared to miss the point, there was the tragic story of the "Ballerina," who went on with her career. The price she paid, of course, was the loss of her lover.[15]

In keeping with this wife-as-romantic-partner image, children were to be kept in the background when husbands were home. According to the expert advisors, the children were to be fed and ready for bed, spend a few minutes with Daddy, and then go on to radio, television, or sleep.[16] Dinner was to be on the stove, ready to serve, and the wife was to be prettily dressed, combed, and made up, ready to greet her husband. Those women who managed to achieve this mythic state of romantic readiness also managed to convey the impression that there was no work involved in keeping house. It was as if they spent their days like Sleeping Beauty, graciously awaiting the return of their men to waken them from their lifeless state. Husbands were never to see them at work.[17] It was as if the work of housekeeping had gone with the servants. The number of articles suggesting handwork to fill the housewife's days matched those that were aimed at the Victorian woman whose staff maintained the household. The successful maintenance of this fiction of the nonworking wife was reinforced by the reduction of the space allotted to domestic work in the new houses.

Paradoxically, at the same time that the production area of the typical house was being radically reduced, women were being urged as never before to a greater level of production, to "accomplish" something at home in their "free" time. The magazines offered a myriad of projects for the new homemakers—redoing furniture; canning one's own produce; making curtains, aprons, overalls, and lace edgings on handkerchiefs, or creating recipes to enter in the Pillsbury Bake-offs. But these activities were presented as recreation; time fillers, rather than meaningful production.

"Pick-up Work," a monthly column in the family-oriented magazine *Household*, offered two activities: embroidery to imitate appliquéd gingham on dish towels, and crocheted lace tablecovers. For those with a social conscience, the work had further implications: "These little cheer-ups sell like hot cakes at your bazaar table too."[18] In its December 1949 issue, *American Home* suggested applying decals to kitchen cabinets and constructing built-in storage cabinets.[19] Home remodeling was the focus of their January issue. Here, the magazine offered tips on basement refurbishing, in "Made Over for Fun . . ." (p. 39), and advised remodeling homeowners to "save the old kitchen" in an article entitled, "A Kitchen Makes a Wonderful Nursery" (p. 88). For the less venturesome, there was an article telling how to turn a wire coat hanger into a hat rack.[20] In February, the cover story featured "A One-Room Camp You Can Build Yourself" (p.24). They also insisted, "You *Have* a Sewing Room! Take a good look around . . ." (p. 33). For those who had no closets to convert into sewing rooms, they offered, "Everyone's Making Rugs Today!" (p.34).[21]

Woman's Day, at the time still a foods-promoting publication of the A&P Supermarket chain, picked up the promotion of handiwork and crafts with, "A Modern Embroidered Screen Adapted from an Old Peasant Design." This piece advised the housewife that "The design is so simple you may be able to work it directly from the picture; for the beauty of this kind of handwork is that you don't have to aim for perfection, but can do it as it pleases you . . . ."[22]

Similarly, their husbands were being urged to spend their weekends making and remaking furniture, or using a can of paint to change anything old and useless into something new and desirble.[23] Yet the only space appropriate to productive work in the four-room houses was in the kitchen.

Thus, the families who lived in these postwar houses were expected to use their kitchen much as our colonial forebears had done, as the semipublic great hall or major gathering room in the house.[24] When the women of the Congress on Housing designed their versions of the economy house, they cut back on the space allotted to the formal living room in order to provide what they considered essential space in the kitchen.[25] This apparently simple transfer of superfluous floor space from the public area to a place of greater need in the semipublic area appeared at the time to be a simple economic decision. One found the needed extra room without having to add to the cost of the basic house.

This would suggest that the FHA/VA and Levitt had overlooked an obvious, cost-free selling point when they designed the houses of the subdivision suburbs. However, such a transformation would have been at odds with an important motivation underlying the programs that funded the postwar subdivision suburbs: the political need to expand the propertied classes.[26]

Basic to an understanding of the distinctions between the consequences of the space reversal and the nature of the houses that were provided at Levittown is a socioeconomic difference in interpreting the uses of domestic space. The difference between the spatial distribution in the deliverer-designed houses, with their large living room and smaller kitchen, and that recommended by the women at the congress reflected several important aspects of the American belief system. The American Character, a useful—if fictitious—entity that has been with us since Tocqueville, denies the existence of a class-stratified society. Americans believe themselves to be either middle- or upper-class—or on their way to being so.

When Alfred Levitt designed his four-room houses, he imposed a middle-class geography on them. The women of the congress, on the other hand, in shifting the balance between public and semi-public space, were designing their economy houses more in keeping with the traditions of the lower-income, i.e., working-class families. Moreover, they were acknowledging, however implicitly, their own 'proletarianization.' For the middle-class wife-as-household-manager had, since the 1920s, been steadily giving way to the 'Jane-of-all-trades' who cleaned, cooked, and laundered.[27]

No such connection between income and lifestyle was made, however, by the providers. From the earliest publications of the FHA, recommending approved designs to the builders, the ideal had been a reduction, rather than a reformulation, of the traditional middle-class floor plan.

Public space is a luxury. The larger public/formal space of the living room thus reflected a middle-class style of formal, if not ritualized, social life. In essence, if not in volume, the spatial designs of Levitt Cape Cods and ranches were symbolically middle-class. Had Levitt been designing a working-class dwelling, he could have replicated the traditional spatial allotment of the working-class tenement, in which formal space was discarded in favor of living space. Such a transition could have been as economical as the floor plan that he chose.

The simple substitution of a kitchen/family room for the living room would have released space for a third bedroom on the first floor. This bedroom could then have been rented to a boarder, thereby increasing the family's discretionary income, until such time as the children of the family needed the space. Had such a transformation taken place, there would have been no loss of real space, since working-class families generally do far less formal entertaining. Sociological studies of working-class suburbs have shown an important distinction in the visiting and entertaining patterns between families in the working and middle classes. Within the working class—particularly among first- and second-generation immigrants—the tendency is to limit entertaining and visiting to a marked degree to members of the extended family. Such interfamilial visiting is appropriate to "semipublic" or "semiprivate" space within the home.[28]

Traditionally, the immigrant family had gathered in the kitchen, the children studying at the table, the father reading his paper, the mother cooking, mending, or washing.[29] All other available space was allocated to sleeping. If there was more sleeping space than the family needed, it was quickly turned to income through the introduction of boarders.[30]

This image of domesticity is qualitatively different from the middle-class Victorian image of the lady at her embroidery in the drawing room, the father smoking his pipe in the library, and the children out of sight in the nursery upstairs. Middle-class entertaining was noted for the degree to which the guests were more likely to be unrelated—friends and acquaintances associated with one's college years, one's business, or one's community associations and clubs. This type of entertaining would take place in the public/formal areas of the home.[31]

The choice of the women of the congress to alter the ratio of space acknowledged these distinctions in economics, class, and lifestyle. At the practical level, a four-room house is insufficient to support a middle-class lifestyle. Since the kitchen was to serve not only as food preparation center, but also as dining room, family room, and entryway, the women agreed that it should take precedence over the less often-used living room, and they enlarged it accordingly.[32]

To have reversed the ratio between living room and kitchen in the actual economy houses—those like Levittown—would have radically altered the socioeconomic implications of their spatial interpretation as well. Such a transformation would have had economic consequences for the builder. Whereas social engineers might have created housing suitable for the lifestyle of workers and their families, private enterprise had to play to the market.[33]

Reversing the ratio between public/formal and semipublic/informal space would have facilitated a different social interaction, which would have identified the houses and their owners as working class. Not only would this have reduced their market value as a status symbol, it would have had political implications as well. "Worker housing" had no place in a democratic republic. Middle-class housing, even rudimentary middle-class housing, was more acceptable. And that is what was built under the terms of both the FHA and the GI Bill. Instead of rooms, the houses offered efficiency; instead of work space, they offered appliances.

Creating an Efficient Kitchen; The Impact of Gender

Even in the economy houses they designed, with their old-fashioned, all-purpose kitchens, the women of the Congress on Housing strongly objected to the use of the kitchen as laundry, arguing that cooking and laundering are incompatible uses of space. Faced with the choice, the women would rather have eliminated the appliances that the builders included in order to have the extra space for a laundry/utility room at the rear of the house. Indeed, many of the

women objected to the inclusion of the appliances as standard components of the houses. Not only would they have preferred to select
their own, but they argued that the builder-provided appliances became inordinately expensive when their initial cost was amortized
over thirty years along with the house. It was also conceivable that
many of the young suburbanites would have had the option to buy
or inherit second hand appliances as older homeowners upgraded
their prewar equipment, thus further reducing the expenditure for
appliances.[34]

This difference in perspective highlights another tension in the
interpretation of domestic space—that between male and female.
The men who designed the kitchen/laundry had a different concept
of spatial efficiency. William Levitt made much of the fact that he
included appliances in each and every house he constructed. Writing an endorsement in an ad for General Electric, Levitt emphasized
the role of the appliances from the builder's point of view:[35]

A dream house is a house the buyer and his family will want to
live in a long time . . . an electric kitchen-laundry is the one big
item that gives the home-owner all the advantages and conveniences that make his home truly livable. [On including the
Bendix washer in the sales price, he continued], . . . it will sell
faster.[35]

Although there is no evidence to suggest that the appliances
did not appeal to the women who bought the Levitt houses, it is
clear from Levitt's remarks that he is selling to the machine-oriented
husband, rather than the wife. The conveniences are intended to
make "*his* home truly livable."

It is also clear from the analysis given by the women at the
congress that they believed including the appliances to be economically counterproductive. Yet, long after the results of the Congress
had been disseminated, Levitt remained proud of having standardized the inclusion of the appliances in the sale of the house:

From the beginning we had thought of the houses we built as
"complete." We still did. No Levitt house was ready for occu-
pants until the kitchen appliances and automatic washer were
in.[36]

Leaving the inclusion of the appliances aside, the location of
the washer in the kitchen was troubling to the women, but not to

the men.[37] Its place in the Levitt house was not mandated structurally or economically, either by the given floor space or by the
layout of the plumbing. It was a design decision; one that could
have been modified with little or no expense. Indeed, it would have
been unnecessary for the women to have had to trade the appliances
for space in order to separate the food preparation from the laundry.
The laundry area of the Levitt Cape Cod could have been separated
from the food preparation area without changing its physical location. By merely opening the washer area to the rear hall that served
both the bathroom and the bedrooms, and rotating the washer 90°,
the laundry area of the Levitt house would have met the demands of
the congress with no alteration in plumbing lines or floor space.

Modifying the ranch to achieve this alteration would have been
only slightly more involved. In the ranch, the washer was already
located at the nexus between the kitchen and the rear hall. It, too,
could have been rotated to face the hall that served the bedrooms
and bath without any structural change, although some form of par-
tition or screen would have been an aesthetic improvement. This
would have removed the soiled laundry from the food preparation
area and placed the machinery closer to the bedrooms and bath, the
source of most household laundry.

Another modification that could have been accomplished with
no economic impact was the location of the kitchen door in the Cape
Cod. The door was located in the center of the side wall of the room.
Thus, all traffic flowed across the kitchen, dividing it into two areas:
the appliance wall and the eating wall. By merely moving the door
to the front corner of the kitchen, a hallway would have been implied directly across the front wall of the room.[38]

The original approaches to interior space contained in the basic
four-room Levitt Cape reveal more about the differences between
the typical male and female interpretations and use of space. The
designers clearly did not work in a kitchen. Their concept of "complete" can be summed up by the number of built-in machines and
cabinets. They did not see the kitchen from within. Only later, when
the Women's Congress analyzed the space as work space would
these subtle distinctions be made apparent. And by then, most of
the Levittown houses would have already been remodeled to reflect
the interpretations of the new homeowners—both male and female.

Meanwhile, the new environmental determinism inherent in
much of the 1950s social analysis was raising specters of feminine—
and, by definition, deviant—ghettos in which husbands and fathers
were reduced to harried visitors who turned over their paychecks to

4.1

Redesigned kitchen layout, showing the ease of turning the laundry and heating equipment toward the bedroom hallway. (a) Cape kitchen as delivered in 1947. (b) Cape with utilities facing bedroom core.

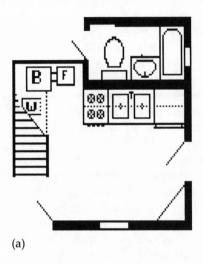

(a)

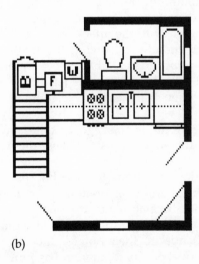

(b)

becurlered, complaining, coffee-klatching wives and materialistic, whining children, whereas wives and mothers were reduced to neurotic, child-driven chauffeurs.[39] And the generic term for this social milieu had become "Levittown."

The Suburban Revolution

The residents of Levittown were well aware of the criticism. According to the experts, their houses were too small and hopelessly repetitive, the layout was counterproductive, and the community was too "suburban" to survive. Moreover, the 'planned' community had been designed for a static population composed solely of young married couples with small children; there was little in the development that offered cultural or intellectual uplift.

Focusing only on the criticism, one might erroneously conclude that the postwar suburbs were indeed a failure, not only to the critics, but to the suburbanites as well. One might expect that the homeowners in Levittown would have had many complaints about their homes and community and, given the opportunity, abandoned them.[40] The Levittowners, conscious of the mounting criticism, responded quite differently to the attack on their homes and community. In 1957, they proudly celebrated the tenth birthday of their community. In addition to a gala ball, a beauty pageant, and a parade that included a float honoring the legendary origins of the development on the "potato fields," the celebration included a house tour.

Still smarting from the barrage of criticism directed against their houses, and the suggestions that Levittown was an incipient slum, the residents opened their homes to visitors and journalists to show how much they had done to their houses in the intervening decade. This combination of celebration and defensive pride in the improved properties became a Levittown tradition, which affords the observer the opportunity to examine what the residents themselves deemed essential to their homes. Indeed, the community's continued sensitivity about its reputation has provided a decade-by-decade documentation of the evolution of their houses. For although the deliverers had neglected to consult the homeowners prior to construction, the homeowners, far from being passive, were more than willing to answer their own needs.

So active were they that their home-remodeling activities supported a quarterly journal within the community. *Thousand Lanes: Ideas for the Levitt Home* concentrated its coverage on the changes that Levittown homeowners had made in their basic houses.[41] By 1954, when the journal was started, the remodeling of Levittown's 17,500 houses had become a big business. The magazine was financed largely through advertisements from local companies connected with the remodeling industry: lumber yards, hardware stores, carpenters, painters, contractors. Whether by doing it themselves or by using contractors, the Levittowners had so thoroughly remodeled their houses by 1957 that the *New York Times* announced that hardly a house could be found that was not altered in some way.[42]

These alterations can be interpreted in several ways. One—and this would seem to be obvious from the criticisms recounted so far—would be that the houses, as delivered, had failed to satisfy the owners. And, based on the expressed desires of the Women's Congress, that may have been true, but it is not borne out by the repeated anniversary celebrations with their house tours, nostalgic references to the "good old days," and the expressions of adulation for the founder of the community.[43]

Rather, the houses of Levittown appear to have been exactly what their owners needed—a start. Most of the early Levittowners were short on money and long on energy and ingenuity. Moreover, they were relatively young and able to wait for the fulfillment of their housing dream. Had the Levittowners been either more affluent or totally dissatisfied with the four-room house, they would have moved on. Most did not.[44] Rather, the Levittowners took their homes quite seriously, and finding themselves with the rudiments of shelter on a considerable piece of land, were able to build their dream from that basic framework.[45]

Their remodeled houses show us how closely the dreams of the Levittowners matched the desires, rather than the needs, established by the women at the Congress; how closely their solutions addressed problems that the social critics had identified; in short, how strongly they conformed to the values of middle-class family life that were part of the American consciousness during the first decade of Levittown.

More important, their houses will show that by investing sweat equity in their houses, the Levittowners raised the value of their homes and their community.[46] For, contrary to the critics' fears for them, the young, lower-income veterans were not saddled with a house they could not manage.[47] Nor, contrary to *Fortune'* fears, was the government saddled with the foreclosures of worthless housing as the developments failed.[48]

Instead, by beginning with only the basic elements, a large number of the Levittowners were able to turn the reductionist houses of 1947–1951 into fully developed middle-class housing by 1957.

5

Expanding the American Dream

Spring, 1957

By the Spring of 1957, tenants and rental units were becoming rare in Levittown. William Levitt had long since moved on. The nearby air base, Mitchel Field, which had supplied his Bethpage Realty—later Junto[1]—with many of its tenants, was scheduled for closing. The few remaining military residents would be leaving. Twelve years after the war the typical resident of Levittown was still the homeowning veteran and, although many of the men still commuted to various parts of New York City, a strong percentage were working in the several defense plants in the Bethpage-Farmingdale area to the east of Levittown.[2]

In the fall of the year, a number of newspapers and magazines revisited the ten-year old Levittown, measuring it against the earlier predictions. Their assessments were largely positive. Even those who had expressed negative appraisals of suburbia, found space during the anniversary display to commend the community for not having become the slum that was predicted.[3]

They took particular note of the number and quality of the renovations and alterations that had been done on the original houses. In-depth coverage of these changes was reported in the local media on Long Island, in particular in the several publications directly aimed at the Levittown population, *Thousand Lanes*, *The Towner*, *The Levittown Tribune*, and *The Levittown Eagle*. The coverage shows that in the area of renovation the later versions of the Levitt houses—the 1949 through 1951 ranches—proved to be more versatile. As part of their redesign efforts in 1949, the Levitts had adapted the concept of transformable space from Frank Lloyd Wright. They installed a pivoting bookcase/partition between living room and kitchen, which could also serve to screen the kitchen from the front entry. They built drawers into closets and walls for storage; installed a television set in the stairwall, and a double-access fireplace between the living room and the kitchen. The rear window of the living room was designed to be removable. The opening where the window had been became an archway between the existing living room and the new extension, and the window could be reused in the new room. Similarly, the 1950 and 1951 carports readily lent themselves to conversion to garages or to additional living space, requiring only the construction of two walls to enclose them.

The Cape Cods were more static in design. Any alterations beyond the finishing of the attic involved some major structural change. The frame-and-shingle construction, however, made even this model easier to remodel than houses of brick or stone. Nevertheless, it remains easier to locate an unmodified Cape Cod than an unmodified ranch even today, although the ranches outnumber the Capes by a ratio of 11 to 6.[4]

Finishing the attic to create one or two bedrooms was almost mandated by the size and number of the original two bedrooms in the Levitt houses. This alteration, in its most basic form, could be easily done by the inexperienced homeowner, since the essential framework was already in place. Even with subcontracting for the electricity and the preliminary heating and plumbing (for adding a future bathroom), the completion of the attic rooms was inexpensive and did not produce a considerable increase in property taxes.[5] Indeed, since the finishing of the attic need not result in any visible exterior structural changes, the owner's surreptitious do-it-yourself conversion could avoid any additional taxes.[6]

The simplest structural change that had been made in the Levitt houses was one the Levittowners called "squaring the kitchen." In the 1949 through 1951 ranch models, the front door had been set into a recess in the left front corner of the front wall of the house. This resulted in the loss of about nine square feet of the corner of the kitchen. The intention of this had been to create a vestibule and visual hallway to direct both the eye and the flow of traffic to the rear living room. This retained a certain amount of privacy for the kitchen, although it sacrificed floor space. Many of the Levittown homeowners rejected the sacrifice. They preferred to use the space for a larger table and chairs or for additional cabinets and counters.[7] Although several of the women were not happy to have the kitchen serving as the main entryway, most still preferred the additional space over the traffic diversion.[8]

As Levittown matured it became apparent that other spatial redefinition would be necessary. Among the other criticisms of Lev-

5.1

"Squared" kitchen. The most common—and least expensive—method of
creating additional space in the ranch models.

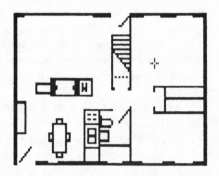

ittown and its counterpart communities, one of the most salient had
been that their design was based on a static view of family life.
Whereas the houses and community might have been acceptable for
young mothers with toddlers, both were now indicted for being inadequate to the social needs of adolescents. This deficiency applied
equally to the houses and to the amenities available in the nearby
community.

Thus, most of the renovations were more complex and reflected the changes in the life cycle through which the family had
moved. Rather than simply adding one room to serve as dining
room, the owners often extended the house across the complete ex-
panse of one wall, adding in the process a minimum of two interior
rooms. For example, a family might add a sidewall extension to the
Cape to produce a garage with a room at its rear. The new room
would then become a dining room, or it might become the new living room, freeing the original living room to serve as dining room.
Other families added a full-width extension across the back of the
ranch model house. This provided a new living room and a second
room that could serve as a master bedroom or a den, depending on
the needs of the family.

In the Women's Congress, much importance had been placed
on the role of the dining table in family life, not only as a place to
eat—the kitchen could serve as well—but as a place in which to
teach the young the manners and mores of middle-class America.[9] In
the Spring 1957 issue of *Thousand Lanes*, the most common major
renovation shown is a large, formal living room to the rear or side of

the original house, with the original living room converted into a dining room. The second most frequently displayed renovation is the simple addition of a dining room, either by constructing an ell, or by converting one of the first-floor bedrooms into a dining room. Other variations included building a new kitchen in order to turn the existing kitchen into a dining room. The plan most frequently chosen was based on a logical sequence of activity flow from kitchen through dining room to living room; less acceptable, but also less costly, was the placing of the dining room in a location one room removed from the kitchen.

Those families who adapted their houses to the most rigid room definitions through door and window placement were often locked into inadequate spatial arrangements later in the family cycle. Those who allowed for more flexible interpretations of space were ready for the changes in social activities that took place when their small children entered their teen years.

As the children of the postwar "baby boom" reached adolescence, they presented a large group with which American society had to contend. The creation of a specially designed place within the home for adolescent children was logically linked to yet another social disorder popular with the social critics of the fifties—juvenile delinquency.[10] In the years after Senator Joseph McCarthy's crusade against Communism had been discredited, the American media rediscovered another cause for concern in one of the most ubiquitous threats to their traditional mores: the teenager.

The 1955 movie *Rebel Without a Cause* dramatized one of the greatest fears of the suburban family with its tale of adolescent *angst* and parental abdication. Teenagers had become the new social anomaly. Their suspected predilections to sex and violence both attracted and repelled their elders, as social 'experts' and commentators identified yet another subject ripe for exploitation. American communities underwent intense self-examination in the light of the growing concern for the survival of family life in the wake of the teenager. Juvenile delinquency, gangs, teenage pregnancy and its concomitant the "shotgun marriage" created a climate of tension and indecision among parents suddenly faced with their responsibilities for providing something appropriate for their restless young to do in their free time.

The widespread condemnation of the suburban habitat broadened to include an evaluation of its nurturing qualities. As with the earlier criticism, this was often contradictory. Mothers were indicted for being both overprotective and uncaring; fathers, for being domi-

neering, but detached and emasculated.[11] The call went out for a
return to the "traditional" values, which centered on the family
home. Whereas some social scientists attacked the family for failing
its young, others indicted the community for failing to provide more
and better activities to keep the young occupied.

During its first decade Levittown had been spared from much
of this tension. The age and life stages of the young veteran families
that populated Levittown were such that only after 1957 did most of
the children reach adolescence. In the June 27 issue of the *Levittown
Tribune* the Levittown Property Owners Association devoted its column to a tenth anniversary re-evaluation of their community's progress over the previous decade. In response to the somewhat hyper-
bolic question "What makes Levittown a miracle community?" they
included:

Levittown is a child-centered community at this time. It is a
veritable wonderland for raising children. Combined with good
schools and highly superior park facilities we have top recreational leaderships, both paid and voluntary. Levittown, with
characteristic foresight, is pioneering in an anti-delinquent program aimed at children who do not respond to normal group
youth activities.

The lack of teen-oriented facilities did not last very long after
that. The Levittown Roller Rink and movie theatre both opened in
1957, providing Levittown teenagers with acceptable alternatives to
the gang and the back seat of an automobile.

In this period, those Levittown families with older children
chose the addition of a second living area—variously labelled a den,
rumpus room, family room, or "rec" room—when they remodeled
their houses. These rooms were intended to provide a separate but
contained area in which the adolescents could entertain safely.[12] It
was apparent in the text that accompanied the remodeling articles
that families at this stage recognized a need for a social separation
from their adolescent children within the family household. For example, in the Fall 1961 issue of *Thousand Lanes*, contributing editors
Yvette Gervey and Mary Graham Bond presented some general remodeling advice in a two-page article, "Letter From A Decorator."
The article was presented in the form of a response to a request for
suggestions from a correspondent. Incorporated in the advice were
some basic assumptions about suburban life in the 1960s, such as

the increasing importance of hi-fidelity music versus the television, the need for the husband/father to have an office or den to which he can retreat, and the nature of the social life of the youngsters.

Specifically, you want to know where to put that beautiful hi-fi console you've just bought. Also, you need some recreation space for your twelve-year-old twins, Ronnie and Rickie. And could television be banished from the living room?

The article sets forth the project limitations, among which is the fact that the family expects to be transferred within three years because of the husband/father's employment.

On the recreation room, the decorator/editor recommends:

The room will be treated without carpeting so there can be dancing. The original tile flooring is in good condition, so that stays. Two reasonably priced couches will be placed at right angles under the ranch windows. There will be 6-foot-long foam rubber couches which can double as extra guest beds. . . . Since the boys bunk together across the hall in the small bedroom, they will no doubt like to have their overnight visiting Scout-mates nearby. Also, a recreation room near the boys' room is a good combination.[13]

For those families who did not, or could not, add a room specifically for teenagers and their activities, carports and garages were often enlisted as erstwhile rumpus or party rooms when the teenagers began to socialize.[14]

Whereas urban, working-class adolescents might move to parks, playgrounds, pool halls—or worse—the suburban middle-class teens were encouraged to stay within the family home, even if walls had to be removed in order to make it possible. Although Levittown was delayed in its encounter with the teenager, the community's response was well within accepted middle-class family practice.[15] For those unsure of how to respond, the answers were as close as their family television set.

Television in the 1950s had discovered suburbia and its problems. The teenager at home became a stock character in many of the medium's family comedies. Suburban living became not only the setting, but the focus of the plot in a variety of these offerings. The suburban families were presented both as idealized, didactic representations of "typical" American family life and as objects of satire.

As this process intensified, the line between commercial productions and suburban family life blurred. Do-it-yourself interior decorating began to take its cue from advertisements and articles in family-and home-oriented magazines. Family life became the subject of an increasing number of television programs, which blurred the line between the domestic economy and the commercial culture. Television families were often shown using the products that sponsored their programs. As these lines became increasingly unclear, Americans and their families were treated to entertainment designed to sell not only a product, but a way of life—a way of life that was reinforced by the design of the very houses in which they lived.

Suburbs, suburbanites, and suburban activities dominated the television situation comedies, many of which had more of situation than of comedy. Plots revolved around "typical" nuclear families. The prewar radio comedies based on urban-dwelling ethnic families were sanitized for the postwar generation.[16] An example of this process can be found in the evolution of the program "The Goldbergs." In 1947, the Goldbergs were one of the many entertainment families on the radio.[17] Molly Goldberg and her extended family lived in a tenement apartment in the Bronx. She was able to interact with her neighbors without leaving her building. Indeed, by utilizing the airshaft window, she could do so without leaving her apartment. This reduced the family's level of privacy, but generated a communitarian sense of sharing among the neighbors. Molly's family was humorous, ethnic, extended, and urban. The Goldbergs moved to television in 1949.

In October 1951, "I Love Lucy" came to television. Lucy and Ricky Ricardo were also urban dwellers; the Cuban-born Ricky, decidedly ethnic. The Ricardos' walk-up apartment in the building owned by their neighbors, Ethel and Fred Mertz, was similar to the Goldbergs'. Shared space, hallways, alleyways, and basements provided the setting for many of the programs. By 1955, less than five years later, the Ricardos had moved to the suburbs and the Goldbergs had left television. In their stead were Ozzie and Harriet, Donna Reed, and Jim Anderson, the father who knew best.

Each of these television families lived in a single-family house in which they practiced middle-class virtues.[18] To establish the suburban context, such programs often began with a full view of the exterior of the house in which the sitcom family lived. The Stones of "The Donna Reed Show" lived in a two-storied colonial. The Andersons of "Father Knows Best" lived in a vine-covered Cape Cod. Although this house was considerably larger than those of Levittown, the architectural imagery was the same. Both the house of the Andersons of Springfield and the house of the Eckhoffs of Levittown followed the configuration of that house frequently drawn by kindergarten children: a gabled, one-story dwelling with a front door centered between two windows in the wider wall.

These programs presented viewers with an idealized view of family life, one that could be emulated in the proper setting. Urban situation comedies, like Jackie Gleason's "Honeymooners," portrayed childless, blue-collar workers as apartment-dwelling buffoons, whereas the suburban world of the Cleavers, ("Leave It to Beaver"), the Andersons ("Father Knows Best") and the Stones ("The Donna Reed Show") was dominated by single-family houses with dining rooms, front yards, basketball hoops on the garage, and at least one car in the driveway. The homes were furnished in an unobtrusive, traditional style, albeit arranged for better camera angles. The families generally consisted of two or three children, a professional father, and a mother whose domestic activities often revolved around serving milk and cookies and/or drying her hands on a clean dishtowel.[19]

The plots centered on the children. The parents' role was reactive. For example, consider the elements of the plot of one airing of "Father Knows Best":

1. Teenaged offspring lose ground in school
2. Father spends time finding solutions
    a. visits teacher
    b. buys tickets to a concert rehearsal
    c. lectures on the need for American students to thirst for learning.
3. Resolution: children discover the beauty of knowledge for its own sake.[20]

The didactic nature of the programming is unmistakable. In many scenes, Jim Anderson would actually address the audience rather than the offspring.[21] In such scenes, the message was often an encapsulation of the values of middle America. The dramatic format, that of teaching a child, allowed the presentation to be pedantic without appearing to talk down to the audience.[22] But the lesson was there; American families—at least good American families—lived, worked, and believed in a certain way.

There were no adult companions; father and mother interacted as equals only with each other. When other adult characters were introduced, they were cast as part of the social support system of suburbia: repairmen, teachers, servants, or policemen. Father did not bowl, play cards, or "hang out" with other men. Mother had no confidante for a morning's coffee-klatch. There were no aunts and uncles, few grandparents, in television's suburbia. The American family was the nuclear family. Their homes and communities had been designed to support them and their way of life.

It was this way of life which had been assumed in the design of the reductionist houses of the subdivision suburbs. It was domestic, traditional, and privatized. It reflected the Protestant ethic, the cult of domesticity, and the rural ideal, all artifacts of the nineteenth century. In addition, it expanded and solidified the American middle class. The success of this expansion became more apparent during Levittown's second decade.

During the decade between 1957 and 1967, the American value system underwent a transformation. The issues swelled gradually, emerging sporadically at various levels of society. For draft-age youth, the pièce de résistance was the war; for the minority poor, it was the disparity between their situation—the continuation of segregation, discrimination, and lack of equal opportunity—and the rising affluence of the white middle class. For middle-class women, it was the rigid reestablishment of the cult of domesticity with its concomitant, the bird in a gilded cage. In part a product of the relative affluence of the postwar decade, in part a reaction to the continuing military involvement in Southeast Asia, the uneasy truce between those in power and those without it began to come undone. The sides shifted as the issues emerged, but at its base, the tension was between those who were part of the establishment and those who felt themselves exploited by it. By the end of the decade, the suburban revolution that had begun with the returning veterans of World War II had given way to an urban counterrevolution rooted in opposition to yet another war.

Levittown was not without its own turmoil during this period.[23] But the nature of the issues that erupted with volatility in Levittown reveals the degree to which the postwar suburbs had reflected and ratified traditional middle-class American values, producing stable, middle-class communities. The residents had put their roots down, investing both economic and physical equity into their properties. In so doing, they justified the postwar housing policies that had made them possible. The built environment of Levittown in the 1960s provided visual evidence of the owners' stake in the society of which they had become an integral part.

The Levittowners' many battles to retain the values of middle-class suburbia erupted more often in school- and library-board elections than in flag burnings and protest marches.[24] The tension between containing the budgets for both systems and improving the quality of their services resulted in a series of compromises. Those who could not live with the compromises took the route so often followed in American history—voting with their feet, moving to areas more compatible with their needs and their values.[25]

The safety valve of this new frontier was an economic one: the ability to resell the Levitt house for enough money to buy into a more expensive development. Those who remained were primarily those for whom Levittown's compromises had been acceptable, if not preferable. The schools were stable, if not innovative; affordable, if not elaborate. The libraries were divided between the two value systems that predominated in the community: the conservative Island Trees library, with its emphasis on preserving traditional family values, and the more liberal Levittown library, with its emphasis on exploring new possibilities.[26]

Spring and Summer, 1967

In the summer of 1967, hippies from across the country gathered in San Francisco for the first "be-in." Young Americans brought their guitars and their love-beads, their flowers and their marijuana, to a massive gathering at which they stressed the values of peace, love, and personal freedom. The experience was repeated across the country; they gathered from San Francisco to Woodstock, singing their folk songs with themes of love, peace, and social revolution, and demanding an end to the war in Vietnam.

For many middle-class Americans in the late 1960s, it appeared that the social threats that had hovered over American society since the end of World War II—juvenile delinquency, political subversion, and communism—were inherent in these civil rights and antiwar movements. Parents, police, and public officials were also concerned about the apparent decadence attached to the gathering. The "love" that many of the young people exalted was overtly sexual and unrestrained; the "peace" they advocated was viewed by their opponents as a surrender to communist-sponsored violence in Vietnam; their social revolution, as a threat to the social fabric of America. In addition, their dependence upon a variety of mind-altering substances was seen as proof that Nikita Khrushchev's threat—to bury American society from within—was indeed becoming a reality.

The traditional values of the American middle class and, in particular, its suburban lifestyle, were under siege, and it was the youth of America who were challenging the values of their elders. The juvenile delinquent of 1957 had become the social dropout of 1967.

The music of the youth culture mocked everything from political complacency to the patios and barbecues of the suburbs; from marriage and monogamy to the relations between the races.[27] Young people were urged to "tune in [to reality], turn on [with drugs], and drop out [of school, society, the bourgeoisie].[28] The generation that had taken pride in serving their country during World War II now found its children opposing the nation's involvement in Vietnam and, along with it, everything that symbolized middle-class America. Traditional mores regarding the "place" of various groups in American society were under attack or overthrown. Rioting broke out in cities across the country as blacks, whose postwar efforts to attain civil rights had been frustrated, vented their dissatisfactions in demonstrations and marches. In the suburbs, women who had accepted the feminine mystique without reservation in the 1950s found themselves challenged to move out of their domesticity and fulfill their personal potential through education and a career; in large numbers they rose to meet the challenge.[29] To many, the nation appeared to be on the verge of self-destruction.

The social revolution of the sixties and the counterculture it produced were not strong movements in Levittown. In general, Levittowners aligned themselves more with the "establishment" than with its opponents in 1967. The youth of Levittown served proudly in Vietnam.[30] The parents continued to enlarge their houses, maintain their lawns, entertain at barbecues, and debate the merits of the schools that consumed such a large part of their property taxes.

In Levittown's second decade those who had rented were gone. Gone, too, were those who had planned to use Levittown as their first stop on their way to larger homes and "better" neighborhoods.[31] The transitory nature of the population had ended.[32] The drastic inflation of house values in the two decades after the war had made selling and moving on not only possible but attractive to those who had sufficient equity in their homes. The basic Levitt house was valued at over twice its original purchase price; the improved houses had almost tripled in value. This increase, coupled with the increased equity due to mortgage reduction, allowed Levittowners to "buy up" as they moved on. As a result, those who remained in Levittown were largely those who had chosen to do so, remaking Levittown itself into their version of a "better" neighborhood.

The new options available to Levittown homeowners did not go unnoted either by the local real estate dealers or the home-improvement industry. Moving 'up' no longer meant leaving Levittown. Several construction companies offered Levittowners moderate-cost expansion options for the Levitt houses.

For those who chose not to remodel, there were other opportunities. Levittown Equities, Inc., for example, specialized in finding homeowners who would rather trade their basic '49 ranch, which the company valued at $14,500, for an already-expanded version of the same model with "4 bedrooms, 2 baths, 2-zone heat, dormer, squared kitchen, center hall, and garage" for $16,990. To sweeten the deal, they offered not only an upgrade in house, but the possiblity of mortgaging the new house for a figure high enough to provide extra cash over and above the cost of the larger house.[33] In the inflationary period of the 1960s, this transaction made good economic sense.[34]

The increased equity also permitted those who elected to stay in Levittown to refinance their houses to underwrite extensive remodeling and expansion projects. The FHA further supported these efforts through its "203K" home improvement loans. These long-term "modernization" loans offered from $2500 to $10,000 for periods ranging from seven to 20 years at interest rates of 6 percent and did not entail refinancing the original mortgages. The alterations were subject to the same FHA inspection and approval that applied to all FHA financing. Levittown's contractors and real estate brokers were quick to incorporate the liberal terms of the program in their ads.[35]

The introduction of this program was instrumental in the decision of Long Island Lighting Co. to cosponsor a pair of "Custom Exhibit Homes."[36] The exhibit houses, two Levitt models, were retrofitted with electric heating as part of the company's campaign to boost electric heat. The interior space in these houses was redesigned to take advantage of the additional kitchen/stairwell space made available by the removal of the original oil burner.[37]

The remodeling projects spawned an industry in the area.[38] Remodelers were so much in demand that they were able to specialize in Levitt houses, producing standardized packages of improvements and alterations at a reasonable cost.[39] The contractors displayed their projects to the community through their ads in the pages of *Thousand Lanes*. The magazine encouraged their advertising by including

5.2

(a) Most common changes and additions to the first floor of the basic Cape Cod model: (1) added living room or den; (2) added master bedroom, freeing up original master bedroom (5); (3) added room, variously used as dinette, mud room, play room; (4) original living room used as formal dining room after additions or attic expansion; (5) original master bedroom turned into living room or den; (6) former children's room turned into play room in conjunction with expanded attic areas. (b) Most common changes and additions to the first floor of the basic ranch model: (1) added living room or den; (2) added master bedroom, freeing up original master bedroom (6); (3) added garage or converted carport, used as intended or converted again into dining room or den; (4) former children's room turned into play room; (5) original living room used as formal dining room.

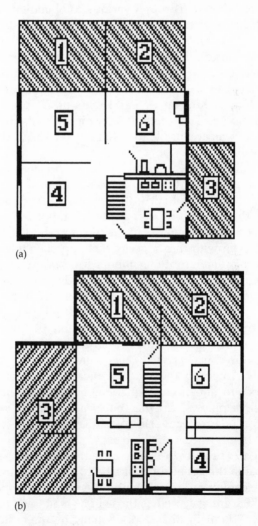

(a)

(b)

three to four such major renovations in each issue. The articles, in turn, served to reinforce the contractor's message. In addition, *Thousand Lanes* offered many examples of homeowners' projects, such as room dividers, built-in storage, homemade furniture, or decorative innovations such as displays of milk glass, found objects, or doll collections.

One of the most energetic of the contractors was Herbert Richheimer. His "Museum of Modern Home Improvements" offered scale models of both the houses and the various additions and modifications he offered. Through various combinations of the stock elements, Richheimer could provide homeowners with a three-dimensional model of how their home improvements would look before they made their decision.[40]

Others created full-size models of the Levittown rooms in their showrooms. Zino Construction, for example, featured an ad promising "Playrooms, Kitchen, & Bathrooms on Display!" at their Levittown showroom. This method was highly cost-effective, since one model room was applicable to either 6,000 Cape Cod or 11,500 ranch houses in the area.[41]

An unintended side effect of this specialization was a subtle shift in the power of design back to a provider. Those homeowners who wanted to individualize their homes either had to do most of the work themselves, or prepare for a tug-of-war with contractors who advocated their own ready-made, standardized designs.[42] Nevertheless, even with this supermarket approach to remodeling, a judicious recombination of the standardized offerings in materials and designs enabled the homeowners to redesign their houses with a certain level of individuality, albeit within certain preset parameters.

The real individuality of the remodeled houses was expressed through the interpretation and decoration of the available space, rather than through a radical restructuring of the building. The houses featured in *Thousand Lanes* were decorated in styles ranging from Early American (heavy pine pieces with fabrics of plaid and patchwork) to Japanese (lightweight furniture lines, with shoji screens, floor pillows, and rice-paper accessories), with a sprinkling of Danish Modern (foam-slab sofas on tapered legs with wedge bolsters and free-formed coffee tables).

By 1967, Levittown had matured. Trees that had been spindly or invisible in the aerial shots of Levittown in 1947 now obscured the view. The configurations of the houses, once described as "like peas in a pod,"[43] were as varied as those in a small town of the nineteenth century. In the main, the work of changing the basic four-room cot-

5.3

Examples of standardized remodeling offerings advertised in the pages of *Thousand Lanes* magazine.

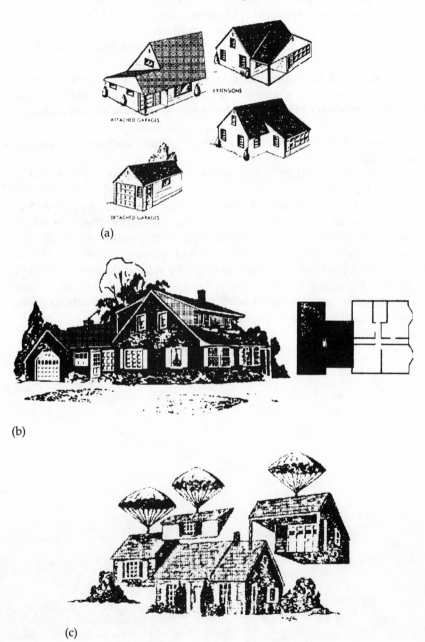

(a)

(b)

(c)

tages into individualized six- and eight-room houses had been accomplished. The remodeling industry that had proliferated for the first twenty years could no longer confine itself to Levitt houses. Their market was dwindling; the original Levitt houses had been enlarged, remodeled, and upgraded.[44]

Although the slum that critics of Levittown had threatened in the forties had never materialized, the scrutiny continued. As the social revolution of the 1960s intensified, Levittown and its residents were now more likely to be under indictment for their 'bourgeois' culture and 'hopelessly middle-class' values, than for the lack of such qualities.

Levittown and its residents were not clustered at either end of the social spectrum.[45] Neither part of the 'establishment' nor opposed to it, the residents of Levittown had achieved the proper balance between rugged individualism and social conformity on which the housing policies of the 1940s had been predicated. Levittown was no longer a question mark; it had arrived. Moreover, it had been officially approved. The community was no longer an oddity, to be scrutinized by the curious or the haughty.[46] Rather, it was looked upon as a source of advertising copy—the ultimate in social acceptability in postwar America.[47]

6

A Closer Look

This chapter examines several Levittown houses in detail. In all but one case, their owners represent the variety and the typicality of present-day Levittowners with more than ten years residence.[1] They are in early middle age; the adults are actively employed outside the home; their children are young adults or late adolescents. In the one case where the homeowners are still in the early stages of family development, they represent the second generation of one family to own the home, and almost all the renovations on their house were in place when they became the owners.

Each of the houses had been structurally completed by 1967, and represents the spatial use and needs of a nuclear family with two or more offspring who are adapting to the needs of the changing life cycle. Thus, each house has experienced some aspect of multigenerational use: in some cases the family maintains sleeping quarters for the long-term vacations of retired parents; in others, two generations of adults share the house. In still others, the adult children maintain a room in the home despite having established a household of their own. In this, Levittown appears to be moving away from the major characteristic that marked its early years, the lack of variety in age and stage in the family cycle among the residents.

Thus, the one attribute of the postwar suburbs that set them apart from earlier communities—the isolation of the nuclear family—may have been an aberration occasioned by the size and nature of the available housing, rather than the beginning of a new trend.[2]

The Colmer House

In an open letter (undated) in the spring of 1967, Hubbard Cobb, editor of *American Home* magazine, invited the homeowners of Levittown to enter their home in a contest focused on home improvements in Levittown.[3] The contest, timed to coincide with the twentieth anniversary celebration of the community, was jointly sponsored by the National Home Improvement Council, Levitt and Sons, and the magazine.

Prizes were offered by 14 of the major manufacturers of products for house and home, from construction materials to appliances. The prizes included a "ten-day, first-class, round trip to Paris, for two, with all expenses paid," donated by Levitt and Sons[4] and "more than twenty major prizes from major manufacturers." Westinghouse color television sets, Kohler plumbing fixtures, General Electric stoves, and U.S. Plywood wood paneling were among the prizes. The prizes and their respective brand names were duly noted in the magazine, as well as in the various local papers that covered the contest.

Improvements of all types, large or small, do-it-yourself or contractor-built, additions or changes, were welcomed in the invitation. In all, some 200 houses were entered in the contest. The winners were featured in the May 1968 issue of American Home.[5]

When the prizes were announced in November, Mr. and Mrs. Dennis Colmer had won third prize—a General Electric Deluxe self-cleaning range, model J757. The nature of the renovations which were undertaken by the Colmers provides a text that reveals the resolution of the tension between self-expression and conformity that was at the heart of the Levittown experience. Retaining the integrity of the exterior of the house was one of Mr. Colmer's underlying principles. Yet the house was being designed "to suit one family's way of life—ours."[6]

The Colmers' house, an original Cape Cod when they bought it in 1960, had been expanded in 1966 to provide room for Mrs. Colmer's widowed mother. Mr. Colmer had designed the renovations and had based his plans on careful study of the way in which the family and the existing house interacted, as well as on anticipated changes that would be brought on by the arrival of Mrs. Colmer's mother.

Working in his office in nearby Hicksville, Mr. Colmer came home for lunch almost daily. Thus, the Colmers' home is atypical in that its homeowner/designer, Mr. Colmer, was a working man who spent a part of the working day at home. When he designed the changes in the floor plan, he did so with a better than average understanding of the functional role of domestic space. His design elements reveal an educated concern for household work and activity, as well as for visual and aesthetic form. As a result, many of his interpretations coincide with the desired changes called for in the Women's Congress on Housing.[7]

When the Colmers purchased their house, it was a basic Cape Cod with only one alteration: the previous owners had sheet-rocked an upstairs room to be used as either a bedroom or playroom for one of their children. There was no heat supplied to this room. However, the rising heat from below kept the room adequately warm for sleeping purposes.[8] The Colmer family moved in with no intention of renovating the house. Rather, they saw the house as an interim home for three to four years, after which they expected to move on to something larger and more suitable.

Their plans for the remodeling evolved gradually. Initially, after the first year they found that they needed more space for storage. "Having grown up in a large house with a large basement and a garage, and all that," Mr. Colmer missed the space of a larger home. His solution was a garage—"a large garage." In his first plan he showed his skill at going beyond standard designs in order to meet his own needs and desires. Because the 60-foot frontage lacked the necessary width for a standard two-car garage, he adapted his plan to the site. Rather than build a single-car garage, he jogged the house-side wall to allow for a room-sized breezeway between the garage and kitchen. The jogged wall provided an extra two feet of floor space within the garage to allow for comfortable access to the car.

The breezeway room was left unheated; the family refers to it as a porch. It has served in several capacities since it was first constructed in 1963. The room, directly off the side of the kitchen, provided an ideal place for the family's two boys to play when they were small. Storage cabinets were added to augment the storage space in the kitchen. The room also provided space for the laundry room/entryway, an element that the Women's Congress had seen as essential to their basic house design. It has also served as breakfast room, in good weather, taking much of the traffic away from the work area in the kitchen.

Mr. Colmer designed it as transitional space, "a room to come into." Its function is similar to that called for by the Women's Congress: a place in which to take off boots and snow, a place between house and garage, between indoors and out, between front yard and back. The original kitchen, which is still intact, is used now primarily as work space. It is "the only thing we've never changed." By 1967, when they entered *American Home*'s contest, they had changed just about everything else.

Mr. Colmer wanted to preserve the integrity of "the original concept of the Levitt house" in his redesign. The one-storied front elevation was retained to keep the house as "cozy and cottagey and

6.1

Front elevation and floor plans for Colmer house. (a) Front elevation.
(b) First floor. (c) Second floor.

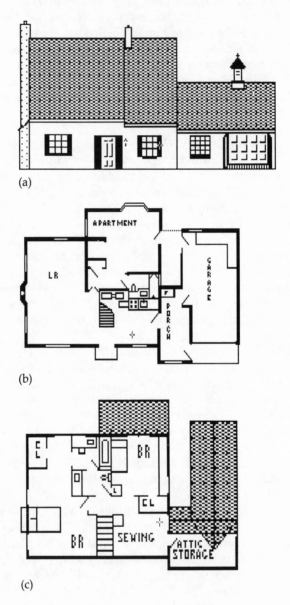

(a)

(b)

(c)

as Cape Cod-like as possible." The Greek Revival flavor of the original Levitt design on the street side was left unchanged, although the rear elevation has been altered. These alterations provided living space both upstairs, through the construction of a full dormer, and downstairs, through the addition of an ell. Mr. Colmer's concern with retaining the integrity of the Cape Cod is a key to the sense of community that most of the Levittown informants expressed. It is their tribute to retaining the visual harmony of the community. The self-expression that the homeowners exhibit on the exterior of their houses is restrained. It is in the interior of the houses, through their spatial and decorative interpretation, that their creativity comes through. In this way they are able to conform to the norms of the neighborhood in their exterior forms, while expressing their individuality and molding their homes to suit their various lifestyles in their interior functions.

When they began the first stage of their alteration, the Colmers saw the garage as a twofold asset. It would provide them with much-needed extra space while they remained in the home, but it would also provide a salesworthy extra when they sold. The area above the garage was planned for deep storage of seasonal items such as winter clothes, or lifestyle-specific items such as playpens and high chairs.

The family's original plan—to remain in the house for a short time—was changed shortly after the garage addition was completed. Mrs. Colmer's mother was widowed in 1962, and the couple found that her living alone in a large house presented several problems for both families. Mrs. Jensen, a retiring woman, became lonely living in the big house alone. In addition, Mr. and Mrs. Colmer had had to undertake the maintenance for both houses, which imposed a drain on their time and energies. As an alternative, they began to consider consolidating the two households in the Colmer's Cape Cod.

Before any changes were made, both Mrs. Jensen and the Colmers spent a good deal of time analyzing the implications of the transition. Each of them had grown up in multigenerational households, and so they had no romantic illusions about the prospects for such a situation. Mr. Colmer began researching both the problems and the benefits of three-generation households. Through his reading and his conversations with friends and colleagues who had some experience with multigenerational living, he found that two areas invariably tended to produce problems and irritations. Attempting to live as a single family unit was one; disciplining the children, the other. His findings "confirmed [his] feeling that the households should be separate." Thus, the renovation was planned from the beginning to enhance the benefits of life in an extended family while minimizing the difficulties.

Sketches were drawn up and family consultations held. Only after they felt that they had worked out most of the pitfalls did they approach Mrs. Jensen with the floor plans. After some discussion and rethinking, they finalized the design for the new addition.

The dwellings would be connected, yet their daily lives would be independent. To achieve this, they included an interior door through which one could enter either household, but they established certain ground rules regarding its use. No one was to open the common door between the units without first asking and gaining permission.

Mrs. Jensen's apartment consisted of the original hall and bathroom, along with the smaller bedroom behind it. To this area they added an extension that reached eight feet into the back yard. This extension and the small bedroom combined to create a large living area that was designed to have the function of three rooms, in terms of space, but remain a single, large room. Because it is located on the normally cooler northwest corner of the house, and because older people often require more warmth in their environment, the apartment has its own thermostat and circulator. The floor plan incorporates an arrangement of walls and closets that was designed to ensure privacy. In the Colmers' section, the original living room was extended into the master bedroom behind it. The new room served as a multi-purpose social area that included seating space before a new fireplace.[9] To increase privacy between the two dwellings, a large dressing room/closet was located along the wall separating the Colmers' living room and Mrs. Jensen's living area. The dressing room was located in the area that had been formed by the original bedroom closets and the original linen closet. This space serves to insulate the living space in the apartment from the noise of activity in the family living room. Parties of as many as 12 people, with music and singing, have been held without disturbing the apartment area. The original chase (plumbing) wall between the kitchen and bath further served to reduce the transfer of sound between the units.

Despite their desire for multifamily, rather than extended family, living, the Colmers had to compromise some of their designs in order to conform to the Hempstead Town building code for the Levittown area. A two-family house was defined in Hempstead as one having two kitchen sinks. The standards for "mother-daughter" houses, on the other hand, had been established to accommodate an extended family, while protecting the area's single-family residential nature. The definition of the mother-daughter house was a multi-family residence with a "shared" kitchen. The test for a shared kitchen was the absence of a second kitchen sink within the structure. As a result, the Colmer addition has a stove and a refrigerator, but no sink in its kitchen area.

Adhering to the building code presented a conflict with the family's intent to maintain two independent households. To resolve the conflict, Mr. Colmer designed and installed a sink in the bathroom that serves as both a kitchen and a bathroom facility. The sink is larger and higher than a standard bathroom lavatory, but lower than a standard kitchen sink. A formica shelf is hinged over the commode which, when lowered, serves as a drainboard for quick kitchen clean-ups in the apartment.[10]

Since the apartment extends into the rear yard, it has windows on three sides that provide both light and cross-ventilation, as well as a feeling of spaciousness. The door to the outside leads to the shared patio, which further extends the available space. This patio can also be approached from the Colmers' breezeway room, which serves to mitigate any sense of isolation while retaining the privacy of both dwellings.

The flexibility of the house is most apparent on holidays when the combined family entertains. At such times, the house is expanded to utilize all lower floor space as if it were a single unit. By setting buffets on bridge tables in the Colmers' extended living room and opening the door between units, they can set up tables for as many as 24 in the apartment's space. Except for such large gatherings, the Colmers have not felt the need for a separate dining room; indeed, they prefer their arrangement. This makes them unlike the women of the Housing Congress; however, a bit of ethnic history explains how they have carried on another tradition.

For a few years after they first remodeled the house, the Colmers set aside a portion of their enlarged living room for a dining area. Here they placed a table and chairs that they used primarily for entertaining. The table was placed at the front wall of the living room, and was visually divided from the living area through the use of two area rugs of different sizes. The larger carpet was used for the conversational area—sofa, chairs, and fireplace; the smaller carpet marked the dining space.

In 1969 the family went "home" to Norway and discovered a

combination coffee/dining table which, when fully extended, can seat as many as 12 people. This unit was used by their Norwegian relatives to make more efficient use of their small apartments. The idea intrigued the Colmers, who bought one for their home. Closed, the table is slightly higher than the standard coffee table, and serves four as a casual eating surface. Extended, it rises to standard dining table height. Despite its usefulness in a small home, this table has not been adopted by any of their neighbors. Although many other of the Colmers' ideas have found their way into the Levitt houses in their neighborhood, for most of their neighbors the formal dining room has been the preferred arrangement.

In their redesign, the Colmers allowed for several stages in the life cycle.[11] The redesign, undertaken when the two children were just entering school, provided the boys with a playroom off the kitchen, just a few steps away from the watchful eyes of their mother. As the boys grew older, this became a second dining area. It provided for two distinct social areas, one for the adolescents and one for their parents; separate spaces, linked by the kitchen. By spatially dividing the two major social areas in the house they allowed for independent activities for the teenagers without sacrificing their own need for informal space.

Similar creative uses of space were incorporated in the upstairs bathroom. With four members, the family needed more than one bathroom. Yet because considerable floor space was needed for the apartment, there was no place for a second bath, even a half bath. They decided on a compromise. Since bathing, washing, and showering were the more time-consuming bathroom activities, the Colmer plan called for a multipurpose arrangement of the space in the bathroom. The plan provided for a tub/shower and lavatory in one half, and a toilet and lavatory in the other, separated by a locking door. Thus, they were able to have most of the benefits of two full baths in little more than the space required for one. The toilet/lavatory area is accessible from the hall; the tub/lavatory area, from the master bedroom. Thus, several benefits derive. Children can be bathed for bed while father is shaving for an evening with guests. Guests can use the hall area lavatory without seeing the upset left by their hosts, who had just showered in the other half of the bath.

The Colmers ran into their first challenge when the contractor encountered their plans for this bathroom. The contractor's sense of economy called for the room to be placed at the front of the house, between the stairs and the small sewing room. There were several reasons for this: connecting the plumbing would be less expensive, since the existing piping was below this area. In addition, this location conformed to the prepackaged plan with which both the contractor and his workers were familiar. Despite the added expense, Mr. Colmer was adamant and insisted on his original design. He ran into further challenges in the location of the windows in the new master bedroom. Originally, the side windows on the second floor had been placed four feet apart. This was part of Levitt's standardized construction. It was highly economical, because it allowed the space between the windows to be filled by an uncut standard four by eight foot piece of sheetrock. To the contractor's dismay, Colmer insisted upon relocating the windows 8 inches further apart. The Colmers' plan for the finished room, however, called for the placement of their four-poster bed between the windows. Since the standard double bed is 54 inches, or four feet, six inches wide, the bed—centered—would extend into the window openings by three inches on each side. The windows were moved.

The renovation, executed while the Colmers' two boys were still of school-age, has continued to serve the couple as the boys matured, left home, and married. Mrs. Jensen still maintains her separate quarters, and Mrs. Colmer has gone into the work force. Mr. Colmer no longer comes home for lunch. Thus, the main part of the house is empty all day. But the arrangement of space serves the couple's empty nest stage in the life cycle today quite as well as it served both their young family years and Mrs. Jensen's widowhood.

The master bedroom, designed 20 years ago, still offers the combination of privacy and intimacy for which it was intended. The faux fireplace set into a paneled-and-shelving wall unit, the pair of chairs for quiet television viewing or reading, the semidouble bathroom with its individual lavatory areas, create the ideal retreat for a couple in the 1990s.

The large living room, with its fireplace, piano, stereo, and multi-use table, is a restful place for a working couple to take a light evening supper. The "porch" still serves as transition space between the outdoors and the semiprivate work space of the kitchen.

Meanwhile, despite the much-examined "generation gap" of the sixties, this couple, who were in their mid-twenties when they created their multifamily household in 1967, has managed to share their home amicably with Mrs. Colmer's widowed mother. Moreover, they have provided themselves with the potential for continuing in their own home should they both retire, or should one of them be left alone.

As Mrs. Colmer's mother approaches her 80th year, she may

find maintaining a separate household a burden. At some point, she will no longer be with them. At that time, they will have the potential for an income-producing apartment with no greater alteration than the erection of a wall where the common doorway stands today.

Should they decide to do so, however, they will find themselves among a large number of Levittowners who are altering the single-family nature of the community. The Colmers will find that such a decision is not without its social costs. Levittown's major community concern in 1987 was the proliferation of *sub rosa* two-family houses. The pioneers have reached retirement age; those who replaced them have different needs and goals.[12]

The nature of Levittown is changing. As its original residents mature, there are fewer young children in the community. The inflation of real estate values in the Northeast, coupled with Long Island's high property taxes, has made Levittown too expensive for its children. They have grown and moved on to less expensive housing. Levittown is also becoming too costly for many of those original residents who retire or find themselves widowed. Those 'pioneers' who wish to remain are beginning to convert their homes to something other than the single-family residence of the postwar years. They are creating small 'apartments' that they rent to young couples who also need basic housing. In doing so, they are incurring the hostility of the third generation of homeowners, those who bought the already renovated houses at middle-income housing prices. This group resents what they consider the devaluation of their investment through the proliferation of two-family houses, almost all of which are illegal and therefore unregulated. This new group of residents are relatively more affluent than either of the first two generations of Levittowners. They have to be. The basic Levitt house, where it can be found, is selling for over $130,000. Remodeled varieties can command figures upward of $200,000.[13]

The Taylor House

Lydia and David Taylor were not the first owners of their Cape Cod on Farmyard Lane. Mrs. Taylor believes they were the third. The house was one of Levitt's original rental units. It was then sold to an intervening owner, who did little or no remodeling. In 1967 the Taylors purchased it.

The couple had one child when they bought the house. They now have three children, two sons and one daughter. The twenty-three-year-old son is not living at home. Mrs. Taylor's parents, who live in Florida, spend several months of the year with the family. Their periodic visits shaped several aspects of the renovation. Mrs. Taylor's father, who was a building contractor before he retired, assisted in both the planning and the design.

Like the Colmer house, this house was custom-tailored to the lifestyle of the residents. Little attention was paid to the market value of the renovations, since the family intended to remain in the house. The benefits they expected to derive from the remodeling would be social rather than economic. The standard 6000-square foot plot on which this house is situated limited the size and placement of any structural additions to the orginal floor space. The solution was to create a new room, which is only 12 feet wide, but which runs the full 24-foot depth of the house and extends an additional seven feet to the rear.

The extension, like the original house, sits on a concrete slab.[14] The front elevation remains that of a one-story Cape Cod, as does the Colmer house, although the addition rises to a second story in the rear of the house.

Because Mrs. Taylor, an only daughter, has assumed full responsibility for the extended family's major holiday celebrations, one of her primary needs was a large kitchen with plenty of seating space. The first floor of the extension, a 12' × 33' "great room," was thus designed to serve as a combination kitchen-dining room large enough for holiday entertaining.

The new kitchen is a working kitchen; its function has not been minimized or disguised in the renovation. The party wall between the original house and the extension now serves as an appliance wall. In keeping with her emphasis on celebratory cooking, there are both a refrigerator/freezer and a full freezer; a washer and dryer complete the appliance wall. The cabinets begin next to the appliances and continue along the back wall of the house. In all, the cabinets provide some 150 linear feet of shelving.

Throughout our interview, Mrs. Taylor explained the many varieties of storage added to the house by pointing out that "these houses have no storage," a complaint echoed by many of the other residents. Indeed, one of the signs of Levittown's continuing affluence is the need for additional storage space that so many of its residents have had to address. The four-room basic house was not designed to hold the myriad items of personal and family possessions that Levittowners of today take for granted.

The new kitchen was designed primarily to serve for extended-family entertaining. To that end, the room is equipped with rolla-way furniture so that when the holidays come, the room can seat and serve the whole family. The dining area at the front of the room is separated from the work area by a six-foot base cabinet, which is on casters. During major entertaining, this unit is rolled to the side wall, where it replaces a desk. The desk, in turn, is moved to the storage wall in the old kitchen, which has become a music center. This allows considerable floor space in the kitchen for several dining tables and chairs.

Although no attempt was made to pretend that the kitchen is not primarily a functional room, it is obvious from some subtle touches that it is also a public room, a room for company as well as family. The kitchen air conditioner is built into the wall behind a cabinet and is accessed through the open door of the cabinet. A strong emphasis on home entertaining permeates the redesign. For example, by extending the kitchen beyond the rear wall of the original house, the Taylors created an ell for a sheltered patio. They included a pass-through window from kitchen to patio to allow for outdoor as well as indoor entertaining.

The original kitchen is now a music room containing an electric organ and several beanbag chairs. Built-in storage units have replaced the original kitchen cabinets. This room is open to both the staircase and the living room beyond, and provides a place for music and relaxation just outside the new kitchen/great room.

The living room in the Taylor house has not been changed structurally. It is the original Levitt living room, even to the faux beams in the ceiling. Its persistence is not readily recognizable, however, since the original kitchen wall has been removed, opening the staircase on both sides. The free-standing staircase now appears to bisect a continuum of space that incorporates the music room.

The removal of the wall between stairs and the music room increases the sense of spaciousness at the entry, creating a wide vista from what had been two small rooms. This sense of space is intensified as the stairs rise without bannisters and are fully carpeted, extending the floor of the music room. Some definition of space is created by the placement of the furnishings, which are arranged to provide a visual pathway through the living room to the den at the rear of the house. A sectional sofa, placed along the front wall, turns at a right angle to the wall and continues parallel to the stairs. This defines the path, without interrupting the visual space of the living area.

The rear of the house has been altered more radically. The for-

6.2

Front elevation and floor plans for Taylor house. (a) Front elevation.
(b) First floor. (c) Second floor.

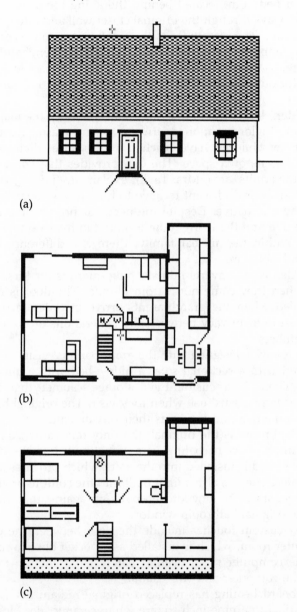

(a)

(b)

(c)

mer master bedroom, located behind the living room, has been extended sideways through the original closet wall and into the former small bedroom. The remainder of the small bedroom was divided to provide a computer/video-game room for the children,[15] and a deep-storage area—"what the Levitt house lacks, we had to give ourselves"—for out-of-season clothing and equipment, and for seldom-used articles such as lobster pots and coffee urns.

The den, larger than the living room, provides the major social space. Mrs. Taylor mentioned privacy as one reason for the den. Now that her children have reached adolescence, their entertainment requires its own space. The den provides that space without invading the adults' area. Mrs. Taylor explained, "I don't want to sit with the kids, nor do I want to have to hide in my room." The den provides an alternative. Despite the need for privacy, the door between the den and the living room is stored in the closet for most of the year. Within the nuclear family, there is a difference between privacy and isolation.

The den area converts into sleeping quarters for Mrs. Taylor's parents when they come north from Florida. The door is retrieved and installed when the grandparents arrive in order to provide a larger measure of privacy between the generations of the extended family members.

The den was designed with the grandparents' visits in mind. It is furnished with a sectional sofa, a hide-a-bed with a queen-sized mattress. There is a custom-built storage cabinet that includes drawers for the parents' use when they visit. The original bathroom opens onto the den and serves as their private bath.

The bathroom is the original; the only renovation, other than the installation of wainscoating, is a soffit, built into the tub area. The shower head is installed into the soffit which provides a vertical flow of water. There is also a light built into the soffit to brighten the shower area, since the new kitchen butts up against this wall, eliminating the original bathroom window.

Other custom touches include the door between the den and the computer room, which is installed as a pocket door to save floor space. The computer room itself is barely large enough to hold a desk for the computer and two chairs.

Baseboard heating has replaced original radiant heat, and the floors are tiled in a nine-inch-square white ceramic tile. Most of the house is carpeted. This is important in a slab house, since without the radiant heat in the floors, the concrete tends to retain the cold and be uncomfortable underfoot. The burner—a replacement—is located in the original space under the stairs, but it is now accessed from a door into the den, rather than from the former kitchen, as was originally designed.

The additions were done when Mrs. Taylor was expecting her third child. Thus, the area over the kitchen was also extended to provide a new master bedroom on the second floor. The double dormer that was already on the house contained two bedrooms. This area now provides a 12 × 16-foot bedroom, originally used for the two boys, and a slightly smaller bedroom for the daughter. Both rooms have full closets, the boys' room with access to the knee wall. Mrs. Taylor repeats her one criticism of the Levitt houses, "There's absolutely no storage in the [original] house."

In addition, the attic area provides a small space for a computer/office and a large, multi-use bathroom. Like the bathroom in the Colmers' house, this single bathroom is designed to provide most of the benefits of two separate baths. It is located in an area that is 14' square, and can be used with some degree of privacy by four people. The basic square has been divided into a T-shape, with a stall shower on the left of the entry and a café-doored commode on the right. The top of the T opens to about 9 by 14 feet. To the right is a sink, with a base cabinet, a hanging basket chair, and a telephone. Across from this is a second sink with both a cabinet and a full wall counter top. With the addition of a small wicker chair, this will become a vanity.

The computer area across from the bathroom includes the original chimney and is open to the stairs and the upper hall.[16] Since the front of the house follows the pitch of the original Cape Cod roofline, this section of the attic has no windows. Indeed, there is no window along the front of the roofline. As a result, the house retains its original Cape Cod appearance from the street. Although Mrs. Taylor did not specifically mention a concern with the integrity of the original Levitt design as a reason for this design decision, she—like Mr. Colmer—did refer to the harmony of the streetscape as a positive effect of that decision.

The master bedroom, which covers the entire second floor of the addition, is 12 feet wide by 21 feet deep. There is reduced usable floor space on the second floor due to the geometry of the extension. Retaining the original slope of the front roofline while extending the footprint seven feet in depth called for some modifications in the pitch of the rear roofline. Even with the shallower pitch, it was necessary to sacrifice some wall height. As a result, the ceiling in this room is slightly lower than eight feet. To compensate for the pitch of the front roof, closets were built across the front wall of the house, which are six feet deep with sloped ceilings. Shelves and storage drawers are built into the rear of the closet where the ceiling slopes downward to meet the front wall of the house.

The Taylors have considered moving, but find that they cannot equal the size and value of their house elsewhere. Nor can they be assured of finding a buyer who can afford to pay what their home is worth. Thus, although more affluent than the widowed and retired members of the first generation who find Levittown too costly to remain, the Taylors, too, are finding that the high cost of Long Island real estate has had an impact on their housing.

The Mendola House

Several blocks away from the Taylor home is the home of Lucy and Jim Mendola. They, too, are the third owners of their home, a 1949 ranch that now has nine rooms and two baths. Other than adding a skylight to the cathedral ceiling in the dining room, the Mendolas did none of the structural alterations.

They bought the house in 1976 from the Ilanos, who were responsible for most of the interior renovations. The house was built on one of several odd-shaped plots that Levitt purchased after his initial large-scale acquisition of land. Because the property did not provide the necessary 200-foot depth for a pair of back-to-back plots, the houses on this street came with extra deep, irregularly-shaped plots. In itself, this quality creates a more desirable area. Those sections of Levittown that do not replicate the 60' × 100' plots are less readily recognizable as postwar tract developments and are in greater demand. The plots have also lent themselves to more individualized redesigning of the original floorplan, which again imparts an upscale quality to the house.

The first owner of the house, a swimming-pool contractor, installed a large, in-ground pool with a small (8' × 10') cabana to the rear. The cabana provided a dressing room and bath for summer use, and winter storage for the garden furnishings. Mr. Rosa also installed pools for several of his neighbors, before selling the house to the Ilanos and moving on. Thus, not only has this property been improved, but it is located on a street in which most of the properties have also been upgraded, thereby enhancing the collective value of the neighborhood.

When they moved in, Mr. and Mrs. Ilano customized the house to reflect their upper middle-class lifestyle. They added a center hall and a bar/den to the left of the original kitchen, which had been squared. Behind this extension, they installed a maid's room and utility/service area with an exit to the back yard. Across the back of the house, they added an extension that was 16 feet deep and 32 feet wide. They opened the rear wall of the original living room to this extension, creating an L-shaped dining/living room. They opened the ceiling above this new dining area, creating a cathedral ceiling. The original staircase rises to a balcony that runs across the ridgeline of the house. At either end of the balcony is a large bedroom, one of which is in the original attic, the other over the den extension. They added a bath to the area over the kitchen, off the balcony.

On the first floor, they eliminated the original utility core, combined the two bedrooms into one large master bedroom, and constructed wall-to-wall closets at either side of this room.

The house was now appropriate for an up-and-coming attorney and his wife. There was considerable space for extensive indoor and outdoor entertaining. There was ample room for their sizable wardrobes. The storage space was tailored to the variety of clothing needed for the many social activities in which they were involved. (Mrs. Ilano had a special closet fitted for her evening gowns, and one under the stairs designed just for her shoes, boots, and handbags).

After ten years, the Ilanos moved on. They, in turn, sold the house to Mr. Ilano's young law partner, James Mendola. With only minor changes, the house suited the Mendolas and their three children quite well. The maid's room became the computer room; the bar/den, the rumpus room.

When Mr. Mendola's mother became ill and moved in with them, the family transformed the poolside cabana into a small apartment for their college-age son, moving the elder Mrs. Mendola into his upstairs bedroom. As her illness progressed, it became necessary for Mrs. Mendola to move to a health-care facility, returning the upstairs bedroom to her grandson.

His 'apartment' has reverted to a cabana. However, it also serves the younger Mrs. Mendola as a study, since she has resumed her academic career. Although small, this area could also become a rental area, if the Mendolas were to decide that they wanted or needed added income. Similarly, had the elder Mrs. Mendola not been ill, it might have served as more private quarters for her.

Right now, however, the Mendolas feel no need for extra income. Their family uses every bit of available space for its own

6.3

Front elevation and floor plans for Mendola house. (a) Front elevation.
(b) First floor. (c) Second floor.

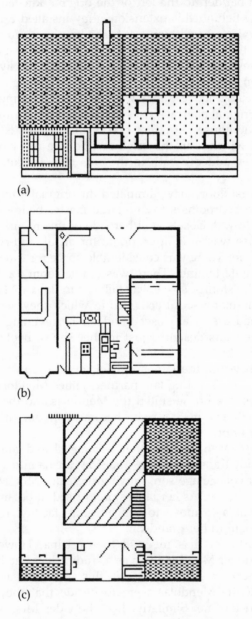

(a)

(b)

(c)

activities. A tenant or boarder would be an intrusion. The section of Levittown in which they live has not yet found itself becoming a two-family neighborhood, and they—and their neighbors—prefer it that way.

For these Levittowners, the house represents more than a place to live. It is an extension of their lifestyle, as well as one of their biggest investments. These couples are generally in the years of their highest earning power. In many cases both spouses have full-time careers. They are still decades away from retirement and old age. Their needs are complex and costly. They express sympathy for the older generation, but little empathy. They worry about their off-springs' ability to pursue a similar way of life in the future. But they do not believe that Levittown can, or should, provide the solution.

Meanwhile, their houses reflect the amenities of the approved lifestyle that has been advocated by American commerce and industry through a wide assortment of media. Fads and trends that appear in house and home magazines are reflected in spatial uses within the Levittown houses. Mrs. Taylor's exercise room/computer office is not unusual in today's upscale homes; nor is her 14-foot bathroom with its hanging basket chair and telephone.[17]

The Colmer's bed-sitting room, with its cozy fireplace and paired slipper chairs, is typical of many of the English country-type rooms showcased in such journals as *Architectural Digest* and *House Beautiful*. Mrs. Mendola's usurpation of the backyard cabana for a private study while she completes a postgraduate degree also reveals the degree to which Levittown and its houses have kept pace with the lifestyle of the American middle class.

Looking Toward the Year 2000

The housing situation in Levittown is somewhat different for the younger members of the baby-boom generation.[18] Martin and Rosemary Stark are among them. Despite her parents' assistance in the purchase of their house, the Starks have had to rent one floor of their home in order to be able to maintain it. Her parents, Tony and Agnes Romeo, converted the 1949 ranch house into a two-family dwelling in several stages. Throughout these stages, the basic arrangement of the original Levitt house was maintained, which resulted in several compromises in layout and design.[19] For example, there is no defined entry hall; one enters the house through a door to the dining room, located in what had been the garage. The original kitchen is to the right of this room, essentially unchanged in arrangement, except for the squaring of the entry corner, which now opens into the dining room. Similarly, the only modification to the original bathroom was the addition of shower doors and wainscoting.

The Romeos' first alteration was the conversion of the garage into a dining room when Rosemary was entering her teens. Later, they undertook the first actual extension of the house to provide room for Mr. Romeo's mother, who was moving in with them. At that time, the second floor was double-dormered to produce three bedrooms and a bath. The first floor of the house was extended across the rear, doubling the floorspace of the living room and original master bedroom and increasing the original size of the house by almost 50 percent.[20] The master bedroom and its extension provided two rooms separated by an archway, with a door to the garden for the elder Mrs. Romeo. The upper floor provided bedrooms and a den for the younger family. In this way, the generations were able to maintain some privacy, although the basic arrangement was that of an extended family.

In 1981, when their daughter married, the Romeos completed the conversion, turning the second floor into a three-and-a-half-room apartment with two bedrooms and a kitchen/living area for the new couple. Two years later, when the Romeos decided to retire to Florida, they sold the house to their daughter. The younger couple was able to afford to purchase the house only because it would produce sufficient income to offset the mortgage payments. They have now moved to the first floor and are renting the second floor to Mr. Stark's younger sister, her husband, and their baby. Although still inhabited by an extended family, the house has become a distinctly two-family residence with separate entrances. It provides for total individualization, should future residents not want to interact.

As the Starks became more economically comfortable, they added a bedroom behind the dining room and converted the original bedroom side of the house into quarters for their three small children. The original master bedroom, once the quarters of their great-grandmother, is now the room of the twin girls. The older woman's two sections—bedroom and parlor—provide sleeping and playing areas. The original small bedroom is used as a nursery for the little boy.

The living room is 24 feet deep, large enough to allow for two distinct seating areas. In one, wing chairs and tables provide a conversational grouping. In keeping with the trend towards privatizing family life, the house is strongly oriented toward the rear garden.

The living room and the master bedroom both have bay windows along the back wall, which overlook a landscaped garden and a large pool, complete with several levels of decking and patios. The seating groups in this section of the living room are arranged so that the chairs face the view provided by the garden.

In the other—original—area of the living room, a sectional couch with a sofa bed faces the fireplace. Here, as in many of the remodeled houses in Levittown, attention has been paid to providing temporary sleeping quarters for the retired parents who occasionally come north from Florida. When the Romeos spend summers in New York, the sofa-bed area can be screened off to provide them with some privacy. The Levitt-designed pivoting cabinet has been removed, the wall extended to replace it, and the fireplace enclosed in sheetrock. The fireplace has taken on a very modern look, with a ceramic tile border flush to the wall and directly on the floor to form the hearth.

The new master bedroom is set off from the rear section of the living room by curtained French doors. A 12-foot closet crosses the bedroom wall, which divides that room from the dining room. This creates a sound barrier between the dining room and the couple's bedroom, although its effect on their privacy is mitigated by the fact that the bedroom opens directly into the living room.

In many ways the latest addition reflects not only the living styles of the baby-boom generation, but a generational shift among Italian-Americans away from the extended family with which their parents had been familiar. When the elder Mrs. Romeo shared the home with her son and his family, she was an interactive part of the household. Despite the privacy afforded by her double room, her meals were family meals, and the living room was open to all members of the household. Mrs. Stark, her grand-daughter, on the other hand, has maintained separate quarters in each phase of her married tenancy in the household. Similarly, Mrs. Stark's sister-in-law maintains her own separate kitchen, and the two families visit rather than interact.

Despite this, however, Mrs. Stark does not consider her home to be one of the new two-family houses that are proliferating in Levittown. The distinctions she makes are important to an understanding of the nature of the changes that are taking place in the community: the rise of absentee and/or commercial landlords. This creates a dilemma for the Starks, who expect to be transferred to New Jersey within the next two or three years. They feel that they will have to sell the house, if their in-laws will not rent the downstairs—more

6.4

Front elevation and floor plans for Stark house. (a) Front elevation.
(b) First floor. (c) Second floor.

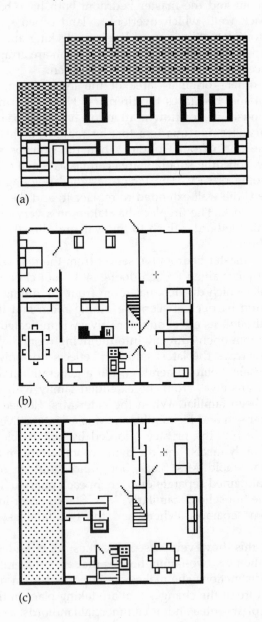

(a)

(b)

(c)

expensive—apartment. The Starks do not want to become absentee landlords, and commented on the problems that such landlords are beginning to cause on their block.[21] Group renting and room renting have become more obvious in the neighborhood as cars proliferate along the streets. In addition, this has given rise to what appears to be a severe absence of owner pride and care.

The Stark's tendency to distance themselves from the landlords in Levittown is not unusual. They draw fine lines between two-family houses and houses in which there are two families in residence. Other Levittowners exempt themselves from the two-family category, too, despite the fact that their households are composed of two and even three generations of adults with a comparable number of cars and activities. If the additional adults are family members, particularly adult children of the homeowners, there is an apparent dispensation. "Tenants" are those who come as strangers and rent quarters from the owners. "Landlords" are those who admit strangers to their homes.

The home of George and Phyllis Donaldson is in transition; neither landlords nor empty-nesters, they find themselves sharing their home with their grown children at several stages of residence. One son is still living at home; a daughter has married, but still has clothing and assorted possessions at home. Another son is divorced, which has had a disruptive effect on the parents. The mother has cut herself off from this son and avoided discussing him in our interview, although she made her disapproval of his lifestyle quite clear. Yet, it appears likely that this son may soon be returning to the nest, at least temporarily, until he can recover from the economic effects of the divorce. At present, the house is not arranged to provide him with private quarters; rather, he will return to find himself once more the younger generation in a nuclear family, at least temporarily.

This family should not find their situation to be too unusual, considering the plight of many of the neighboring families. Nearby, the Cotanis are also coping with adult children living at home. Like the Donaldsons, they had expected to be spending the final preretirement years in an empty nest. Contrary to the received wisdom of the fifties, however, the Cotanis—like most of their neighbors— were looking forward to the experience. They saw it as an opportunity to reestablish their own adult relationship, and to expand their living area to reflect the interests that have developed as their parental responsibilities diminished. However, the economics of the eighties have forced their two children to remain at home several

Front elevation and floor plans for Donaldson house. (a) Front elevation.
(b) First floor. (c) Second floor.

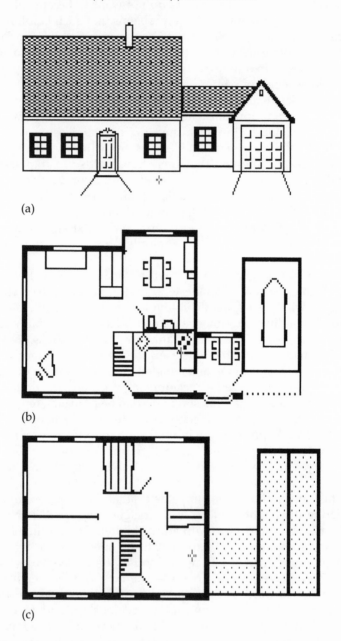

(a)

(b)

(c)

6.6

Cotani floor plan. (a) First floor. (b) Second floor.

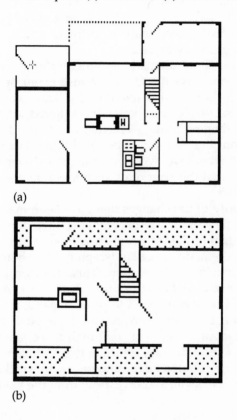

(a)

(b)

years beyond what was the norm for the parents' generation. As a result, the potting shed/laundry that Mrs. Cotani had added to the rear of the house now stores her son's hunting gear, her daughter's skiing equipment, and the extra furniture which had been intended for the bedroom-turned-den that has reverted to a bedroom for the son. The Cotanis have come to accept the fact that one or both of their offspring will probably be with them for several years longer.[22] Their situation is made easier by the fact that many of their neighbors share in it.

The O'Kanes, for example, have their three adult children and one son-in-law still living at home with them. Mr. O'Kane appears to find this situation surprisingly pleasant, commenting that he enjoys having the kids around. His attitude toward a large family circle is reflected in the history of the family's experience in the house. Since the O'Kanes moved in in 1963, they have also shared their household with members of their extended family. At one point Mrs. O'Kane's father lived with them for several years; at another time, her brother-in-law moved in.

Although it is not dramatically different in the most important aspects, in several ways the O'Kane house is out of harmony with other houses in the area. For one thing, it has never been enlarged in any way. Essentially, except for the squared kitchen and some superficial rearranging of the elements, this house has not been altered at all. Considering the number of children raised in it, as well as the relatives who have lived with the family over the years, it is unusual to find that the exterior of the house remains as it was originally constructed.

The majority of the changes that have been made to the house reflect the family's emphasis on enjoying their home as the focal point of their family life, rather than competing for neighborhood honors through remodeling or landscaping.[23] The house is located at the corner of a curved intersection. This creates a plot with more yard area to the side and the front than to the rear. A major portion of the side yard has been paved to provide parking for the family's eight cars. And, to provide privacy for their pool, they have surrounded the backyard with a six-foot-high fence, above which they have attached a second fence, which is five feet high. This does not result in the same suburban demeanor as a white picket fence, but it allows the family to swim and dive away from the view of the neighbors.

Of all of the houses visited in the course of this study, the O'Kanes' was the only one that remained true to the original geography provided by Levitt in 1949. Yet even here, modifications have been made that are specific to the family's lifestyle, rather than to some external norm imposed by the various governments that have jurisdiction over it. Indeed, the multilayered, 11-foot fence is almost certainly illegal within the building codes of the town. At the whim of a disgruntled neighbor or a cruising building inspector, the family could be made to remove the upper level fence.[24]

Similarly, Mrs. Cotani's potting shed encroaches seriously on the established building lines, and her husband admits that most of his modifications to the house should have been done under a town building permit. Although their improvements may be technically illegal, these families are protected by the fact that their modifications to the houses fall within the accepted limits for suburban residential architecture. Their neighbors, themselves probably vulnerable to the building inspector's scrutiny, are unlikely to register a complaint until and unless the modifications or the lifestyles violate the community's norms.[25]

The built environment of Levittown is also being altered by an influx of new construction, most of which is in the form of two-family houses on undersized plots. Speculative builders are buying up what little available land remains. This is generally found in the smaller, more irregular plots that were rejected as building lots in earlier, more affluent times. The houses built on these plots are designed for high density—large, narrow-line houses that consume as much as 60 percent of the lot, and even more where building and zoning boards are accommodating. The resulting configurations tend to diminish the suburban demeanor, creating instead what the residents of Levittown disdain as the "Queens look."[26] Narrow lots and two-family houses result in an increase in the number of cars parked along the streets and in the driveways. Areas of Levittown where public transportation is uneven are particularly vulnerable to this problem.[27] The proliferation of cars along the streets is also viewed as an urban artifact encroaching upon the suburbs, and has been the subject of restrictive zoning and housing legislation in other Long Island communities that are trying to retain their suburban qualities of life.[28]

Recently the Levittown Property Owners Association took legal action to stop a developer who was building two-family houses on scattered plots in Levittown. Along with the increased traffic and local congestion resulting from the concomitant increase in cars, two-family houses create the potential for an increased number of absentee landlords and a lowered sense of interest in maintenance and landscaping. These trends threaten to diminish the quality of suburban life in Levittown, thereby decreasing the property values the homeowners have worked so hard to maintain. Thus, the homeowners' major objection to the new construction was their perception that the middle-class suburban qualities of the neighborhood were being devalued by the introduction of this new form of affordable housing, even though it met the legal requirements for building and zoning within the Town of Hempstead.[29]

The Levittown Property Owners Association is determined not to let that happen. The Association has fought the construction by attempting to block any further development within the community's borders, armed with the special zoning legislation that incorporated Levitt's restrictive covenant almost verbatim into the Hempstead Town building and zoning codes.[30] But they recognize that this is simply a holding action; they, too, are finding the high cost of living in Levittown to be a burden. Limited forms of two-family housing may soon be needed even by its strongest opponents.[31]

7

Myths and Meanings

For all the faults attributed to them by their critics, the houses of the postwar subdivisions had a widespread appeal. They may have been small and repetitious to their observers, but to their owners they represented something more than basic shelter—they were an opportunity to build a better life, a first step on the road to success. It is at that level that the housing programs of the 1940s made their greatest achievement.

Contrary to the expectations of its critics, Levittown did not become a slum. Rather, the houses evolved into a solidly middle-class suburban development of homes complete with country kitchens, center halls, second and even third baths, dining rooms, vestibules, family rooms, computer rooms, and dens. Although not every home in Levittown can be said to reflect quite the level of comfort and individualization to be found in the homes of the Taylors, Colmers, and Mendolas, the community, with its blending of variety and harmony, is far removed from the slum that was predicted in 1947.

This chapter examines the deeper meaning of the houses of Levittown by isolating common elements and significant themes in two versions of the Levittown story, each of which draws on the same basic information to reach radically different conclusions. The first version is that which has become the folkloric history of the community. The second is that of the outsiders—generally professional observers such as journalists, sociologists, and urban planners. These contrasting versions, which are referred to in this chapter as the myths of Levittown, have persisted for more than 40 years, and have settled on the one hand into a form of traditional history or civic belief and on the other into a form of pseudo-intellectual disdain for suburban life in general, with Levittown serving as its archetype. As it is used here, the word *myth* refers to a group explanation of an experience informed by shared perception, rather than by systematic inquiry into accuracy of detail. With repetition, the explanation acquires a patina of authenticity.[1]

In 1957, when Levittown celebrated its tenth anniversary, the local papers provided extensive coverage for all the events, from the parade to the house tour. In a special section devoted to "The Levittown Decade," *Newsday* restated the essence of the myth.

> First there were only potato farms and then came the day veterans moved into the homes they had dreamed of, homes they could afford. . . . "Levittown—A screaming black headline on the front page of *Newsday*, May 7, 1947, struck Long Island's veteran population with more hope and elation than they had felt since the news that the Second World War had ended. . . . "2000 $60 Rentals Due in L.I. Project" . . . You had to be a veteran who had returned to a homeland that could not provide you with a home to feel the full impact and promise of the headline. It was 1947, a year in which there was a crying need for 5,000,000 new homes in the U.S. It was the year of the great housing shortage. Families had doubled up. All you had to do to visit your in-laws was walk into the next room. . . . Suddenly, like a Christmas present in the spring, William J. Levitt, dynamic, young (37), self-assured president of Levitt & Sons (he was one of the sons) announced his dramatic, partial solution to Long Island's housing need. On the open Hempstead Plains in the potato farm area of Island Trees, he would build 2000 four-room Cape Cod houses which veterans could rent for $60 a month.[2]

The folkloric version is retold on such occasions by the long-term residents of the community who refer to themselves as the "pioneers," and are largely those early residents who persisted past the rental days and became the first homeowners.[3] One such pioneer— now widowed and no longer a resident—repeated the essence of the myth to explain the meaning of Levittown to an exchange student:

> The war was over, and we were living in one room in my parents' apartment. . . . Think of it, Wei Ren, we were living in *one* room with *two* children. The boys had come home from overseas and all we wanted was a home of our own. Then Mr. Levitt turned all these little potato farms into Levittown, and we got a piece of the American Dream.

We were all in the same boat; we didn't have much money, but we worked together; everybody pitched in. We shared everything; we shared tools and cars, minded each others' kids, passed play-pens and high-chairs from house to house—everything.
It was—at least to us—a Paradise.[4]

Mrs. Klerk's reference to "a piece of the American Dream" is evocative of a larger myth—the American belief in the socio-political importance of homeowning as a concomitant of the republican ideal. This belief, variously referred to as the Jeffersonian ideal, the yeoman myth, and the rural ideal, equates the privately-owned house and lot with family virtue, political stability, and civic responsibility.[5] The equation of Levittown with the American Dream is a persistent element in the community's self-description—past and present. The linking of the house and community to that dream has been repeated by the Levittown residents over and over, not only in interviews throughout the course of this study, but in news coverage, letters to the editor, and publications of the Levittown Property Owners Association.

The myth has a number of components: the rural roots of the community, the benevolent builder, the pioneer spirit among the residents, the joy of single-family dwellings, the collective activity among the homeowners as they worked to impart an individuality through remodeling and landscaping, and the struggle for upward mobility through material goods. Within these are a number of stock elements that express a larger belief system: the strength and youth of American society; the quest for freedom and independence that lured the early settlers, and the benevolence of the founding fathers who established the nation; the rural ideal in which the yeoman farmer tills his own soil; the rugged individualism of the pioneer family, coupled with the collective nature of the trek west (circling the wagons against attack; nuclear families banding together against the natural forces of the west); and, most important, the attainment of upward mobility through equal opportunity.

Levittown, an area of some seven square miles with retail stores, recreational centers, and 17,500 houses, thus has meaning far beyond shelter, commerce, and amusement. The mythic version of the Levittown experience testifies to the importance of homeowning in the American mentality.[6] The myth's emphasis on gardening and the rebuilding of the houses roots the Levittown experience in the Arcadian myth and the pioneer saga, and the emphasis on the days when the couples were young correlates to the American sense of a new beginning and eternal youth. In short, the Levittown myth is the American myth.

In 1985, W.D. Wetherall captured this version in his short story, "The Man Who Loved Levittown." Told as the narrative of Tommy DeMaria, a widowed Levittown homeowner of retirement age, the story is the encapsulation of the myth. It opens with De-Maria's recollections of the spring of 1947 when, as a newly discharged veteran, he came "out on Long Island" from the Brooklyn home of his in-laws in search of a job and a place to live. Stopping at a local diner, he is surrounded by bitter farmers, complaining about being driven off their farms by the developers. He has little sympathy for the farmers, believing instead that they had made a fortune from the sale of their lands. DeMaria then tours the area to find a boarded-up old farmhouse with

> an ancient Chevy piled to the gunwales with old spring beds, pots and pans. Dust Bowl, Okies, *Grapes of Wrath* . . . just like that . . .[7]

His description recreates the image of the postwar rural-to-suburban metamorphosis that is one of the basic components of the myth.

The story continues with the arrival of the veterans—like De-Maria—and their young families. They find themselves living like "pioneers," one for all and all for one in their "cute, little" houses. The men gather to do battle with the crabgrass and the snow, to share their tools, and to expand their houses; for relaxation, they coach the Little League teams, toss balls on the lawns with their children, share a beer in the carport. The women gather to share their recipes and their appliances; they keep their eyes on the ever-present children while they plant flowers, decorate the newly expanded houses, shop, and participate in PTA activities.[8]

In the residents' version, as in Wetherall's story, the barbecues, parties, and local events take on a new dimension in which simple hamburgers become epicurean delights; house renovations and car troubles become adventures, and casual acquaintances lead to life-long friendships. DeMaria is particularly saddened by the trend among his former neighbors to retire to Florida, abandoning him and his beloved Levittown for a condo in the sun. The story ends on a dismal note; the pioneers are leaving in increasing numbers, driven out as much by the rising property taxes as by the new-comers who do not understand the Levittown way of life. Renters are moving in; they and their children have no respect for the traditional values of the early Levittowners. There is little to celebrate in Tommy DeMaria's contemporary Levittown; Camelot is gone.

Although Wetherall's 'man who loved Levittown' is a fictional character, the sentiments he expressed are resonant of those expressed by Levittown residents throughout the course of this study. Their memories of the beginnings stress the same elements: Bill Levitt took care of the veterans, providing everything they needed; his houses were well constructed; the community was a rare combination of youth and cooperation; people worked hard to maintain their property; and everyone took care of each other in times of need. It is an idyllic story, in which much tribute is paid to William J. Levitt. He is credited with inventing everything about Levittown—and by extension, the postwar suburb—from the curvilinear roadways to the inclusion of educational sites and buildings for public recreation; from the on-site factory method of construction to the provision of trees and landscaping.[9]

This version of the history of Levittown has been told so often that it has taken on a transcendent reality. It is repeated at 10-year intervals when the anniversary of the community is celebrated. It has been made into slide programs and videotapes; it has been repeated on network news programs and in the national press.[10]

The persistence of the myth among residents past and present is a significant part of the history of Levittown. Outsiders may have seen only the monotonous rows of boxlike houses; it was they who wrote of social malaise, rigid conformity, or divisive school-related struggles.[11] The residents saw the myth; for them it contains the essence of the Levittown story. As Tommy DeMaria expressed it,

You talk about dreams. Hell, we had ours. We had ours like nobody before or since ever had theirs. SEVEN THOUSAND BUCKS! ONE HUNDRED DOLLARS DOWN! We were cowboys out there. We were the pioneers.[12]

Although these versions are in many respects idealistic, they express a reality that is summed up in the statement, "We got a piece of the American Dream." It would be a mistake to disregard the truths of the myth in a search for greater accuracy. Rather, we should try to grasp the underlying meaning to those whose myth it has become.[13] On one level, the Levittown story is the story of politics, of housing policies and demobilized veterans, of real estate development and construction technology; on another, it is the story of

7.1

Aerial view of Levittown taken after construction of the first 6000 houses in 1948, and before construction of the 1949 ranch models. (NCM) Area east of Wantagh Parkway, north and south of Hempstead Turnpike.

young families, hard work, and realized dreams. But it is always a story of houses and homes. And those houses are an important key to understanding the persistence of the myth.

The story began even before the overturning of the first acre of ground as a chronicle of events based largely on Levitt's press conferences and the company's press releases. The groundwork for it was laid in 1944 in an article in the *Saturday Evening Post*, based on an interview with William Levitt in which he revealed his plans for the future.[14] The author, Boyden Sparkes, provided a history of the firm into which he wove the elements that would eventually be codified into the basic outline of the myth. Among these are the roles and personality traits of the three principals in Levitt and Sons. Abraham, the father, a semiretired lawyer, serves as the landscaper

for the developments. Alfred, the younger, more retiring son, is the
architect for the firm, whereas William is the innovative business-
man and builder.

Sparkes detailed Levitt's plans for the postwar model community in which he would build

> the swimming pool, then the community house, then the base-
> ball field, then the handball courts and then a pathway for bi-
> cycle riders. A boy will be able to get on his bike and ride for
> five miles or more without crossing a vehicular road. Such lux-
> uries, previously provided with houses of ours costing up to
> eighteen thousand dollars, we now intend to provide also for
> those who will buy our four-thousand dollar houses.[15] We can
> find plenty of customers who will feel that so much for four
> hundred dollars down and twenty-seven dollars a month will
> really be like a miracle.[16]

This use of phrases such as "like a miracle" was typical of Levitt's interviews. Although the exaggerations were his, they were
quoted freely by the press. This type of coverage of both the Levitt
firm and its products set the tone for most of the Levittown story in
the early years: Levitt would build a miracle. The repetition of the
exaggerations gave a ring of authenticity to claims by both his ad-
mirers and his detractors that he had singlehandedly invented the
postwar subdivision suburb.[17]

Actually, Levitt's promise of postwar miracle houses, pre-fabri-
cated with all new, built-in components and innovative materials,
echoed those made during the World's Fair of 1939. The fair's
"Home of Tomorrow" would be made from inexpensive, easy-care
materials; it would be bathed in sunlight, and—thanks to modern
technology—within the reach of "all but the lowest classes."[18]

The reference to class raises another element of the myth—
albeit a complicated one—the social status of the Levittown population. Levitt's interviews and subsequent press coverage make its
clear that the houses were intended for a lower-income group from
the start. Yet, in restrospective analyses, Levittown has generally
been treated as if it had always been a middle-class community.[19] In
part this is due to a widespread conflation of the meanings of 'average' and 'middle' as terms for describing relative standing in income
and class in a society that believes itself to be classless.[20] Of equal
importance, however, is the traditional role of home ownership as a

symbol of the middle class status, which has caused a retrospective attribution of that standing to those for whom Levitt was building.[21]

Throughout the construction period, the term "lower-income" was frequently used to identify the market for the houses of early Levittown, not only by Levitt, but also by the press and by those in Washington whose housing policies would fund the construction.[22] Levitt repeatedly referred to the cost-efficiency of his materials, and to the fact that he was building for those whose incomes were in the range of $3000 a year.[23] Moreover, he was building originally for a tenant class.[24] That he was successful in reaching them is supported by the fact that several of the studies found that the median income in Levittown during its first five years was between $3000 and $3750 per year.[25] In 1951, the census bureau located the "average American" in Levittown. This man, among other characteristics, "had an approximate annual salary of $3000."[26] Such an income was typically earned by those in blue-collar, service, and clerical positions in the period.[27]

Neither Levittown nor its residents were perceived as being solidly middle-class in 1947. Despite repeated approval for the project expressed in the editorials of the local press, there was also a strong, if little-recorded, local opposition to the proliferation of this low-cost housing project in its preconstruction phase, and much of this opposition was grounded in class. The combination of lower-income constituents and mass-production materials and techniques sparked serious opposition to the project among the older residents of Nassau County, concerned with retaining their way of life and their property values.[28]

Levitt's innovations also caused serious concern among those with an interest in housing and planning, particularly among those in the building trades.[29] The local press defended the construction as sound, lauded the innovations as cost- and time-effective, and accused opponents of "elitism and cronyism." This coverage also repeated and reinforced that element of the myth which presented Levitt as an innovative creator of the mass-produced suburb, the answer to the veterans' housing shortage. Levitt and his technology became rallying cries as the local press sensed in the homeless veteran and his champion a powerful issue.[30]

The Levittown myth is so strong that many of its elements have found their way into the more exacting scholarship without qualification. Consider, for example, the belief that the houses "sprang up" from potato farms. This version of the construction process has been repeated so often that the accepted image of the preconstruction area has become that of a rural farming village.[31]

Yet, although a large portion of the acreage at Island Trees was engaged in the production of potatoes at the time of the construction, commerce and industry had been making inroads in the area for several decades. The hamlet was situated within four miles of Hempstead, a suburban commercial center with branches of several major metropolitan department stores. Within five miles in several directions were four major industrial plants: Grumman Aircraft, Republic Aviation, Sperry Gyroscope, and Liberty Aircraft Products, as well as the seat of the government of Nassau County in Mineola.[32]

The population of the county in 1940 was 406,748—roughly 1130 people per square mile. The census for that year lists only 636 farms in Nassau County, a total that included nurseries and florists. This figure differs considerably from the number of farm dwelling units (1377) and slightly from the number of owner-occupied farm *houses* (608) listed in the same census. The discrepancies can be explained by the existence of migrant worker housing on owner-occupied farmland on the one hand, and by the number of nurseries or florists where there was no farmstead on the other.[33]

Nassau County, an area of some 360 square miles, was listed in the census for 1940 as one of the "urban and non-farm places." In that year there were 122,024 "non-farm dwelling units" among more than 108,000 residential structures in Nassau County, as compared with some 1377 "rural farm dwelling units" (only 608 of which were owner-occupied farm houses).[34]

In addition, the golden nematode had seriously reduced the productivity of the area's remaining farmland. Headlines in the *Nassau Daily Review Star* for April 16, 1947 shouted, "2600 Acres Made Useless by Nematode." The story included interviews with Hicksville farmers who were conceding defeat to the pest after a five-year battle to control it.

Island Trees was small and underdeveloped, but its setting was no longer rural. The rural-to-suburban element of the myth hinges on the difference in connotation between the words *fields* and *farms*. Potato 'fields' can be used in any number of types of agriculture, from subsistence farming to agribusiness. Potato 'farms,' on the other hand, suggest a rural community with family farms and perhaps a small crossroads with a general store and a tavern.[35] This bucolic image of the preconstruction Island Trees is the one that persists in the myth and is doggedly defended by old-timers from Levittown who weave the theme into their community's heritage.

The suburban mythology is not unique to Levittown. The proliferation of subdivision suburbs in the postwar period and suburbia's consequent position in the mythology of America can be seen

7.3

Long Island, showing distances from Levittown to industrial plants in
1947. Levittown is just to the east of Hempstead. Grumman Aviation (3) is
to the east of Levittown, in Hicksville, and Republic Aviation (4) is to the
east of Grumman in Farmingdale. Sperry Gyroscope [now Unisys] (5) is
northwest of Hempstead in Lake Success. (Scale = 1 inch = 30 miles)

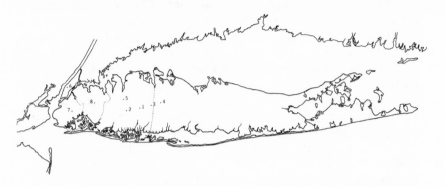

in such widely separated communities as Midwest City, Oklahoma
and San Lorenzo, California. The generation that fought the Second
World War and bought the postwar tract houses were the beneficiaries of domestic policies which fostered an important transition in
American society. By 1956, over 60 percent of the houses in America
were owner-occupied, as compared with 43.6 percent in 1940.[36] In
large measure, this shift in tenure was the result of domestic policies
that made the construction of affordable housing for veterans a reality.[37] As a secondary and perhaps unintended result, it served to
expand the American middle class. It is this factor, more than any
other, that underlies the persistence of the myth.

There is, however, a countermyth that was generated among
the social scientists and professional observers who monitored the
postwar suburban experience. Suburbia, particularly the development or subdivision suburb of the postwar period, became the ob-
ject of widespread scrutiny almost as soon as the first tract house
was occupied. As if in reaction to the residents' heroic story version,
the observers' myth has been relatively harsh in its treatment of suburbia, the residents, and the community.[38] In this version, Levittown
is frequently used as a type for the postwar suburban community.[39]

At first the attention of the commentators was focused on the
sheer size and scope of the subdivisions and the housing production.[40] The qualities found in the new subdivisions were compared to

the ideals that had been promoted during the Progressive Era for 'planned' or 'garden' communities. For the most part, they failed the comparison.[41]

As postwar suburbanization intensified, the critical posture of the commentators toward the subdivision suburbs gradually changed to a concern for what was perceived as the loss of social community inherent in the unrelieved rows of housing. The early interest in the construction, business, and planning aspects of the postwar suburbs quickly gave way to concern for the inner workings of the social groups within the new communities, as other writers took up the question of the suitability of these suburbs as social environments.[42]

Throughout this period the supposedly more objective, analytical scholarship was actually generating a mythology of its own. Based on random-sample questionnaires, the studies of the suburbs began to focus on a perceived suburban pathology, which was often reinforced by the thrust of the questions: the loneliness and the social dominance of the women, the extended absence and moral abdication of the men, and the resultant dysfunctional behavior of the children, particularly the adolesents.[43]

The celebration of Levittown's tenth anniversary sparked a second round of scholarly analysis, much of it locally generated. This work was more positive—some of it almost defensive—in nature. Much of it originated with scholars who were themselves suburban residents.[44] These studies argued that the critics had fallen into the *ad hoc, propter hoc* fallacy, in which two events that coincide in time are assumed to be causally related, and that rather than generating the ills of postwar American society, suburbia merely mirrored them. Harold Wattel, a Levittown resident and professor of economics at nearby Hofstra College, pioneered the supportive scholarship. In his article "Levittown: A Suburban Community," published in 1958, Wattel made three main points. First, he held that Levittown was a "realistic housing alternative for the thousands . . . of families who wanted to raise children on something other than the streets of our major metropolitan population areas." He argued further that the indictment of suburbia "should have been directed instead at our national culture." And third, he indicated that the true assessment of the new suburbia could only come from an evaluation of its major product, the generation of Americans being raised in these communities.[45]

Herbert Gans added the element of a participant/observer to the study of the suburban development. The New Jersey Levittown on which he based his study *The Levittowners* was the third of Levitt and Sons' development suburbs. Gans moved into the development and set out to study the process of community development in a subdivision suburb. Like Wattel, Gans found his Levittown to be more of a piece with American society as a whole, and less a unique environment. To the degree that the environment of the new suburb had an impact on the residents, Gans saw it as a positive influence, related to the fact that the new homeowners had attained their goals—that piece of the American Dream.

College students from Levittown took up the defense as well. Ann Robinson's 1958 term paper for her sociology class at N. Y. U.'s School of Education, "Levittown, U. S. A.; A Biased Sociological Study," was in fact a remarkably unbiased account of the Levittown story. She attributed much of the negative stereotyping of life in Levittown to the media and its unrelenting focus on the community. Robinson refuted the positions taken by the media in covering such supposedly "Levittown" issues as conformity, social competition, juvenile delinquency, religious bigotry, and education. Like Wattel, she measured Levittown and its problems against the reality of life in other communities, rather than an ideal, and found Levittown and its imperfections to be typical of American society in general. By 1969, the revisionist studies of suburbia had shown that most of suburbia's ills were also attributable to American society as a whole.[46]

As Levittown moved into its third decade, other issues such as the civil rights movement and the rising antagonism toward the war in Vietnam eclipsed suburbia as topics of controversy. It wasn't until the late 1970s and early 1980s that suburbia came under scrutiny once again. By then, the newness of what Mumford had dubbed "mass suburbia" had worn off.[47] Americans had adjusted to their little houses, the shopping malls and supermarkets, commuting, and the other aspects of modern life formerly lumped together as "suburban living."

Indeed, by the middle of the 1970s, it had become apparent to most analysts that the evolution of the American suburb had reached a climax. The residential nature of the suburban communities had given way to a more complex organization. Commentators spoke more of the "megalopolis," of "exurbia," and—more recently—the "techno-burb."[48] The Highway Acts of 1944 and 1956, which encouraged commuting from and within the suburbs, had also made it practical to truck urban amenities to the suburbs. No longer definable by their dependence on the urban core, most suburbs had become self-sufficient. Employment could be had in the

many industrial parks and office complexes spotted throughout "exurbia." Shopping malls had brought all but the most exotic goods to
the suburbs. Universities, colleges, and community colleges had established major cultural and educational centers in suburban set-
tings. Thus, although the postwar subdivision suburbs were highly
viable, they were no longer suburban. They had evolved into a new
form of city.

On the surface, the two interpretations of the suburban myth
appear to have little in common. In each of its versions, however,
the Levittown myth has several constant elements. There is, for example, the farms-to-houses phase in which William Levitt plays a
key role. In the first version, Levitt "invents" the suburban subdivision by generating new technologies for house building that make
possible a well-built, affordable, single-family residence for young
veterans and their families. To his credit are the curvilinear roads,
which restrict traffic; 'his' on-site, factory method of production
which made affordable houses possible; facades individualized by
variation in color and ornamentation; and green spaces and recreational facilities expressly designed for the children.[49] In the alternate
version, these same elements are interpreted quite differently. Here,
Levitt is portrayed as a despot, imposing conformity not only
through his restrictive leases and covenants, but through the mass-
produced houses in which the same floor plan is replicated thousands of times with only minor variations. His single-function dormitory suburb with its overemphasis on children and their needs is
cast in this version as the progenitor of a cultural and intellectual
wasteland. But in both versions, Levitt is portrayed as larger than
life. He is the patriarch and prime mover; the residents, his subjects.

The second aspect of the myth centers on family life in the
community. In the residents' version, the focus is on the early days
when the young residents, suffering from lack of funds, compen-
sated for that shortage by "making do." Their expressions of mutual
concern, through their sharing of tools, telephones, and cars, and
their cooperative babysitting, carpooling, and social experiences,
create a memory of halcyon days. The contrasting version general-
izes the same experiences into a suburban mystique of collectivity
and conformity that borders on a total loss of individuality and in
which those who resist the mystique are punished for it.[50]

The Levittown myth of the social analysts is based on the purported pathology of suburban society: the rows of replicated houses,
the crying babies, the absent fathers and lonely mothers. The myth
of the Levittown residents, on the other hand, is based on nostalgia,

recounting their early period through their remembered experiences. But in each version, whether they are portrayed as the culmination of the American Dream or as rows of little boxes imposed on the residents by the builders, the postwar suburbs are treated as static environments—the FHA-approved, subdivision tracts of the 1940s.[51]

How are we to reconcile these conflicting visions of suburbia? Where is the common ground between the antipathy of the critics and the esteem of the residents? If the postwar suburbs were as destructive as their critics implied, why is the nostalgia so strong? What are the links between the experience of the participants and the criticism of the observers?

Regardless of the bias of its adherents, each of the suburban myths is predicated on several common elements: the small, single-family house; the nuclear family with commuting father, housekeeping mother, and young (preschool to early elementary school) children. But these elements are frozen in time. In the real world, husbands retire, wives take jobs, children grow up, and more important for this essay, the built environment changes. These changes do not figure largely in either version of the Levittown myth, but they are an important component in the overall satisfaction the residents feel for their community. The reality of the suburban experience is as much the product of the redesigned environment as it is of the FHA-designed, builder-delivered subdivisions that formed its roots. Indeed, the reshaping of the environment by the residents was a key factor in the postwar suburban experience.[52]

From the personal interviews I conducted, to the various events celebrating Levittown's fortieth anniversary, to accidental conversations sparked by the mere mention of my study of Levittown, the residents conveyed a remarkably similar attitude toward their homes, their community, and the builder.[53] The homeowners, particularly those original owners who take pride in calling themselves "pioneers," referred to the developer in heroic terms. There is an underlying gratitude toward the man who "made it all possible."

This attitude is not found among the homeowners in Levitt's older and considerably more expensive developments. Indeed, many of the residents at Levitt's Strathmore Vanderbilt community did not know that he had built their houses.[54] Nor is the attitude shared by the owners of his later developments on Long Island, who may be aware that he built their development, but apparently see no reason to celebrate the fact.[55]

What, then, is the importance attached by the Levittown residents, both male and female, to their suburban houses? By disregarding or minimizing this attachment, we overlook a significant part of the postwar experience, the upward social mobility implicit in home ownership. We underestimate the value of home ownership, particularly during inflationary years, as an economic investment for young workers. Moreover, we miss the role of the "household economy" in increasing that investment through home remodeling, and the concomitant sense of empowerment as these homeowners shaped both their environment and them selves.[56]

Although these factors have been present in middle-class suburban developments as well, they did not play as pivotal a role as they did in Levittown. In large part this is due to the disproportionate symbolic value of homeownership in assigning *de facto* middle-class status.[57] The myth of Levittown is the community's tribute to that process. But it is also tribute to a larger political reality, for the *de facto* membership in the middle class brought with it the fulfillment of the republican ideal.

8

The Politics of House and Home

The qualities that defined the suburban myth—domesticity, cooperation, and conformity—were not the characteristics of a social revolution. Nor were the qualities that defined the suburban home-owner—home-loving, industrious, and child-centered. Indeed, the suburban home-owners would prove to be the ideal counterfoil to the social revolution of the 1960s. Perceiving themselves to be neither oppressed nor powerless, the suburbanites internalized the message, but not the medium of social revolution.

As if to justify the republican tenets of Jefferson's ideal, the so-called "Happy Days" of the 1950s witnessed the rise of a mentality dominated by nationalism and conformity.[1] That the mood was tenuous is evidenced by its brief duration—less than a generation. Yet, during that period the power of the American consensus was sufficient to support the creation of a number of agencies of ideological leveling such as Joseph McCarthy's Senate subcommittee, the House Un-American Activities Committee, and the McCarren Act.[2]

By the end of the 1950s, any lingering, postdepression fears that American workers might embrace a socialist agenda appeared to have been without foundation. Despite sporadic outbursts of worker dissatisfaction, American labor had settled into comfortable coexistence with the social and political traditions of American capital. This mood is highly correlated with the increase in suburban residence by lower-income workers who were enabled—some would argue even forced[3]—to move to the affordable proprietary houses in the suburbs that were built under the terms of the VA and FHA housing programs.

The housing program may have been intended primarily to stabilize the postwar society on a structural level as it converted from a wartime to a peacetime economy; nevertheless, its proprietary component had political as well as economic implications. Many of those reformers who advocated a wider expansion of the homeowning class, both before and after the war, had proposed it as a means of diffusing the values of the republic among lower-income, blue-collar workers and their economic counterparts in clerical and middle-managerial positions.[4] In this they echoed those housing reformers of earlier generations, from Catharine Beecher to Ebenezer Howard, who had promoted better housing as a form of social engineering.[5]

The twentieth-century version of this form of environmental determinism was succinctly expressed by William Levitt in his oft-quoted comment of 1948, "No man who owns his house and lot can be a Communist; he has too much to do." More important, he had too much at stake; responsible for the welfare of a family and committed to a 30-year mortgage on a house whose value was dependent on continuous maintenance, the homeowning veteran was unlikely to have the time or the inclination to social revolution. Although the housing policies of the postwar years were intended less as a form of social engineering than as a resolution to the housing crisis, the provision of basic houses on a proprietary basis provided an important social benefit, one that was not lost on those who developed the programs.

In the closing months of World War II, the federal government turned its attention to the postwar economy. Among the concerns was the need to implement a reconversion that would reduce the appeal of the socialist agenda which had gained strength during the Depression.[6] A well planned program of reconversion would avert the type of social unrest that had been generated among the returning soldiers of World War I, both in Russia and in Germany, giving rise on the one hand to a Communist revolution and on the other to National Socialism (Nazism).

Housing, or the lack of it, was one of the issues that the Truman administration addressed. The doubled cohort of young people ready and able to establish their own households and the limited supply of existing housing quickly became issues around which various factions rallied as they prepared for the reconversion society. "The need for housing" became "the housing shortage" which in turn became "the housing crisis" as demobilization intensified.[7]

The American housing crisis, however, had not begun with the veterans who returned after World War II, nor would it end with the construction of Levittown. Rather, what began in the postwar years was a shift in the politics of housing in America. The government's financial involvement in the consumer side of residential construction—formerly suspect as a form of socialism—gained new legitimacy as the numbers of homeless veterans and their families reached epidemic proportions.[8] Housing, home ownership, the American home itself, became the mobilizing themes for a wide range of interest groups, each of which presented ideological arguments stressing the need to preserve the American way of life. The fact that the images presented by many of these advocates were mutually contradictory did not reduce the intensity of their rhetoric.

By 1945, the problem was larger than simply finding housing for the veterans. The fear of possible postwar unrest had taken on some substance. Workers began to agitate for pay increases, which they had patriotically foregone "for the duration." Mutterings about industrial profiteering and workers "cheated" out of their fair share grew louder and accompanied increasing numbers of strikes and walkouts.[9] Despite the optimistic, if somewhat self-serving, tone presented in the media during the waning years of the war, many serious social commentators were concerned about the possibility of a postwar American version of the veteran-generated socialist revolutions that had plagued so much of Europe in the years following World War I. The lack of adequate housing, in this context, was cast as a contributing factor in the unrest that had preceded the European upheaval in the earlier period. The combination of labor unrest and the shortage of housing loomed as a genuine threat to the peace, a threat that had to be addressed.[10]

Anticipating the possibility of such postwar problems, the policymakers in Congress had begun working on solutions during the closing years of the war.[11] Housing received considerable attention. Typically, the solutions offered split along political lines. (Less obviously, they split along regional lines, with representatives of urban areas in the Northeast more likely to advocate legislation that included slum clearance and public housing.) On the one hand, the Progressive/New Deal reformers favored a program of public rental housing constructed at government expense. The conservative opposition, on the other hand, favored much more limited government involvement. They preferred either government subsidies for privately owned-and-operated rental construction, or federal insurance for privately contracted mortgages for individual home buyers. Although the wartime construction of housing for defense workers and for military personnel and their families had set a precedent for direct federal involvement in residential construction, attitudes toward such involvement changed slowly. Despite the intensification of the housing shortage and the existence of New Deal precedents for resolving it, there remained in 1946 a strong ideological opposition to direct federal aid to individuals, even homeless veterans. Yet, even the most conservative granted that the problem was too large for private industry to overcome alone. Advocates on both sides of the housing issue advanced their particular position under a banner of patriotism: direct federal aid to the individual was tantamount to overthrowing the social and economic system; not to provide housing for those who had fought to preserve the American way was tantamount to treason.[12]

Thus, the planners faced an interesting dilemma: in order to stave off a socialist revolution, they might have to adopt a socialist solution. The dispute was not in *whether* the government should fund, but *whom*—and how.

When the battle was over, the proper role of government in the field of housing had been refined and reinterpreted. Federal intervention in providing the construction of domestic residential housing had settled into a pattern that would remain dominant until well after the social upheaval of the 1960s. This change in attitude eventually led to the housing programs that funded the construction of the final 13,500 of Levittown's 17,500 units.[13] Federal support would be in the form of economic supports directed toward the large developer, the lending institutions, and the individual home owner.

By October 1947, when the rental section Levittown was ready for occupancy, the direction of the suburban housing industry was clear. From coast to coast, the operative builders who had developed their variations on "industrialized" construction methods during the war created the "rows of ticky-tack"[14] that would be both praised and damned in the years to come.

The newly constructed houses of the postwar subdivision suburbs served to introduce homeowning on a gradual basis. Those who could not have afforded to purchase the standard, prewar suburban houses in the middle price range were able to live modestly and affordably while gradually upgrading their holdings. Their monthly payments were reducing their mortgage rather than going to a landlord, as they added rooms, appliances, and amenities to the basic house, which was not only livable as delivered, but expandable as well. As the houses of the postwar suburbs increased in economic, social, and aesthetic value, the residents, in turn, derived their class identity from the enhanced status of the communities in which they lived. More important, they derived their political identity from their new status as landowning members of the American middle class.[15]

Although it is difficult to demonstrate a causal relationship be-

8.1

Housing starts by funding type.

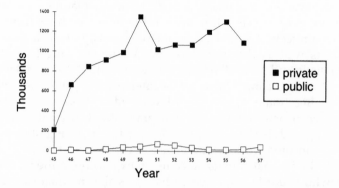

Based on figures in Series N 29–54; "Value of Private vs Public Residential Construction in millions of dollars, 1947–1949 prices" *Historical Statistics . . . Colonial Times to 1957*, p. 381.

tween the rise of lower-income homeowning and the political consensus of the postwar period, nevertheless the consensus was particularly strong among those members of the lower-middle class who made their homes in the development suburbs that proliferated after World War II. They were generally well satisfied with their portion of the American Dream. Their houses and the communities in which they stood had risen in real economic terms as well as in symbolic value. On the one hand, inflation had increased the property owners' relative equity in their real estate. On the other, by expanding and remodeling the basic houses the owners had increased the real value of their investment. The opportunity to enlarge and modify the basic houses, inherent in the later versions of the housing programs, upgraded the original subdivision suburbs into middle-income neighborhoods, thereby solidifying the economic upward mobility of the homeowners. In effect, they had created middle-class homes out of what had originally been built as lower-income housing.

In the end, the policies developed in the postwar years were even more effective than they had been intended to be. They were successful not only in housing lower-income Americans—albeit with certain restrictions—but in promoting new communities that reinforced the dominant value system of the country.[16] While this study was not undertaken to test the environmental determinism theories of either the Romantic or the Progressive housing reformers, nor to serve as a history of community planning, the findings appear to have implications for social as well as urban planners. The social engineering of those who created the nineteenth-century rental housing projects, typified by Pullman, Illinois, and Vineland, New Jersey (as well as the first phase of Levittown, Long Island), was paternalistic and controlling, aimed at "uplifting" the residents.[17] In contrast, the housing policies of the later 1940s, by underwriting and encouraging home ownership, developed a process of inclusion. The lower-income homeowner was gradually drawn into the newly expanding middle class; the provision for full financing of mortgages for lower-income workers succeeded in expanding the homeowning class, and with that expansion came an expansion in the numbers of those who could be expected to have a stake in American society. Rather than imposing them, the proprietary experience reinforced and rewarded the traditional American values of cooperative individualism, industry, and thrift.

9

POSTSCRIPT

In 1987, Levittown celebrated its fortieth anniversary. The celebration occasioned a number of retrospectives during which many of the pioneer members of the community expressed dissatisfaction with the changes taking place in their community and its residents. In particular, the residents deplored the loss of that sense of community which had made their years in Levittown so special. Like Tommy DeMaria, they found the old spirit of camaraderie missing; neighbors no longer gather for coffee or to share their tools and labors.[1] Preschool children are seldom seen in the backyards or playgrounds of Levittown. In addition to the nostalgia for the long-ago Levittown, there were more serious complaints. Many pointed out that the sense of pride for which the community had once been noted appears to be slipping. Some homeowners are failing to maintain their gardens, and the exteriors of many houses are in need of repair. Other houses have been subdivided in order to provide rental income. They, who were once the vanguard of the suburban revolution, now feel as if they are attending at its wake.

Of course, part of the problem these Levittowners face is due to the fact that they themselves are no longer the same. After 40 years, even the same people living in the same houses do not make the same community. Family lives have changed; many of the Capes and ranches of Levittown now house empty nests. Others have become extended households. There have been economic changes: two-career households are more the norm than the exception, and two cars are parked in every driveway, at least when the residents are at home. In general, there is more affluence in Levittown. Few residents have a need to borrow tools or supplies; the landscapers' trucks arrive in Levittown with the first robin. But that, too, is changing. As the "pioneers" approach retirement, they are finding that the costs of upkeep, both physical and economic, are becoming a serious burden.

The houses of Levittown that were built originally as affordable housing for young nuclear families have been remodeled and expanded to the point where they are no longer within the range of lower-income buyers.[2] The sheer numbers of the remodeled houses have had an economic effect on the entire community. Their dominance has elevated the socioeconomic level of the neighborhood so that even those few houses which remain unaltered have had their values inflated. Many basic houses command selling prices ranging from $125,000 to $150,000.

Other factors have affected the economics of housing in Levittown, along with the rise in the real value of the houses. The steady inflation in real estate prices, which once worked to the advantage of the homeowners, has reached the point where it now makes it harder for them to sell. Meanwhile, property taxes in the region have risen to the point that many widows and retirees cannot afford to keep the houses that they are unable to sell. In response, some have created illegal apartments in order to be able to continue to afford to live in the house they own. Other retirees have moved South, renting their houses to the young couples who cannot afford to buy them. Still others have sold their homes to real estate agencies and other speculators, who lease the houses while waiting for their price. These tendencies have increased the percentage of houses owned by absentee landlords.

The processes that Levittown is experiencing are at work in many areas of the country. The rows of little houses filled with young nuclear families that constituted the mythic image of the postwar subdivision suburbs have been replaced by more complex communities with new and often contradictory problems. The situation is in part the result of the economics of housing. The inflation of land costs, particularly in the Northeast, has made the construction of entry-level basic houses, such as those originally built in Levittown, unprofitable even on such a massive scale. An inexpensive house is a poor investment if the building plot consumes more than half the final selling price of the house. A rudimentary $25,000 house on a $50,000 lot must sell for $75,000 in order for the builder to break even. Even lower-income consumers are reluctant to pay that price for what they recognize as a cheaply constructed house. On the same plot, a builder can construct a $150,000 house and sell the package to an upscale client for $250,000 with little difficulty. As a result, few builders are willing to take the risk of building "affordable" housing—particularly in great numbers, and fewer lending institutions are likely to agree to fund them in the undertaking.[3] Moreover, local building codes often set costly minimums in spatial dimensions, design, and materials for any new construction in order to retain the particular socioeconomic level of the community. Thus, high land costs impel the construction of larger, more expensive houses or of multifamily dwellings that double the investment return on the land.

As this book goes to print, less than half of the American population resides in suburbs, and many of those who do are now tenants.[4] The promise of the postwar housing policies—the American Dream of a vine-covered cottage of one's own—is becoming more and more unattainable for the children of the postwar baby boom. The nation of homeowners that appeared to have been so essential to the growth of a democratic society, not only to Jefferson in 1800 but to Truman in 1947, is no longer in the forefront of domestic policy. Forgotten is the folk wisdom of the thirties and the forties: Roosevelt's assertion that "a nation of home owners, of people who own a real share in their own land, is unconquerable";[5] Peter Bailey's insistence that homeowning produced a better working class;[6] or Levitt's assurance that "no man who owns his own house and lot can be a communist."[7]

Meanwhile, our cities—and, increasingly, our suburbs—are plagued with growing numbers of homeless people—families as well as individuals. A large underclass is developing as the middle class has begun to contract.[8] Across the country the numbers of homeless families have increased as the distance between haves and have-nots has increased. Those who cannot afford any form of housing are using the streets and doorways of our cities for their shelter. The market in luxury housing for the few has diminished the number of affordable houses being started for the many. The problem is more ominous as the homelessness rises through the classes and a larger proportion of the homeless population is composed of formerly middle-class families dislocated by the lack of affordable housing.

Paradoxically, this situation is strongly related to the success of the housing policies that produced the postwar suburbs. Within a single generation the mass-produced suburbs with their identical rows of inexpensive tract houses have been transformed, like those of Levittown, into middle-class communities of individualized, often commodious homes. Through a combination of renovation and expansion, the entry-level houses of the 1940s have increased in value to the point where they are now beyond the reach not only of many of the children who were raised in them, but even of the generation who effected the transformation.

Although it might appear at first glance that the affordable housing of the forties was an aberration and that the programs which funded them were failures, it would be a mistake to rush to that conclusion. Rather, it may be the abandonment of such programs that is the failure.

The success of the housing programs of the 1940s in redefining and expanding the middle class was limited to the target constituency of those programs: lower-income and working-class family men—primarily white. For today's housing problems to be solved, new programs would have to accommodate also those groups who were largely excluded from the postwar policies: minorities, single parents—especially working mothers—and the elderly, especially the single or widowed. These are the groups who are most heavily impacted by today's housing shortage. Their housing needs differ in many respects from those of the veterans.[9]

Objections to government-provided solutions to the crisis voiced today are similar in nature to those of the 1940s. That is, such programs are socialistic and in their collectivity tend to erode the initiative and moral vigor of their target population and, by extension, of the nation. Yet, closer examination of the housing produced under the programs of the FHA and VA indicates that although they may have contained elements of socialism, it was a socialism which was reinterpreted to conform to the values as well as the needs of a capitalist society. It combined the mythic elements of American rugged individualism with the pragmatic elements of cooperative effort—a collective individualism.

The Levittowners are undoubtedly correct in their claim that Levittown neither can nor should provide the solution to today's housing crisis. Levittown, and the other postwar tract developments, despite their relatively low density, are overbuilt. Row upon row of single-family houses utilizing only 12 percent of their plots are no longer feasible in today's land market; they are anachronisms.

By looking more closely at the Levittown experience, however, it may be possible to abstract some workable elements of a solution to the housing situation we face today. Although the freestanding, single-family suburban houses of Levittown may no longer be the only—or even the best—pattern for affordable housing, Levittown and its houses can provide a model for that solution—a model of process rather than product.

Appendix I
The Sale of the Rental Units

At the end of 1949, the Bethpage Realty Company, the rental agent subsidiary of Levitt and Sons, still owned 4028 rental units in the 10,000 unit community. All of these units were Cape Cods from the first section of the development. Bethpage Realty had $5,500,000 in working capital that "presumably had been put into Bethpage by the Levitts at some stage."[1] The units were mortgaged—in the name of Levitt and Sons—for $25,000,000. Effectively, the $5,500,000 was the construction profit on the 4000 units.

Junto, a nonprofit educational group in Philadelphia, heard that the Levitts wanted a capital gains tax arrangement.[2] They agreed to purchase the Bethpage Realty and its rental units for $5,150,000. To finance the purchase, they took a short-term (five days) loan of $1,500,000 from the Fidelity-Philadelphia Trust Co.[3] This they gave to Levitt and Sons as a down payment on Bethpage Realty Company. Along with the company they acquired the $5,500,000 working capital, the 4028 rental units, and the $25,000,000 mortgage. They used the working capital to repay both the bank loan of $1,500,000 and the balance of $3.4 million to Levitt and Sons. At this point, they had paid a total of $4.9 million for the package. They withheld another $250,000 to be given to Levitt in December. This transaction enabled Levitt to withdraw the $5,000,000 in profits from the rental housing, unload the burdens and responsibility of a landlord, and avoid up to 71 percent tax on the dividends earned by the original investment by taking instead a capital gains break on the sale.

Junto, on the other hand, would have the rents to use to pay off the original mortgage of $25,000,000. Meanwhile, they would use the profits of $75,000 a year—tax free—for educational purposes.[4] The Levitts, in turn, were said to be putting their proceeds into building the 1950 models of the ranches—some 4000 of them, "complete with built-in television" on the 1400 acres that they had recently purchased. The new models would sell for $7990.[5]

Appendix II
The Women's Congress on Housing

The participants in the Congress were selected from among some 4300 women who responded when the Director of the Housing and Home Finance Agency held a press conference on March 15, 1956. He requested letters from women who would provide the benefit of their experience as homemakers to those who would design better homes. From the respondents, 103 were selected to participate in the Congress, which was held in Washington on April 23, 24, and 25, 1956.[1]

The women ranged in age from 25–45. More than 85 percent held no outside employment. More than 99 percent had children; 87 percent had at least two, and of these 239 children, most of whom were under 16, 65 percent were under 10. Their educational level was above average; 77 percent had attended college and 44 percent had completed it. Family incomes were also above average—one-third had incomes over $10,000; one-quarter were in the area of $8,000 to $10,000 a year. Another 15 percent fell into what was called "lower-income groups," those having annual family incomes of less than $5000.

Although they represented both urban and rural areas, about 95 percent of them lived in single-family structures. Their houses were essentially based on the prewar middle-class model, with only sixteen percent having fewer than six rooms. Sixty-four percent had a basement; 68 percent, a separate dining room; and 75 percent, a garage or carport.[2]

In comparison, the Levittown housewife was typically between 30 and 45 in 1956. Family incomes were generally neither as high nor as low as those at the conference; by 1960, only 20.3 percent had incomes over $10,000; 20.9 percent had incomes between $8000–$10,000; and only 12.1 percent had incomes lower than $5000.[3]

In contrast to the women at the Congress, the median for years of school completed by residents over age 25 was considerably lower in Levittown, although at 12.2 years, it was still above average for the nation in 1960.[4]

The educational standard is strongly related to the relative youth of both groups of women. Postwar young adults were expected to remain in high school and attend some college, whereas people of the same socioeconomic level one generation earlier were not.

There is no way to correlate exactly, since we do not know the various regional representatives in the Congress, and we do know that the Northeast in general, and Nassau County in particular, have registered higher in cost of living and in income since at least 1947. For a comparison of Levittown with New York State, Nassau County, and several nearby communities, see Appendix III.

Appendix III
Comparative Social Statistics
on Levittown over Time

Estimated Total Population[1]	1960	68,000*
Estimated Total Population[2]	1980	80,000
Median Household Income[3]	1959	$ 7467
Median Household Income[4]	1980	25,493
High School Graduates[5]	1960	82.9%
High School Graudates[6]	1980	78.4%

*These figures reflect differences in identifying "Levittown." The 1960 figure is based on the 17,400 houses that Levitt built and called Levittown, whereas the 1980 figure is based on the whole geographic area now identified as "Levittown," regardless of whether Levitt built the houses.

Comparisons with Selected Areas

1980

	Median Household Income[7]	Income Per Capita	High School Grads
Levittown	$25,493	$ 7830	78.4%
Other Nassau Communities[8]			
Roosevelt	$21,780	$ 5,999	66.8%
Garden City	$36,477	13,567	90.2
Muttontown	$50,531	19,582	91.8
Sands Point	$75,001	29,741	94.2
Nassau County	$26,090		
New York State		$16,647	

	1959/60[9]
Levittown	$ 7467
Garden City	13,874
Nassau County	8515
New York State	6371

High School Graduates	*1980*[10]	*1960*[11]
Levittown	78.4%	82.9%
Roosevelt	66.8	
Garden City	90.2	
Muttontown	91.8	
Sands Point	94.2	

Employment Distribution in Levittown[12]

Total number employed in Levittown	27,618
Total employed females in Levittown	11,365
Managerial and Professional Specialty Occupations	5408
Executives, Administrative, Managerial	2854
Professional Specialty[13]	2554
Technical, Sales, and Administrative Support Occupations	11,431
Health technologists and technicians	109
Technologists and technicians	531
Sales occupations	3176
Administrative support (includes Clerical)	7531
Service Occupations	3415
Private household occupations	92
Protective services	1103
Other services	2216
Farming, Forestry, Fishing	219
Precision Production, Craft, Repair	3575
(Mechanics, Construction workers, Precision workers)	
Operators, Fabricators, Laborers	3567
(Includes truck drivers)	
Machinery & Heavy Equipment Operators	72
Handlers, Helpers, Laborers	982

NOTES

Preface

1. In addition to their other subdivisions, the firm of Levitt and Sons built three developments that they called "Levittown" in the period between 1947 and 1958. The first of these is the Long Island community that is the subject of this study. After Long Island they built a second Levittown in eastern Pennsylvania and a third in southern New Jersey. The New Jersey Levittown has since reverted to its earlier name, Willingboro. Herbert Gans, *The Levittowners* (New York: Vintage Books, 1969), p. viii.

2. Charles Edouard Jeanneret, *Vers une Architecture*, (1923).

3. This study of Levittown was aided immeasurably by the work of the small but growing number of scholars whose interest in the social history of American domestic architecture has opened up a new perspective in the field of architectural history. In addition to the work of Dolores Hayden [*Grand Domestic Revolution* (Cambridge, MA: MIT Press, 1983), *Seven American Utopias; The Architecture of Communitarian Socialism, 1790–1975* (Cambridge, MA: MIT Press, 1976), and *Redesigning the American Dream* (New York: W.W. Norton, 1984)] and Gwendolyn Wright [*Building the Dream* (New York: Pantheon Books, 1981) and *Moralism and the Model Home* (Chicago: University of Chicago Press, 1980)], among the works that were most rewarding were Clifford E. Clark, Jr., "Domestic Architecture as an Index to Social History . . . ," *Journal of Interdisciplinary History* 7:1 (Summer 1976), pp. 33–56, and *The American Family Home, 1800–1960* (Chapel Hill: University of North Carolina Press, 1986); Alan Gowans. *The Comfortable House; North American Suburban Architecture 1890–1930* (Cambridge, MA: MIT Press, 1986); David Handlin, *The American Home* (Boston: Little, Brown & Co., 1979); Roy Lubove, *The Progressives and the Slums* (Pittsburgh: University of Pittsburgh Press, 1962); Elaine Tyler May, *Homeward Bound; American Families in the Cold War Era* (New York: Basic Books, Inc., 1988); Daniel Schaffer, *Garden Cities for America; The Radburn Experience* (Philadelphia: Temple University Press, 1982); and Sam Bass Warner, Jr., *Streetcar Suburbs* (Cambridge, MA: Harvard University Press, 1963).

4. Although many of the reformers advocated environmental determinism, they offered few floor plans to indicate how the houses were laid out and fewer photographs of rooms to show them in use. The interest of the housing reformers had been on societal rather than individual improvement. As a result, they centered on externals—the visual landscape and the

planned or garden community. When they looked to the interiors their interests were on hygiene at the low end of the economic spectrum or—at the high end—on the aesthetics of interior design, rather than on family function. [One notable exception to this generalization is Catharine Beecher, who treated the *American Woman's Home* as a total environment, paying as much attention to the implements of housekeeping as to the arrangment of space. (New York: J.B. Ford, 1869)].

5.   Among the pioneers in the history of folk housing and vernacular architecture are Henry Glassie, *Folk Housing in Middle Virginia: A Structural Analysis of Historic Artifacts* (Knoxville: University of Tennessee Press, 1975) and James Deetz, *In Small Things Forgotten: The Archaeology of American Life* (Garden City, NJ: Anchor Books, 1977). Although some attention to the vernacular forms was evident as early as 1924, when Lewis Mumford published the first edition of *Sticks and Stones* (New York: Dover Publications, Inc., 1955; Boni & Livright, 1924), it was not until after the introduction of the new social history in the late 1960s that academic historians were attracted to the field. For a representative collection of the writings in the field see Dell Upton and John Michael Vlach (eds.), *Common Places; Readings in American Vernacular Architecture* (Athens, GA: The University of Georgia Press, 1986).

6.   The work of several scholars from different fields reveals a persistence in the spatial distribution of the middle-class house after 1750. Although many of these studies are concerned with change rather than continuity, they all point to an evolution toward a norm that they identify as middle-class and American. See, for example, the works included in Upton and Vlach, *Common Places*, especially Edward A. Chappell, "Acculturation in the Shenandoah Valley . . ." (pp. 27–57); Clay Lancaster, "The American Bungalow" (pp. 79–106); Abbott Lowell Cummings, "Inside the Massachusetts House" (pp. 219–39); Kenneth Ames, "Meaning in Artifacts; Hall Furnishings in Victorian America" (pp. 241–60); and Lizabeth A. Cohen, "Embellishing a Life of Labor" (pp. 261–78).

7.   In his article "Alley Landscapes of Washington," James Boschert points out the key role the residents can play in reshaping their environment and controlling its impact. (Upton and Vlach, p. 282)

8.   The fieldwork included visits to literally hundreds of houses— spanning some three centuries—from Vermont to Virginia, Long Island to Memphis, Minneapolis to Oklahoma. Most of the houses were still functioning. Others were the ruins of long-abandoned homesteads, one of which had been left with food still in its canisters. Many were restorations. Still others had been renovated for adaptive reuse. Most were—or had been— the homes of the "middlin' classes." Some were mansions; few were shacks. One was a tenement apartment; one a *pied-à-terre* in Manhattan's Trump Tower. There were rural farmsteads on Cape Cod and urban town houses in Brooklyn. There were suburban bungalows in California and military

housing in Oklahoma City; small-town Victorians on Long Island and eight-
eenth-century row houses in Pennsylvania. Even dollhouses were not
spared. Only after the houses had been scrutinized as artifacts—photo-
graphed, analyzed, experienced, and interpreted—did the more formal research begin.

   9. Although access to the traditional archival sources would have
enhanced our understanding from the builder's perspective, no such ar-
chive exists. In 1961 the firm of Levitt and Sons was sold to International
Telephone and Telegraph, which in turn sold its interest to the developer,
Starrett. A spokesman for Levitt indicated that the records of Levitt and
Sons for the period prior to the I.T.T. sale were either discarded or subsumed by those of the successor companies. Personal communication from
Edward Cortese, Senior Vice-President, International Chairman] September
17, 1984, and follow-up phone call September 21, 1984. See also Eichler, pp.
158–59.

   Levitt was not interested in making his records available to scholars
even before the company was sold. As early as 1951, John Liell found that it
was impossible to gain access to company records. In his study he quotes
the reply he received to his request for access to Levitt & Sons' "immense
amounts of data." The reply, in its entirety, read

   We have your letter of June 3rd. It is similar to a great many we receive constantly and we are sorry that we have no way of complying
   with your various requests.

Liell, "Levittown; A Study in Community Planning and Development,"
diss., Yale University, 1952, p. 26.

   The one small bit of "archival" material that is available is a scrapbook
which contains Levitt & Sons' clipping file for the construction period. The
organization of the clippings in the file, combined with the absence of any
clippings with a negative cast, creates a document that is somewhat larger
than the sum of its parts. In addition, William Levitt has, over the years,
been remarkably forthcoming in presenting his opinions in the public forum
through press releases, media interviews, and public testimony. Levitt's
pronouncements in the media often revealed more than he intended, and in
composite create a rather clear picture of his relationship with his houses
and their tenants. Thus, despite the lack of archival evidence on the economic and political aspects of his role in creating Levittown, it is possible to
infer from his official statements—if not what he actually did and believed—at least the public image he hoped to create.

   10. This combining of approaches may not sit well with purists in
any of these fields. However, purity of method can shade the meaning and
even impose distortions on the findings.

   For example, relying on traditional sources such as land deeds, many
historians have treated Levittown as a form of "initial occupance" which
Fred Kniffen has defined as "the first post-pioneer, permanent settlement

imprint established" in a region ("Folk Housing; Key to Diffusion," in Upton & Vlach, pp. 3–26). This leads logically to two conclusions that, although technically correct, distort the reality of the Levittown story. First is
the belief that the area was in a rural state prior to construction; second is
the concomitant assumption that the community was built primarily as a
bedroom for commuters to Manhattan. However, although the acreage at
Island Trees was still under cultivation when Levitt bought the land, the
surrounding areas of Nassau County were in the final stages of suburbanization. Agriculture had been moving steadily eastward into Suffolk County
since the middle of the 1920s. Similarly, though a percentage of the Levittown residents were employed in Manhattan, a far greater number of them
worked on Long Island, many within the borders of Nassau County.

The use of a source more suited to the genealogist, the yellow pages
of the Nassau County phone books for the decades preceding World War II,
resolved the apparent contradiction. The listings confirmed that the farms in
the Island Trees area were already anachronistic when the war broke out.
Levittown—erected in the center of Long Island's "cradle of aviation"—was
surrounded by the incipient military-industrial complex even before ground
was broken for the first Cape Cod. Thus, although many of the early residents did commute to Manhattan, they did not constitute a majority of the
residents. Levittown supplied workers for Grumman, Republic and Sperry's
in far greater proportions.

Introduction

1. The relationship between government-sponsored architecture
and political philosophy in twentieth-century Germany is explored in Barbara Miller Lane, *Architecture and Politics in Germany*. (Cambridge: Cambridge University Press, 1968); Ronald Wiedenhoeft, *Berlin's Housing Revolution: German Reform in the 1920s* (Ann Arbor: UMI Research Press, 1985) and
Robert Taylor, *The Word in Stone* (Berkeley: University of California Press,
1974).

2. For an examination of the political philosophy surrounding the
postwar American housing policies see J. Paul Mitchell (ed.) *Federal Housing
Policy and Program: Past and Present* (New Brunswick, NJ: Rutgers University,
1985) and Richard O. Davies, *Housing Reform During the Truman Administration* (Columbia, MO: University of Missouri, 1966).

3. To a degree, the terms lower-income and veterans are redun-
dant. The GI Bill was *de facto*, if not *de jure*, aimed at the American working
class. 'Veteran' generally refers to the soldier—the man who has seen active
service. Upper-income Americans are not the population from which the
enlisted men of the armed forces are drawn, especially during wartime. Military men from the upper-middle class are more often the career officers
who leave the service as 'retirees' rather than veterans.

For in-depth analyses of the postwar housing programs, see Rachel G.

Bratt, Chester Hartman, and Ann Meyerson (eds.), *Critical Perspectives on Housing* (Philadelphia, Temple University Press, 1986); Davis R. B. Ross outlines the background of the veterans' housing programs in *Preparing for Ulysses* (New York: Columbia University Press, 1969); Richard O. Davies provides an analysis of the political culture surrounding the adoption of the housing programs in *Housing Reform During the Truman Administration*; see also Dolores Hayden, *Redesigning the American Dream* (New York: W.W. Norton, 1984); Joseph B. Mason, *The History of Housing in the U.S. 1930–1980* (Houston: Gulf Publishing Company, 1982); Marc A. Weiss, *The Rise of the Community Builders* (New York: Columbia University Press, 1987); and Gwendolyn Wright, *Building the Dream* (New York: Pantheon Books, 1981).

4. See for example, the letter to the editor of *Newsday* from Mrs. Helen Murray, which accused Councilman John McConnell of "short-sightedness" for his criticisms of the Levittown lease restrictions. October 9, 1947.

The local press was the more common source of the laudatory comments on Levitt and his houses. In her weekly column, "Woman to Woman" in the *Island Trees Tribune*, Elizabeth M. Adams introduced her article on housekeeping in this way: "When we finally got settled in a real house, my enthusiasm ran high." [She then went on to advocate both moderation and organization in housekeeping.] (January 29, 1948, p. 6.). See also "The Poet's Corner" for February 5, 1948, "Snow Thoughts" :

> Consider the plight of the much-abused Vet;
> With houses and apartments impossible to get,
> Levitt provided the best answer yet,
> We wouldn't have missed this deal on a bet!

5. Andrew Jackson Downing, *The Architecture of Country Houses* (New York: Dover Publications, 1969/1850). Gervase Wheeler, *Homes for the People in Suburb and Country; The Villa, the Mansion and the Cottage* (New York: Charles Scribner, 1855).

6. The camaraderie of the do-it-yourself project was not confined to the houses. The process was an important element of community development as well. Speaking of the establishment of the Israel Community Center, the oldest Jewish congregation in Levittown, one of the founders recalled:

> We cleaned the hangar, swept, washed, and patch painted. We borrowed chairs from I. J. Morris [a local funeral director]. . . .

From a transcript of the talk given by Dr. Sam Cytryn, Sabbath Service celebrating the fortieth anniversary of I.C.C., June 11, 1988 (Levittown Public Library collection).

7. A number of the homeowners interviewed, for example, had become heavily involved in school politics. Several had developed close ties to

the dominant political party in Nassau County, and one of those had risen to the top of the party, becoming county chairman before he had reached the age of 45.

8. In so doing, it reflected the beliefs of one of the foremost proponents of a republic as a nation of homeowners, Thomas Jefferson. Jefferson's Republican Ideal was rooted in the concept of the yeoman farmer—independent, virtuous, and landowning. *Notes on the State of Virginia* (New York: Furman and Loudon, 1801). See also Loren Baritz, *The Good Life; The Meaning of Success for the American Middle Class* (New York: Alfred A. Knopf, 1989), pp. 8, 11.

9. Mabel O'Donnell, *Down the River Road*, The Alice and Jerry Books. Reading Foundation Series (Evanston, IL: Row, Peterson and Company, 1938), p. 5, 46, 101.

10. William H. Elson and William S. Gray, *Elson-Gray Basic Readers, Book One*, Curriculum Foundation Series (Chicago: Scott, Foresman and Company, 1930/36).

11. A. Sterl Artley and Lillian Gray, *What Next?* Reading for Independence. Curriculum Foundation Series (Chicago: Scott, Foresman and Company, 1952/1947), p. 6.

12. A. Sterl Artley and Lillian Gray, *We Three.* Reading for Independence. Curriculum Foundation Series (Chicago: Scott, Foresman and Company, 1952/1947), p. 4.

13. David Marc, "Comic Visions of the City: New York and the Television Sitcom." Paper delivered at the American Studies Conference, New York, November 24, 1987.

14. Richard Severo and Lewis Milford point out that this treatment of returning servicemen after World War II was atypical of American policy toward its veterans. More typical, they argue, was the apparent disdain for the Vietnam veterans. *The Wages of War* (New York: Simon and Schuster, 1989).

15. The phrase is from Reynolds' song "Little Boxes." It was one of a number of popular songs in the 1960s that denigrated the environment of the mass-produced housing tracts of the postwar suburbs. *Little Boxes and Other Handmade Songs* (New York: Oak Publishing Company, 1964). Among the others was The Monkees' recording of "Pleasant Valley Sunday," which satirized such staples of suburban life as barbecues, lawn mowing, and parent-child relationships.

16. For a discussion of the criticism levied against the postwar suburbs see Scott Donaldson, *The Suburban Myth* (New York: Columbia University Press, 1969). Some examples of the genre include John Keats, *The Crack in the Picture Window* (Boston: Houghton Mifflin Co., 1956); David Boroff,

"Suburbia—Levittown, Long Island" series in the *New York Post,* April 14 through April 20, 1958; and Ralph G. Martin, "Life in the New Suburbia" *New York Times Magazine,* January 15, 1952, pp. 16–42.

17. Among their responses, they initiated home and/or grounds beautification contests and wrote letters to editors defending their homes, their neighborhoods, and even the developers. See, for example, letters to the editor throughout the 1950s and 1960s in the local suburban press. For example, *The Levittown Eagle, The Levittown Tribune, The Midwest City News* and *The Midwest City Leader* (Midwest City, OK), and articles in such house-and-home publications as *McCall's Magazine* cited in Chapters 4 through 6.

More scholarly responses were generated by Harold Wattel and William Dobriner, both residents of Long Island's Levittown, who presented a positive interpretation of the new suburbs and their residents (Dobriner, *The Suburban Community* (New York: Putnam, 1958). In a similar vein, Herbert Gans' work followed the development of community in the New Jersey Levittown from the perspective of a participant/observer. *The Levittowners* (New York: Vintage Books, 1969).

18. The phenomenon of the postwar middle-class expansion is examined in Kenneth Fox, *Metropolitan America; Urban Life and Urban Policy in the United States, 1940–1980* (Jackson, MS: University Press of Mississippi, 1986), pp. 50–52, and in Baritz, *The Good Life.*

19. With neither a peasantry nor a nobility, social standing in America is measured instead by such acquired attributes as wealth and occupation, education and culture. Sociologists rely on clusters—or 'constellations'—of these status indicators that, on reaching a particular critical mass, determine class.

The weight and meaning attached to various symbols of class also change over time. A marked change in the number or weight of the status symbols signifies a move to the next higher (or lower) group. One of the problems in comparative analyses of social class from an historical perspective, therefore, has been to determine precisely those indices of status which have remained constant from era to era. Technology and mass production have combined to make former luxury items readily available to the mass market. As a result, not only do individual members rise and fall within and through the classes, but the status value of the indicators themselves varies over time.

Although landowning and home ownership have been among the more persistent indicators of American social status, even these have experienced fluctuations in value. The increase in railroad and trolley lines in the late nineteenth century allowed the middle class to commute from greater distances. Thus, residential location assumed connotations of social standing: inner-city neighborhoods—abandoned by the middle class—lost status, whereas the new suburban communities gained it.

20. The expression of this identification in the redesigning of the basic houses will be discussed in Chapters 4 and 5.

21. Levittown was funded at first under the terms of the Veterans' Emergency Housing Program, and later under the terms of the Housing Act of 1949, with assistance from both the FHA and the VA.

22. Indeed, if anything, the population profile was less middle class in terms of income and social status than when the development was first constructed. By 1970, Peter O. Muller found the median family income in Levittown to be $13,083. Sixty-four percent of the families earned less than $15,000, the lower-middle income range. Only 23 percent of the working population in Levittown held positions in professional, technical, or administrative categories, which was highly correlated to the figures for his working-class example in Milpitas, California, of whom 22.1 percent fell into those categories. "Everyday Life in Suburbia," *American Quarterly*, Vol. 34, 1982, p. 273.

23. The houses of Levittown currently command prices considerably above the national average, even when the geographic differentials of the Northeast are factored in. As of this writing original Levitt houses—that is, those which have not been structurally modified—are selling for upwards of $140,000, whereas those that have been remodeled and/or extended reach higher than $200,000. (Figures based on weekly monitoring of house sales in Nassau and Suffolk Counties, published in *Newsday*'s Saturday real estate sections.)

Both Michael Dukakis and Mario Cuomo have made political, photo-opportunity visits to Levittown; Dukakis, to woo the "middle-class" voter, and Cuomo to express his concern for the housing plight of the "middle-class." Paul Vitello, "Home is Where High Taxes Aren't," *Newsday*, June 25, 1989, p. 6.

24. The evolution of the American suburb is best delineated in Kenneth Jackson, *The Crabgrass Frontier* (New York: Oxford University Press, 1985). Other studies that treat the structural and geographic elements of American suburbs include Robert Fishman, *Bourgeois Utopias* (New York: Basic Books, 1987); David Handlin, *The American Home* (Boston: Little, Brown & Co., 1979); Sam Bass Warner, Jr. *Streetcar Suburbs* (Cambridge, MA: Harvard University Press, 1978) and Gwendolyn Wright, *Building the Dream*.

25. Houses of this order were built before the war, but for a different market. Individual landowners could hire a carpenter to build a small bungalow or cottage to order—or, in many cases, build it themselves. Mail-order houses could be set up on a small lot, either by contract or by the landowner.

There was also, in the 1920s and 1930s, a spate of building of small, inexpensive cabins intended for summer use by apartment-dwelling urbanites. Among its more substantial residences, Sears, Roebuck and Company offered this type of cottages, "suitable for woods, lake or seashore. [These houses made] comfortable homes in which to live happily during vacation periods and weekends." Katherine Cole Stevenson and H. Ward Jandl, *Houses by Mail; A Guide to Houses from Sears, Roebuck and Company* (Washington, DC: The Preservation Press, 1986), p. 343.

The vacation cottages were often more like unfinished shells than year-round houses, but provided more than adequate shelter as an alternative to camping for those with a desire for vacationing in "the country." Many of these are still in use as summer retreats in the midst of the postwar suburbs; others have been converted to permanent residences. See, for example, the illustrations in Barbara M. Kelly, "The Story of Beaver Pond" in *The Long Island Forum*, February 1980, pp. 24–28.

26.   Ned Eichler discusses the role of the FHA in shaping the postwar subdivision in *The Merchant Builders* (Cambridge, MA: The MIT Press,1982), pp. 3–130. See also Weiss, *The Rise of the Community Builders*, pp. 148–58.

Chapter 1   Construction

1.   Davis R. B. Ross, *Preparing for Ulysses; Politics and Veterans during World War II* (New York: Columbia University Press, 1969) discusses the intellectual and cultural background of the policies designed to assist the returning veteran. Richard Severo and Lewis Milford, *The Wages of War* (New York: Simon and Schuster, 1989) contrast the generosity of these policies with those provided for veterans of other wars, both before and since World War II.

2.   Significantly, the New and Fair Deal housing policies were developed within the congressional committees on banking and currency, rather than a special committee established to address housing problems. The idea of a Department of Housing and Urban Development was more than a decade away.

3   The phrase "American worker and *his* family" was not chosen to perpetuate sexist attitudes toward working women. Rather, it is used to reflect the contemporary concerns of policymakers who viewed family life from the perspective of the nineteenth century. Despite the reality of their experiences as workers, women in 1947 were locked into a tradition in which they either did not constitute the primary wage earner in a family, or—if they did—were not so acknowledged by those in a position to determine policy.

4.   The symbolic veteran continued to be used to promote the postwar housing developments long after reconversion was in place. For example, when William Levitt offered his 1949 model houses for sale, his ad was addressed to "Mr. Kilroy," a play on the fictive character used by the sol-

diers of World War II to lighten the burden of the war. Along with the slogan "Kilroy was here," his caricature was drawn on walls, fences, and aircraft wherever American soldiers were based.

5. For the history of the postwar construction industry see Marc A. Weiss, *The Rise of the Community Builders.* (New York: Columbia University Press, 1987; Ned Eichler, *The Merchant Builders* (Cambridge, MA: The MIT Press, 1982); and Joseph B. Mason, *The History of Housing in the USA 1930–1980* (Houston: Gulf Publishing Company, 1982).

6. The firm was composed of Abraham Levitt and his two sons, the business manager, William and the architect/designer, Alfred. Soon after the war, however, Abraham went into semi-retirement. Although Alfred was the firm's primary architect and Abraham took responsibility for the landscaping of the community, the driving force behind the company's postwar enterprises was William.

7. Boyden Sparkes, "They'll Build Neighborhoods, Not Houses," *Saturday Evening Post,* October 28, 1944, pp. 11, 43–46. Harold Wattel, "Abraham Levitt," *Dictionary of American Biography,* Volume VII, s. v. See also "Up from the Potato Fields," *Time,* July 3, 1950, pp. 67, 68.

8. William J. Levitt, "A House Is Not Enough," in Sidney Furst and Milton Sherman (eds.), *Business Decisions That Changed Our Lives.* (New York: Random House, 1964, p. 64).

9. *Thirteenth Annual Report of the Federal Housing Administration,* Washington, DC, 1946. This program was based on the war emergency title of the National Housing Act (Title VI), which had been established in 1941. Sections 603 and 608 of this title were altered in 1946 from war housing to veterans' housing, and were continued only on an emergency basis.

10. United States Statutes at Large, Volume 61, Part I, (Public Laws, Reorganization Plans, Proposed Amendment to the Constitution). (Washington, DC: Government Printing Office, 1948), p. 193.

11. Although the firm remained a partnership among the father and the two sons, the business management and the construction oversight were the work of William. For that reason the surname "Levitt" will be used in the text to refer to William. Abraham and Alfred will be identified by both given and surnames.

12. There was some opposition to Levitt's bypassing of the unions, notably from the sheathers' union. Berni Fisher, "Plywood or Sheathing? Battle Stalls 4,000 Rental Job." *Newsday,* June 25, 1947. However, the high wages and guarantee of steady work attracted hundreds of workers to the project.

13. For examples of the premature reputation, see "Nation's Biggest Housebuilder," *Life,* August 23, 1948, pp. 75–78, and Joseph M. Guilfoyle

and J. Howard Rutledge, "Levitt Licks the Housing Shortage," (*Coronet*, September 1948), p. 112.

For a detailed study of the production process see Liell, "Levittown; A Study in Community Planning and Development" (dissertation, Yale University, 1952). See also Eric Larrabee, "The Six Thousand Houses that Levitt Built," *Harper's Magazine*, September 1948, p. 82; "A Complete House for $6,990," *Architectural Forum*, May 1947, p. 70.

14.   Levittown, as a type for the postwar suburb, has been examined by journalists, sociologists, geographers, and architects, as well as by writers of fiction. See, for example, William M. Dobriner, *Class in Suburbia* (Englewood Cliffs, NJ: Prentice-Hall, Inc., 1963); Dolores Hayden, *Redesigning the American Dream* (New York: W. W. Norton, 1984); Gene Horowitz, *The Ladies of Levittown* (New York: Richard Marek Publishers, 1980); Kenneth Jackson, *The Crabgrass Frontier* (New York: Oxford University Press, 1985), Jenni Buhr, "Levittown as a Utopian Community," in Barbara M. Kelly (ed.), *Suburbia Re-examined* (Westport, CT: Greenwood Press, 1989), and Guilfoyle and Rutledge, "Levitt Licks the Housing Shortage," *Coronet*, September 1948, p. 112.

15.   This speed—impressive as it was in its own right—was subjected to the typical Levitt public relations twist. The 'completion rate' was expressed as one house every 11 minutes (stated figures vary from 10 to 30 minutes, depending on the publication).

The completion rate was therefore easily misinterpreted to mean a production rate of six houses per hour, 40 hours per week, or 240 houses per week. (see, for example, the section "How to Build Forty Houses a Day" in John D. Allison's dissertation, "An Analysis of Levittown, New York . . . ," (New York University, 1956), p. 61). Alfred Levitt estimated that the rate of construction reached 35 per day in "A Community Builder Looks at Community Planning," *Journal of the American Institute of Planners*, Spring 1951, p. 283.

By starting a house every 11 minutes and keeping the construction pace constant, he was indeed able to turn out a completed house every 11 minutes, once the full cycle of the construction process had taken place. This in itself was no small undertaking, but the actual production rate is closer to half that suggested by the publicized completion rate.

16.   In doing so, Levitt was using the old Stewart railroad line, which was discontinued shortly thereafter. The elimination of the railroad line suggests that Levittown was not expected to be a bedroom community for city-bound commuters. This is further supported by Alfred Levitt's later article on Landia, in which he spells out the firm's plan to create homes for workers at assorted Long Island defense plants.

17.   William J. Levitt, "A House Is Not Enough; The Story of America's First Community Builder," in Sidney Furst and Milton Sherman (eds.), *Business Decisions That Changed Our Lives* (New York: Random House, 1964). This technique of building a vertical monopoly on materials had been imple-

mented during the war by William Atkinson at Midwest City, Oklahoma, as well as by a number of the other contractors with whom Levitt had worked during his time at Norfolk, Virginia. Ned Eichler provides an analysis of these changes in construction methods in *The Merchant Builders*.

18. *Harper's Weekly*, April 7, 1869, n.p.

19. Mildred Smith, *The History of Garden City* (Manhasset: Channel Press, 1963). See also "Garden City Is Part of Big Tract Sold to Merchant 90 Years Ago," *New York Times*, October 4, 1959 (clipping in the "Garden City" vertical file, Long Island Studies Institute, Hofstra University).

20. Of the 1259 acres on which Levitt would build in 1947, Merillon owned 775 acres (61.5 percent) in 1942. By 1946, Levitt and Sons had bought from Merillon some 222 acres (13.9 percent) and Merillon retained 553 acres (47.6 percent), which were sold to Levitt in early 1947. Thus, together these two corporations held 61.5 percent of what would become Levittown.

Local landowners initially held back 414 acres, which were gradually surrounded by the Levitt houses. Many held out until long after Levitt had ceased building in 1951, and their tenacity accounts for the several pockets of non-Levitt houses within the community. Indeed, some of these plots are only now being developed as this book goes to print.

Hagstrom, *Atlas of Nassau County*, 1942 and 1946 editions; Nassau County Grantor/Grantee records for 1946.

21. Dobriner's comparison of the two communities in his *Class in Suburbia* showed, for example, that whereas 61.3 percent of the Garden City residents held positions above the level of "clerical and kindred workers," only 30.1 percent of the Levittown residents did so. Conversely, 27.1 percent of Levittown residents held positions at or below the level of "operators, foremen, and kindred workers," whereas only 10.4 percent in Garden City did. William M. Dobriner, *Class in Suburbia*, p. 97.

22. The houses Stewart built were of two levels: the "apostles," which cost about $15,000 to build, were for middle management, and were designed to rent for $1200 a year. They later sold for $17,000. The lower-level houses, the "disciples," were for clerical workers, and cost about $5000 to build, renting for about $750 a year. These were later sold at prices ranging up to $12,000. The figures cited represent costs in 1869.

The contrast between the two communities is also indicative of the economic changes that had been occurring in residential architecture in the decades between 1920 and 1950. Stewart's six-room "Disciples," the houses he had intended for his working-class rental market, had been steadily inflating in status as well as value. This was due in part to the contrast between their size and that of their four-room postwar counterparts, and in part to the maturation of the Garden City setting. The raw, new Cape Cods were no match for the massive trees, trimmed lawns, and shrub-framed houses of the older community.

23.   Hubbell had served as a member of the Hempstead Town development commission in 1930 when the town's building code was drawn up, and again in 1942, when it was revised, and had been an important contributor to the Long Island Real Estate Board. Hubbell became general manager of the Garden City Company, another of the Stewart Estate holdings, in 1897 (Smith, *History of Garden City*, p. 63.). His obituary outlined a long career in Nassau County's political and economic power circles (*Long Island Daily Press*, May 15, 1959).

Klapper served on the veterans real estate committee and the parks, parkways, and highways committee. *Real Estate Yearbook* (Garden City: Long Island Real Estate Board, 1948), p. 45.

24.   The Merillon Corporation was one of several real estate firms formed in 1893 by the heirs to Mrs. A. T. Stewart. They consolidated the easterly [that is, Levittown] acreage of the original "Stewart Purchase" under two holding companies, the Hempstead Plains Company and the Merillon Estate. At the time of the founding, the move was lauded by the *Building and Loan News* as a strategy to "keep the town out of the hands of speculators." Smith, *History of Garden City*, p. 44.

25.   Both men were clearly in a position to have blocked both the land sale and the building codes changes Levitt needed, had they chosen to do so. Since they did not, it is logical to assume that they, too, were, if not active supporters, at least not opponents of the project.

26.   Guilfoyle and Rutledge, pp. 112–16.

27.   *Island Trees Eagle*, Vol I, No. 1, November 20, 1947, p. 1.

28.   See Robert Caro's biography of Moses, *The Power Broker* (New York: Alfred E. Knopf, 1978), for a discussion of Moses' treatment of those whose plans he opposed.

29.   *Nassau Daily Review Star*, May 2, 1947, p. 1.

30.   The sheathers' union was organized under a powerful labor boss, "Big Bill" deKoning. Berni Fisher, "Plywood or Sheathing? Battle Stalls 4,000 Rental Home Job," *Newsday*, June 25, 1947, p. 2.

31.   "1000 of 2000 Houses Rented as Work Begins," *New York Herald Tribune*, Friday, May 9, 1947, p. 5. *Architectural Forum* noted that the test houses sold out the first day, without benefit of advertising. "A Complete House for $6,990," May 1947, p. 70.

32.   In part this favorable press coverage may be due to the economics of journalism. *Newsday* was in its infancy in 1947. By accepting and publishing prepackaged press releases, the paper could expand its material while keeping staff costs to a minimum. Many of the uncredited pieces on Levitt and his project have more the tone of press releases than of news reports, and may be more indicative of Levitt's version of what the public response should be than of what it actually was.

33. "G.O.P. Gazes in Alarm at Levitt-Type Homes, Leases." "Pride and Prejudice," *Newsday*, October 2, 1947, p. 3.

34. "Big Rental Housing Job to Start," *Newsday*, May 7, 1947; "Work is Begun on 2000 Homes on Long Island," *Herald Tribune*, May 7, 1947; "OK on 2000 Rent Homes Up to Town Law Change," *Newsday*, May 8, 1947; "Construction and Obstruction," *Newsday*, May 8, 1947 (Source: Levitt and Sons corporate clipping file. [N.C.M. L.63, 63.1]).

35. See, for example, *The New York World Telegram*, June 6, 1947, "2000 Modest Cottages in a Model Community at Island Trees Some Four Miles East of Hempstead," "These FHA units to rent for about $60 or $65 monthly will be coming on the market shortly."

36. These terms conformed to VEHP legislation: the houses would be offered first to veterans. Those that weren't taken by veterans after 30 days could then be offered to civilians.
     Almost all of the first 6000 units were occupied as rental housing, managed by Levitt through the Bethpage Realty Corp., which he owned with his brother Alfred.

37. Advertisements that ran throughout July 1947 in *Newsday* featured the selling price of $7500, with a down payment of $500. In pre-construction coverage in trade journals as well as in his earlier press releases, the price had been quoted as $6,990. But by the time the houses were ready to be sold, the cost had been revised.

38. "Will Raise Rents to $65 at End of Lease," *Levittown Eagle*, February 19, 1948, p. 1.

39. For the construction, Levitt originally financed the project under the terms of Title VI, Section 603 of the National Housing Act as amended in 1941, establishing the War Housing Insurance Fund. This title was originally intended as an emergency measure to underwrite the construction of war housing, and provided mortgage insurance for one- to four-family homes. The GI Bill took over when Levitt sold the houses to the original tenants, all veterans. On resale, the houses were mortgaged under section 505 of the GI Bill of Rights, which provided that the Veterans' Administration underwrite an equity loan of up to $2000 while the primary loan was insured by the FHA. *Eleventh Annual Report of the Federal Housing Administration* (Washington, DC, 1945).

40. Despite the strong emphasis on private enterprise in the VEHP and the Taft-Ellender-Wagner housing bill, the building industry had continued to oppose public housing titles as unfair competition for private industry. The social similarities between private and public rental housing, combined with the nature of the arguments against public housing, suggested that if the industry's lobbying succeeded, proprietary housing would be the beneficiary. Not only was government production of housing at-

tacked as socialistic, but multifamily housing, with its implications of collective living, itself came under attack as socialistic and therefore, un-American.

Public perceptions of tenants as socially less desirable further reinforced the consensus that owner-occupied houses were the higher form of residence. See Constance Perin, *Everything In Its Place* (Princeton: Princeton University Press, 1977); John Dean, *Home-ownership, Is It Sound?* (New York: Harper and Brothers, 1945).

41. *New York Herald Tribune*, Tuesday, July 1, 1947, p. 16. Truman was clearly dissatisfied with the provisions for rent control, which he considered woefully inadequate. Nevertheless, as he pointed out, "had [he] withheld [his] signature, national rent control would [have] die[d]" that night.

42. See *The Levittown Eagle* headline for December 11, 1947, "Levitt May Offer to Sell Homes Next Year to Present Tenants; Will Continue to Rent."

43. See House of Representatives Conference Report No. 1611 [Series 11210], "Housing and Rent Control Act of 1948," p. 1. See also "Text of the New Law Extending Rent Controls and Permitting an Increase of 15%," *The New York Times*, July 1, 1947, p. L2, and "Truman's Rent Bill Message," *New York Herald Tribune*, July 1, 1947, p. 16.

44. See Appendix I for a discussion of the process by which Junto was able to take control of Bethpage Realty in what was in effect a leveraged buyout.

45. Despite such articles as *Life's* "Nation's Biggest House Builder" (August 23, 1948) and *Coronet's* "Levitt Licks the Housing Shortage" (September, 1948), Levitt was, in 1948, still not the leader in total houses built. He had completed 4000 houses and was projecting a second 4000 for the following year. A number of builders across the country, particularly on the West coast, had exceeded his 1948 unit total. For a discussion of these builders and the numbers of their units, see Mason, *The History of Housing*.

Chapter 2   The Plan in the Planned Community

1. For a survey of the history of model communities see Gwendolyn Wright, *Building the Dream; A Social History of Housing in America* (New York: Pantheon Books, 1981), pp. 193–214. See also Daniel Schaffer, *Garden Cities for America; The Radburn Experience* (Philadelphia: Temple University Press, 1982); Roy Lubove, *The Progressives and the Slums* (Pittsburgh: University of Pittsburgh Press, 1962); and Kenneth Jackson, *The Crabgrass Frontier* (New York: Oxford University Press, 1985), p. 195.

For an examination of the underlying motivation in one of the planned communities, see Stanley Buder, *Pullman; An Experiment in Indus-*

trial Order and Community Planning 1880–1930 (New York: Oxford University Press, 1970).

2.   The reforms ranged from the simplicity of Catharine Beecher's concept of "an American woman's home" to the complexity of LeCorbusier's plans for a "radiant city." Catharine Beecher and Harriet Beecher Stowe, *An American Woman's Home* (Watkins Glen, NY: Library of Victorian Culture, 1979/1869) and Robert Fishman, *Urban Utopians in the Twentieth Century; Ebenezer Howard, Frank Lloyd Wright, LeCorbusier* (Cambridge, MA: MIT Press, 1976). See also Dolores Hayden, *Seven American Utopias; The Architecture of Communitarian Socialism 1790–1975* (Cambridge, MA: MIT Press, 1976).

3.   *Levittown Tribune*, December 12, 1947, p. 2.

4.   *Island Trees Eagle*, Vol. I. No. 1, November 20, 1947, p 2.

5.   Although Levitt and Sons had not built any of the defense plants in the area, there were three major industries—Republic Aviation in Farmingdale, Grumman Aircraft in Bethpage, and Sperry Gyroscope in Lake Success—and an army air base—Mitchel Field in Hempstead—within ten miles of Levittown. By 1951, when Liell was studying the community, the number of residents who worked at Grumman had increased from 192 to 324. A larger number of Grumman employees—492—whose post office addresses were listed as Island Trees (which is actually Levittown) or Hicksville (which at the time was largely Levittown) were probably Levittown residents, but it is impossible to reconstruct those figures, since Grumman employee records are either classified or destroyed. Similarly, the Sperry Corporation used the availability of rental houses in the area to attract employees from other areas of the country. John Liell, "Levittown; A Study in Community Planning and Development," diss. Yale University, 1952)p. 137.

6.   Alfred S. Levitt, "A Community Builder Looks at Community Planning," *Journal of the American Institute of Planners*, Spring 1951, pp. 80–88.

7.   William J. Levitt, "A House Is Not Enough," in Sidney Furst and Milton Sherman, *Business Decisions That Changed Our Lives* (New York: Random House, 1964).

8.   *Strathmore Vanderbilt; A Great Place to Be* (Manhasset, NY: Strathmore Vanderbilt Civic Association, Country Club, and Women's Club, 1983). See also Boyden Sparkes, "They'll Build Neighborhoods, Not Houses," *Saturday Evening Post*, October 28, 1944, pp. 11, 43–46. Sparkes celebrated the Levitts' intention to incorporate modern technology and social concepts into their postwar construction program. Many of the elements discussed were those which had been developed and advocated by the Progressive housing reformers and community planners. However, neither Sparkes nor the Levitts applied the term *planned* to Strathmore.

9. Liell, "Levittown."

10. The high point of this type of architectural reform came in the years between the turn of the twentieth century and the Depression. Wright, *Building the Dream*, pp. 155–214, and Roy Lubove, *The Progressives and the Slums* (Pittsburgh: University of Pittsburgh Press, 1982).

11. The phrase is from Robert Woods Kennedy, *The House and the Art of Its Design* (New York: Reinhold Publishing Co., 1953).

12. For an analysis of the needs of various classes of home-owners, see Kennedy, p. 14. For the impact of "trickle-down" middle-class housing, see Sam Bass Warner, Jr, *Streetcar Suburbs* (Cambridge, MA: Harvard University Press, 1978), p. 98.

13. There were a number of successful attempts at building such housing. In almost all cases, however, the dwellings were rental units, rather than proprietary houses. For the most part, their success depended on a willingness of the developers to limit the return on their investments. Wright, *Building the Dream*, especially the chapter "Planned Residential Communities," pp. 193–214, and Lubove, *The Progressives and the Slums*.

Andrew S. Dolkart and Sharon Z. Macosko discuss the successful City and Suburban Homes Company, which produced some 13 model tenement/ apartment buildings in New York between 1901 and 1913, a number of which are still operating. *A Dream Fulfilled; City and Suburban's York Avenue Estate* (New York: Coalition to Save City and Suburban Housing, Inc., 1988). For an alternative interpretation of the success of the York Avenue project, see Gina Luria Walker & Associates (ed.), *The City and Suburban Homes Company's York Avenue Estate: A Social and Architectural History* (Kalikow 78/79 Company, 1990).

14. *Newsday*, May 7, 1947; *Journal-American* and *The Sun*, May 8, 1947.

James L. Holton, "Real Estate" column: "New Levitt Project to House 2000 Vets." *World Telegram*, May 9, 1947. "The $16,000,000 project will be built under FHA sponsorship, as to home design and community planning. Moreover, all 2000 of these 4 ½ room cottages are to be financed with FHA-insured Sec. 603 loans. Mr Levitt said today that he expected this new operation of his firm would furnish employment to an additional working force of from 1500 to 2000 skilled mechanics."

These articles were clipped and filed in the Levitt & Sons scrapbook, which is accession L63.63.1 in the manuscript collection of the Nassau County Museum Reference Library.

15. Liell, pp. 98,99. For an account of the transfer from the Levitt subsidiary Bethpage Realty to a nonprofit organization named Junto, see Appendix I. See also Liell, p. 139; "Whence Comes the Dew," *Time*, March 13, 1950; and "How the Levitts Played Safe," *Business Week*, pp. 25–26, March 18, 1950.

16.   J. Normile and R.M. Jones, "$50,000 Worth of Ideas in a Low-Cost Home: Cape Cottage Brought Up to Date," *Better Homes and Gardens*, Aug. 1949: 37–41.

17.   See *American Builder*, June 1946, p. 96 and March 1949, p. 79 for comparative floor plans. The 1947/48 Cape is 30' wide by 25' deep, whereas the 1949 ranch is 32' wide by 25' deep.

18.   "Home Models Accelerate Sales," *American Builder*, March 1949, p. 79.

19.   This ideology is delineated in Gwendolyn Wright, *Building the Dream*, pp. 73–89. See also Loren Baritz, *The Good Life; The Meaning of Success for the American Middle Class* (New York: Alfred A. Knopf, 1989), pp. 8, 11.

20.   A vestige of this belief persisted well into the twentieth century in the form of voting requirements for local school elections. Since school budgets are funded primarily through property taxes, it was believed that only property owners should vote on their expenditure. The interplay between property ownership and rising class status in America is discussed in Loren Baritz, *The Good Life* (New York: Alfred A. Knopf, 1989), esp. pp. 72–76.

21.   Thomas Jefferson, *Notes on the State of Virginia* (New York: Furman and Loudon, 1801).

22.   Downing, *The Architecture of Country Houses* (New York, Dover Publications, 1969/1850), p. xix.

23.   For example, when, on the occasion of Levittown's twentieth anniversary, Lewis Mumford was asked his opinion of the community, he replied, "It's a suburb, and suburbs are just an expansion of a mistaken policy to build without industry. We have to build complete, well-integrated 'new towns,' not monotonous suburbs with great picture windows that look out onto clotheslines." Cited in a news article announcing Mumford's death, *Newsday*, January 28, 1990, p. 6.

24.   The earliest proponents of planned communities in America included the Owenites, Fouriers, Shakers, etc. Dolores Hayden, *Seven American Utopias; The Architecture of Communitarian Socialism 1790–1975.* (Cambridge, MA: MIT Press, 1976).

For the diffusion of the idea throughout the wider culture, see the writings of Andrew Jackson Downing, Horace Bushnell, and Catharine Beecher and Harriet Beecher Stowe. For a fuller discussion of the strength of the ideological link between the social order and the pattern and form of domestic architecture, see Buder, *Pullman*; Daniel Schaffer, *Garden Cities for America* (Philadelphia: Temple University Press, 1982); Lubove, *The Progressives and the Slums*; Dolores Hayden, *Grand Domestic Revolution* (Cambridge, MA: MIT Press, 1983); Gwendolyn Wright, *Moralism and the Model Home*

(Chicago: University of Chicago Press, 1980); and David Handlin, *The American Home* (Boston: Little, Brown & Co., 1979).

25. Although there were provisions for multifamily dwellings in the early versions of the VEHP, the FHA designers strongly "suggested" that they take the form of the two-storied garden apartment complexes, rather than high-rise buildings. Even more strongly suggested, however, was the freestanding, single-family residence. Federal Housing Administration Land Planning Bulletin No. 1, *Successful Subdivisions Planned as Neighborhoods for Profitable Investment and Appeal to Home Owners.* (Washington, DC: U.S. Government Printing Office, 1940).

26. This group was composed primarily of the lower-echelon clerical staff, service personnel, and middle managers, the rise of which was the result of the increasing bureaucratization of commerce and industry after the Civil War. Robert Wiebe, *The Search For Order* (New York: Hill and Wang, 1967).

27. Since economic advisors recommended a ratio of one week's wages for one month's rent, the Levitt houses were ideally aimed at the worker whose wages were $60 a week.

If no other evidence of the economic level of Levittown's target constituency were available, the point was made by William J. Levitt himself when he was interviewed by *Newsday*. "This [the development at Island Trees] is aimed at the needs of the middle-income group who earn $50 ($2600 per annum), $60 ($3120 p.a.), or $70 ($3640 p.a.) a week." ("Big Rental Housing Job to Start," *Newsday*, May 7, 1947, p. 2.

For some of the socioeconomic characteristics of Levittown, see Appendix III. For assessments of the class composition of Levittown, see Dobriner, *Class in Suburbia* (Englewood Cliffs, NJ: Prentice-Hall, Inc., 1963), John Liell, "Levittown; A Study in Community Planning and Development," diss., Yale Univ., 1952), and Herbert Gans, *The Levittowners* (New York: Vintage Books, 1969).

28. The pilot models for the houses were originally built to sell for $6990, and much of Levitt's early media coverage was centered on that price as an example of bone-cutting building. However, by the time he was ready to sell the houses in Levittown the price had been raised to $7500 for the Cape Cod models. His ranches would sell for $7990 in 1949.

29. Dorothy R. Rosenman, *A Million Homes A Year* (New York: Harcourt, Brace and Co., 1945), p. 17. This ratio was used by banks in determining eligibility for a mortgage. It allowed for ability to repay the loan while maintaining the property in reasonable condition.

30. Further evidence that the houses were intended for workers at the lower-income level can be inferred from the fact that Levitt's $7500 houses were advertised in the *Daily News* and in *Newsday*, newspapers that were aimed at the blue-collar worker with some high school education,

rather than in the *New York Times* or the *New York Herald Tribune*, which had their readership among the middle and upper-middle class—and in which Levitt continued to advertise his Strathmore and Country Club developments on the North Shore of the Island.

31.   The bathroom, although constituting another 'room,' had become a prerequisite for standard housing by 1945. Thus, in real-estate parlance, it was assumed, rather than stated, and a "four-room house" was taken to mean four rooms other than the bathroom.

32.   Indeed, Levitt was building such a house some five miles to the west of Levittown in Westbury. It was these houses which he chose to advertise in the *New York Times*. (Sunday, May 18, 1947, p. R5). The Westbury houses, which sold for just $10.00 below the V.E.H.P. limit of $10,000, included in the purchase price three bedrooms, one and a half baths, a "dinette," garage, and air conditioning. This house, after "a nominal down payment," would cost approximately $70 per month—$18.00 a month (roughly 25 percent) more than the mortgage and taxes on a Levittown Cape Cod, but only $10.00 per month more than *renting* it.

33.   A sense of income-to-occupation ratios can be gained by consulting the New York State Civil Service standards for the period. In 1946, head cooks employed in the private sector earned $3125 a year; in federal employment, $2646; and in New York State, $2684. Average salaries for prison guards in New York were $2806; social service workers without a specialty earned between $3061 (private sector) and $3234 (NY). Bank examiners earned between $5309 (U.S.) and $9003 (NY); associate attorneys, $7581 (U.S.) and $6641 (NY). State of New York Department of Civil Service, *Survey Report of the Salary Standardization Board* (Albany, 1947, pp. 119, 127, 171, 199, 217).

34.   In his defense of suburbia, Harold Wattel has argued that Levittown has been a middle class community from the beginning. However, Wattel's interpretation of the community is a rather subjective one, based primarily on his experience as an early resident there. Moreover, as a college instructor, he was in a group that straddles the classes. College professors tend to be both highly educated and underpaid. In 1947, when Levittown was built, college teachers earned an average annual salary of $3736, whereas nonsalaried lawyers averaged $7437 and nonsalaried physicians, $10,726. [Figures drawn from Series D 728–734, "Earnings in Selected Professional Occupations: 1929–1954," *Historical Statistics of the United States; Colonial Times to 1957* (Washington, DC: U.S. Department of Commerce; Bureau of the Census, 1957), p. 97.]

The college professor was therefore lower-middle in terms of earnings, comparing more closely with head cooks ($3125 p.a.) than with other professionals, but middle-class in terms of education, and presumably, interests. Since Wattel would have been more likely to seek out congenial social groups within the community, his assessment of its socioeconomic makeup may be skewed. "Levittown; a Suburban Community" in William M. Dobriner, ed., *The Suburban Community* (New York: Putnam, 1958), pp. 287–313.

35. The term was coined by Michael Schudson, to "label a set of aesthetic conventions" which he then "link[s] . . . to the political economy whose values they celebrate and promote." Schudson compares his version, Capitalist Realism in advertising, to Socialist Realism in art, the process by which officially approved art serves to transmit the officially approved political system. Michael Schudson, *Advertising, the Uneasy Persuasion: Its Dubious Impact on American Society* (New York: Basic Books, 1984) pp. 214–218.

36. *Successful Subdivisions.*

37. Eric Larrabee, "The Six Thousand Houses That Levitt Built," *Harper's*, September 1948, p. 81.

38. "Levitts Quit Low-Priced House Field," *World Telegram*, August 10, 1947. (N.C.M. L.63.63.1) James L. Holton, Real Estate column, "Levitts Halt Sales for Low-cost Homes But Plan Higher-Priced Roslyn Project," *World Telegram*, August 14, 1947. [N.C.M. L.63.63.1]

39. "Levitt May Offer to Sell Homes Next Year to Present Tenants; Will Continue to Rent," *Island Trees Eagle*, Volume I, No. 4, December 11, 1947, p. 1

40. "Will Raise Rents to $65 at End of Lease," *Levittown Eagle*, February 19, 1948, p. 1.

41. Clipping from a 1949 newsreel in which William J. Levitt addressed the housing shortage. Shown on ABC Television Network's "Our World, 1949," February 12, 1987.

42. Given that builders, bankers, and developers were well represented as consultants for the Congressional committees charged with shaping the housing policies, it is not surprising that the finished products reflected their position. "Hearings before the Committee on Banking and Currency, United States Senate, Eightieth Congress, First Session, in *S. 866* et al.
Although Levitt's name is not actually used, the testimony of "a Long Island industrial builder who erected 2,867 houses in 1947 and who schedules 5,000 in 1948 . . ." is included in the Report of the Joint congressional Committee on Housing Report, *Housing*, 1948, p. 114.

43. John M. Gries and James S. Taylor, Foreword in *How To Own Your Own Home* (Washington, DC: Government Printing Office, 1925).

44. W.W. Jennings, "The Value of Home Owning as Exemplified in American History," *Social Science*, January 1938, p. 13, cited in John P. Dean, *Home-Ownership; Is It Sound?*, p. 4.

45. A.S. Freed, "Home Building by Private Enterprise," Address before the Cambridge, MA League of Women Voters, February 26, 1936 (p. 3
of mimeograph). Cited in Dean, *Home Ownership*, p. 4.

46. Quoted in Cleo Fitzsimmons, *The Management of Family Resources*
(San Francisco: W. H. Freeman & Co., 1950), p. 38, 39.

47. Larrabee, p. 84.

48. Frank Capra, *It's A Wonderful Life*, RKO/Liberty Films, 1946.
Capra's film presents the character of George Bailey as the American Every-
man. The plot is set against a matrix in which home ownership through the
beleaguered Bailey Building and Loan Company is the honorable, albeit
humble, institution, whereas tenancy under the malevolent banker/landlord
Mr. Potter represents the evils of a failed society.

49. See, for example, Peter Marcuse, "Housing Policy and the Myth
of the Benevolent State," Jim Kemeny, "A Critique of Homeownership,"
and Dolores Hayden, "What Would a Non-Sexist City Be Like?" [All in
Rachel Bratt, Chester Hartman, and Ann Meyerson (eds.), *Critical Perspectives on Housing* (Philadelphia: Temple University Press, 1986)].

50. In its January 15, 1948 issue, the *Levittown Tribune* ran an editorial
announcing "what is promised to be a weekly press conference between the
local weekly newspapers and Mr. William Levitt, president of the construction firm." It was at these conferences that Levitt would inform or remind
tenants of various community regulations (p. 4).

51. Editorial, *Levittown Tribune*, April 1, 1948, p. 1. It is unclear
whether the statement quoted came from Levitt or from his spokesperson.
    The editor of the *Tribune* remembers this transition rather differently.
In a telephone interview in May 1989, Robert Abrams recalled that he and
Ira Cahn (publisher/editor of the *Levittown Eagle*) would meet Levitt each
week to receive the firm's press release. At one of those meetings, at a time
when Abrams' income from the paper was insufficient to keep him solvent,
Levitt offered to buy the paper and permit Abrams to run it as he had been
doing.
    Abrams believes that there was no interference from the Levitt organi-
zation in his running of the paper. Indeed, the only Levitt input Abrams
recalls after the transfer of ownership was the gardening column, which the
elder Levitt wrote and delivered on a weekly basis, and the continuing press
releases.
    He did not speculate on the possible impact of the fact of Levitt own-
ership on his own sense of editorial autonomy.

52. The name change was initiated by a semianonymous letter to the
editor in the *Eagle*. Signed "Mac," the letter proposed that the community
be named in honor of Levitt. The idea was taken up enthusiastically in an
editorial column in the same issue. December 11, 1947, p. 2.

At the opening meeting of the Island Trees Community Association, Lt. Steve Rakita, a columnist for the *Island Trees Tribune*, objected vehemently to having been "railroaded into the name change" and accused the *Eagle* of being the "mouthpiece" for the Levitt organization. (In this, he may well be on target, although the paper denies any connection with Levitt and Sons other than "good reporting," which they define as going to Levitt to see what is new). In its report, *The Eagle* (which has changed its name to *Levittown Eagle* in support of the name change) is very conciliatory in tone, and the letters to the editor are generally supportive of the organization and critical of Rakita for his protest. *Levittown Eagle*, January 15, 1948, p. 1.

Throughout the following weeks until the name was finalized, the *Tribune* printed letters opposing the change or offering alternative names, whereas the *Eagle* ignored any opposition, reporting instead on what it saw as a groundswell of support for the name change honoring Levitt.

53. Liell, pp. 185, 186. The rent increase was a more volatile issue. The implied threat of a Communist Party interest in keeping the rents low convinced at least one couple that the rent increase was acceptable, since they were opposed to any positions that had communist support. The thrust of the letters was suggestive more of fear of contagion than of support of the rent hike itself: "If the members of the so-called Island Trees Communist Party do not like the increase in rent or anything else, let them move and not jeopardize the status of others." This letter from Mrs. Jean Copp, as well as the letter from her husband, was signed. *Levittown Tribune*, March 4, 1948, p. 4.

In contrast, there is a marked increase in the number of anonymous letters opposing Levitt's policies that began to be submitted at this point.

54. "May Park Cars on Lawns During Three Snow Months," *The Island Trees Eagle*, Volume I, No. 2, November 27, 1947, p. 1.

55. Tenants were advised to avoid paste wax with a turpentine base or plastic waxes, which would dissolve and soften the asphalt tiles, causing them to discolor. Not mentioned in the text was the impact of the tiles on the homemaker. Once dissolved, the tiles stained everything they touched: the hands and feet of crawling children, as well as socks and pajama knees, etc., adding not only to the workload of the mother who had to clean them, but to the cost of replacing stained clothing. "Those black floors . . ." are commented on in almost every interview with the early residents, even now. *Eagle*, January 1, 1948, p. 3.

56. Ibid., December 24, 1947, p. 6.

57. For Henry Ford, see Anne Jardim, *The First Henry Ford; A Study in Personality and Business* (Cambridge, MA: MIT Press, 1970) and Allan Nevins, *Ford* (New York: Scribner, 1954). For Pullman, see Stanley Buder, *Pullman; An Experiment in Industrial Order and Community Planning, 1880– 1930* (New York: Oxford University Press, 1970). Mr. Atkinson discussed his

newspaper in a personal interview on August 1, 1986, at Midwest City, Oklahoma.

58.   In 1952 the Levittown Property Owners Association published a booklet that restated the Levitt "reminders" under the chapter title, "Community Appearance." "Such things as hanging wash on Sunday might annoy your neighbors, who are probably entertaining friends or relatives. Why not save it for Monday or hang it in the attic?" The article adds, "Fences may not be erected without permission from Levitt & Sons. Even if you get authority to erect a fence, consult your neighbors before you go ahead. Many fences have become complete barriers to friendship." *Our Town—Levittown* (Levittown: Levittown Property Owners Association), pp. 11;16.

59.   Sparkes, p. 45. See also *Strathmore Vanderbilt; A Great Place to Be.*

60.   The Levittown (formerly Island Trees) Community Association was apparently founded under Levitt's direction, since Ira Goldman, attorney and spokesperson for Levitt & Sons, was active in its establishment. Goldman presented himself at the meeting as "the people's advocate" in dealing with the organization, and—at least initially—the association was permitted to hold its meetings in the Levittown community hall.

61.   Later, when the group persisted in retaining "Island Trees" rather than adopting the new name of the community, they were denied the use of the community hall, and Levitt officially recognized the newly formed "Levittown Property Owners Association" as the authentic civic association in Levittown. *Levittown Eagle*, January 1, 1948, p. 8. As John Liell noted, Levitt preferred to deal with his tenants as individuals; when they opposed him as a group, he found them difficult and refused to deal with them. Liell, p. 186.

62.   Sparkes, p. 44.

63.   In some areas, such as West Hempstead and Garden City, selling prices as high as $20,000 were not unusual.

64.   Larrabee, p. 87.

65.   *Island Trees Eagle*, Volume I, No. 3, December 4, 1947, p. 2 (editorial, "They Have So Much Enthusiasm").

66.   These criticisms will be discussed in some detail in Chapter 6. See also Liell, "Levittown," pp. 343, 344.

67.   See, for example, Bernard Rudofsky, *Behind the Picture Window* (New York: Oxford University Press, 1955) or Robert C. Wood, *Suburbia, Its People and Their Politics* (Boston: Houghton Mifflin Co., 1958). Peter De Vries examined the image of the suburban wife and mother as a child-centered drone in "Humorists Depict the Suburban Wife," *Life*, Vol. XLI, No. 26, December 24, 1956, pp. 150, 151.

68. See, for example, Gans, *The Levittowners.*

69. David Boroff, *New York Post,* April 15, 16, 1956. p. M1.

70. Gans, *The Levittowners,* page (v).
As recently as April 1987, *Esquire* used the reference in an article on modern suburban subdivisions, "Leaving Levittown Behind," p. 95. The implication was that such a leaving was appropriate. p. 95.

71. Wilson (New York: Simon and Schuster, 1955).

72. *Island Trees Eagle,* Volume I, #3, December 4, 1947, p. 2.

73. *Levittown Eagle,* January 15, 1948, pp. 1,2.

74. John Keats' alliterative reference to the poor construction of the postwar developments, for example, used "Levittown" as a generic term. "It's sufficient at this point to suggest the rooftrees of the nation's Levittowns are held up by levitation." John Keats, *The Crack in the Picture Window* (Boston: Houghton Mifflin Co., 1956), p. xiii.

75. In 1952 a broad-based investigation into housing for the veterans was conducted by a House Select Committee. They reported all manner of problems, from shoddy workmanship to downright fraud on the part of the builders, and concluded that the GI Bill was "a builder's program, rather than a veterans' program." Keats, p. 25–27.

76. The economic corners Levitt chose to cut were primarily in the nature and amount of the space he provided. Even today, the basic structure of the Levitt house remains generally sound.

77. For a balanced discussion of the houses of Levittown, see Eric Larrabee, "The Six Thousand Houses that Levitt Built," *Harper's Magazine,* September 1948. For a detailed examination of what a house should be and do according to 1950s architectural wisdom, see Robert Woods Kennedy, *The House and the Art of Its Design.* New York: Progressive Architecture Library/Reinhold Publishing Co., 1953.

78. Lewis Mumford, *The City in History; Its Origins, Its Transformation, and Its Prospects* (New York: Harcourt Brace & World, Inc., 1961), p. 486.

79. The evolution of the suburban analysis is revealed in the evolution of the articles cited in the *Readers' Guide to Periodical Literature* in the years following the building of Levittown. Between 1947 and 1949, there were four citations for *suburban development,* which focused on the building of new subdivisions. The only entry under *suburban life* was entitled, "Take Time to Enjoy It." (G. T. Kellogg, *American Home,* May 1947, pp. 46ff). (*RGPL* May 1947–April 1949, p. 1937.)
In 1951 the titles began to reveal a shift in attitude. Under *suburban development* there were five entries, two of which bore the titles, "Build and

Be Damned" (Robert Moses, *Atlantic* 186, Dec. 1950, 40–42), and "Suburbs are Strangling the City" (W. Laas, *New York Times Magazine*, June 18, 1950, pp. 22–23). The number of entries under *suburban life* had increased to three. (*RGPL* May 1949–April 1951, p.1932.)

The 1952 titles under *suburban development* included "Challenge to the Cities" (*Newsweek*, 40, July 28, 1952, p. 68); "Cities versus Suburbs" by W. Zeckendorf (*Atlantic*, 190, July 1952, pp. 24–28); "Does Your City Suffer from Suburbanitis?" ed. by M. T. Bloom, T. H. Reed, and D. D. Reed (*Collier's*, 130; October 11, 1952, pp. 18–20) among its seven entries. The three entries under *suburban life* included "Satan in the Suburbs" by S. Stylites (*Christian Century* 69, November 26, 1952), *RGPL* p. 1375).

By 1953, both the numbers and the intensity of the articles had increased. "Flight to the Suburbs" (*Time*, 63:102, Mar. 11, 1952); "Suburbia; Its Taxes Ache" (*Business Week*); "Suburban Growth, Metropolitan Impact" (*Boston Herald*, editorial); and "To Save the Suburbs from Overdevelopment" were among those listed under *suburban development*, and "Has Your Child Room to Grow in School?" (*House and Gardens*), "Homogenized Children of New Suburbia" (*New York Times Magazine*); "Mass-produced Suburbs" (*Harper*); "Some Drawbacks of Suburban Life" (*Science Digest*) signaled the beginning of the assault on "suburban life." (*RGPL*, p. 2268.)

The category *suburban development* was not included in the 1955–57 *Reader's Guide*. *Suburban life* had expanded to 22 titles, and a new category, *suburbs*, included an additional 22. The titles continue to reveal some of the negative attitudes toward suburbs and suburban living: "The Church in Suburban Captivity" (*Christian Century*); "Look at Suburbanites" (*Science Digest*); "No More Suburbs for Us" (*Cosmopolitan*); "Mass-produced Individuality" (*Harper's*); and "Trouble in the Suburbs" (*Saturday Evening Post*).

The late 1950s emphasis on children and child rearing was reflected in the *Readers' Guide* titles of 1957–59, a total of 27 titles. By this time the subject of suburban life had become a stock item for periodicals. Titles such as "Adolescents in Suburbia (*National Education Association Journal*); "Children within Suburban Limits" (*New York Times Magazine*); "Is Youth Lost in the Wilds of Suburbia?" (*National Parent Teacher*); and "Suburbia, Is It a Child's Utopia?" reflect this trend and also the tendency to link the topics of children and suburbs. Other titles were more directly concerned with the suburb itself: "Is It True What They Say About Suburbia?" (*Parents Magazine*); Stress and Strain in Suburbia" (*National Parent Teacher*); "Chaos in the Suburbs" (*Better Homes and Gardens*); "Trouble in Suburbia" (*Senior Scholastic*); and "Suburban Sadness" (*Annals of the American Academy of Political and Social Science*) continue to foster the link between social malaise and suburban life.

80. The impact of the new suburban life on the housewife and mother was more closely scrutinized by Betty Friedan in 1962. *The Feminine Mystique* (New York: Laurel, 1983). Contemporary critics attacked the suburbanites themselves as having abdicated their autonomy. Two major critics of these changes in the "American Character" were David Reisman, *The Lonely*

Crowd; a Study of the Changing American Character. (Garden City, NY: Double-day-Anchor Books, 1953) and William H. Whyte, *The Organization Man* (Garden City: Doubleday-Anchor Books, 1957).

81.   Keats, p. xiv.

82.   John P. Dean. *Home Ownership; Is It Sound?* (New York: Harper and Brothers, 1945); Dorothy R. Rosenman, *A Million Homes a Year* (New York: Harcourt, Brace and Company, 1945).

83.   In 1949, for example, Babylon Town, some 10 miles southeast of Levittown, found itself "threatened" by the construction of Legion Park, a development of houses that were only 24' by 24' overall—even smaller than Levitt's Cape Cod, which was 24' by 30', or his 24' by 32' "49er" ranch. Unable to prevent the construction of Legion Park, the town quickly moved to create the legal barriers that would ensure that it would be the last of the small-house subdivisions erected within the town. The new building code, enacted in December 1952, called for a minimum of 1000 square feet (which could include 200 feet on a second story) per dwelling and 6000 square feet of lot. The dwelling was not to "exceed 27 1/2 percent of the lot area."

Chapter 3   Houses Fit for Heroes

1.   The pull was provided by the resurrection of the Victorian doctrine of 'separate spheres,' which rewarded women who "chose" to return to the home after the war by praising their femininity. The push was more overt. "Rosie the Riveter," who had been something of a heroine during the war, suddenly became something of a pariah; her job was needed by the returning veteran. (Alex Blair, "'Women Wake Up'; The Struggle for Equal Pay in the U.E. and the I.U.E.," and Joy Scime, "Public Policy and the Married Working Woman in the Great Depression." Papers presented at the annual convention of the Organization of American Historians, April 13, 1986.[Panel, "Wage-Earning Women in the Twentieth Century."]

2.   Despite the traditional emphasis of architectural history on the visual elements of the built environment, domestic architecture is more than just the sum of its aesthetic parts. Domestic space, both interior and exterior, interacts with the lives of the residents, not only reflecting but imposing a particular way of life. Houses become "machines for living," creating a physical environment in which the functions of family life are shaped by the form of the space provided for them. Although the environment does not determine human behavior, it provides a strong influence.

3.   Loren Baritz, *The Good Life* (New York: Alfred A. Knopf, 1989), pp. 166–224. See also Elaine Tyler May, *Homeward Bound; American Families in the Cold War Era* (New York: Basic Books, Inc., 1988).

4.   Although there are exceptions to this economic breakdown, in general the population of Levittown was composed of people whose economic level was lower-middle income. See Appendix III.

5.   It was argued by Levitt that integration would lead to a rapid and permanent white exodus, whereas the FHA argued that good communities resulted when people of similar background were allowed to remain together, and it legislated that belief into its funding regulations. See Gwendolyn Wright, *Building the Dream* (New York: Pantheon Books, 1981), p. 247.

The FHA also included a recommendation for "adequate zoning and protective covenants" among its "Subdivision Standards." Federal Housing Administration, Land Planning Bulletin no. 1, *Successful Subdivisions* (Washington, DC: U.S. Government Printing Office, 1940), p.28.

6.   The modernists' version of this phrase, "Form follows function," refers to the function of the materials used. Thus, structures composed of bricks and mortar should be designed to emphasize the bricks and mortar, rather than disguise them. Supporting pillars should look like supporting pillars rather than be hidden under ornamentation. It is a tribute to their lack of concern with domestic space that they overlooked the relationship between their forms and the lives of the families for whom they built. For a delightful, if biting, critique of the modernists, see Tom Wolfe's *From Bauhaus to Our House* (New York: Farrar, Straus & Giroux, 1981).

7.   In all the interviews, both formal and informal, that fed into this study, there was only one resident who indicated that the conformity ("herd mentality," in her words) was uncomfortable. She believed herself to be an outsider for the six years during which she lived there. In part, this may have been due to the fact that she moved in later and was younger than her neighbors.

8.   "May Day Parade Photos Taken to Cite Army Men For 'Treason'," *New York Herald Tribune*, May 4, 1947, p.1; "Monsignor Sheen Offers Plan to Curb Reds," *Ibid.*, p. 34. In a letter to the editor captioned "Citizen Joe Writes on Americanism," a correspondent stated, "As an American, I don't believe in talking down businessmen—or capitalists, as some call them. That's Communist talk which divides our people along class lines." *Long Island Press*, May 7, 1947, p. 18.

9.   Those intellectuals who attempted to defuse the tendency toward labelling nonconformists as traitors were themselves often accused of deviance, or worse. See, for example, "College Dean Sees Hysteria in War on A[merican] Y[outh for] D[emocracy]." *Long Island Press*, May 2, 1947, p.1. The Dean's tolerance for the AYD was viewed with strong suspicion of communist leanings by that group's opponents.

10.   "Stepping Stones to Happiness; a test of adaptibility [sic] to people and to situations," *Household*, May 1948, pp. 7;80ff.

11.   Liell, pp. 259–62. Indeed, Tom Carroll, Chairman of the Levittown 40th Anniversary celebration committee, was roundly applauded when he spoke of that group's goal being to revive the "pioneer" days, when everyone interacted with everyone else. September, 1987, Levittown Public Library.

12. *Levittown Eagle*, January 15, 1948, p. 1.

13. *Levittown Eagle*, January 22, 1948, p. 2.

14. John Liell recounts the tale of a woman who knew her neighbor was 'one of them' because, among other nonconforming behaviors, he allowed his dog to tear up "Mr. Levitt's grass" (p. 260).

15. *Newsday*, October 2, October 9, 1949. This theme was still readily apparent in the many meetings held to prepare for the celebration of Levittown's fortieth anniversary, which included a parade featuring the guest of honor, the aging William J. Levitt. For many of the residents Levitt was as important a symbol of Americanism as the proverbial Mom and apple pie.

16. In the tenth anniversary issue, under the heading "Community Appearance," the brochure modified the Association's 1952 statement forbidding fences. Since Levitt & Sons was no longer in control, the brochure simply pointed out that "Fences are restricted by covenant" and "suggest[ed]" that they not be built, lest they "become a sore point between you and your neighbor." L.P.O.A., *Levittown—Our Town*, Tenth Anniversary Issue, 1957, p. 14.

In case the "suggestion" was not strong enough, the article continued, "The L.P.O.A. has a standing committee on Community Appearance. It is the duty of this committee to investigate and report on any matter which pertains to the community's overall appearance, or property, the streets, shopping centers, or the parks." It concluded by advising the newcomer to "Be a good neighbor and a wise citizen. Do your share in keeping Levittown a 'Garden Community'" (p. 15).

The L.P.O.A. persists in its activities to this day, overseeing community appearance with great vigilance. Over the years it has organized to resolve traffic problems, to demand the removal of 'eyesores' in the community, and to protest both fluoridation of the water and the increase of multiple-family dwellings in Levittown.

17. The emphasis on normative behavior as an indicator of mental health went beyond the social behaviorists in the early 1950s. Sloan Wilson's fictional 'man in the grey flannel suit' was assigned to create a good image for his company's chief executive and decided that a campaign advocating mental health is the ideal method of doing so. The "mental health" he defined stressed "adaptability." *The Man in The Gray Flannel Suit* (New York: Simon and Schuster, 1955).

18. Joan Kron distinguishes between "geography," that is, the interrelationship of space as constructed into the floorplan, and "topography," which is the "scheme" of the house: "color schemes, ambience, style, patterns, and collections"—that is, the personalization of the structure. *Home-Psych; The Social Psychology of Homes and Decoration* (New York: Clarkson N. Potter Publishing Co., 1983), p. 45.

19. Robert Stern, *Pride of Place*, P.B.S. Television series, March, 1986.

20. A "Live Heat" [oil company] ad contains a Thanksgiving message to the new residents: "To you people in Island Trees—you are just as much pioneers as the Pilgrims who years ago settled in New England." *Levittown Eagle*, November 27, 1947, p.1.

21. The Cape Cod itself was a twentieth-century attempt to recreate the eighteenth- and nineteenth-century houses of New England. It was only one of a long line of reinterpretations of 'traditional' architectures. Here again, the re-creation was in the external appearances. No attention was paid to the role of the original floorplan in supporting colonial family life. Robert Woods Kennedy, *The House and the Art of Its Design* (New York: Progressive Architecture Library, Reinhold Publishing Co., 1953), p. 13.

22. Even the recreation provided by Levittown had strong traditional elements. The bowling alley in Levittown's Village Green may have been a far cry from the hills of Rip Van Winkle's Catskills, but Washington Irving had established the game's credentials as part of the American heritage.

23. These fences in particular served only as symbolic elements, since the use of actual fencing to delineate property lines or other spatial limits was forbidden by the Levitt covenant. This restriction extended as well to "natural fences" or hedgerows.

24. Nor were such facilities mentioned in the FHA bulletin. Yet, the feasibility of shared domestic facilities—and the inherent waste in duplication of facilities for individual families—had been in evidence since 1868, when Melusina Fay Peirce began publishing her work on cooperative housekeeping. See Dolores Hayden, *The Grand Domestic Revolution*. Cambridge, MA: M.I.T. Press, 1983).

25. Elizabeth Sweeney Herbert, "This Is How I Keep House." *McCall's*, April, 1949, pp. 41–44.

26. "Cross-and-bible" is a nineteenth-century term used to describe panelled doors whose design implies a cross over an open book. The raised panel that separated the two small squares at the top from two long rectangles beneath formed the cross. The third pair of panels, two shorter rectangles beneath the cross, suggested an open bible. The style is generally referred to today simply as a "colonial" door.

27. An earlier commentary had described the kitchen as "The focal point [of the house] . . ., at the front of the house . . ., which is full of cabinets and designed with a sharp eye on the magazine-reading, ruffled-chintz housewife." Larrabee, p. 82.

28. One of the visual indicators of urban blight frequently used in the movies of the forties was that of the slatternly housewife hanging wash out the back window of a tenement. Many of the old "East Side comedies" used this device, as did the movie *A Tree Grows in Brooklyn*. The film *Hester*

Street, although much later, also made use of the image of hanging laundry to evoke the intimacy and squalor of life in the urban ghetto.

This sense of laundry as a private matter underlies one of the metaphors for embarrassing one's family: "Don't hang your dirty linens in public."

29.   This is not at all unusual, since automatic dryers were still a luxury item for the private home in this period. Nevertheless, they remained the only logical alternative to hanging wash outdoors.

30.   When asked if the residents took such rulings seriously, one early renter in Levittown responded, "We took *everything* seriously; we were so grateful to have a place of our own after living in one room in my parents' home, that we didn't want to risk anything." Interview with M. F. Klerk, former Levittown resident, Hempstead, New York, June 18, 1986.

31.   Middle-class women up to this period frequently sent their laundry to a commercial "wet wash" or employed a local woman to come in and do their laundry. The five-day week was relatively common by 1947, so that domestic work done by outsiders was generally limited to Monday through Friday (although, no doubt, the laundresses did their own wash on the weekends).

32.   For a sense of Levitt's attitude toward nonconformity, see his continuing press releases and advice to his tenants in the Levittown weekly newspapers.

John Liell and Eric Larrabee both report his negative reactions to "insubordination" on the part of the Island Trees Community Association and the Island Trees Tenants Council. His later treatment of the editors of the two Levittown newspapers further reveals his aversion to deviation from his norms on the part of his tenants. Liell, p. 184; Larrabee, p. 84.

33.   Arlene Skolnick, *The Intimate Environment* (Boston: Little, Brown and Company, 1983) p. 26, 27. See also James Gilbert, "Confusing Young Rebels with Their Cause," *Newsday*, June 17, 1986, p.65.

34.   Abraham Levitt, "Fruit is Fine for Little Gardens," *American Home*, January, 1950, pp. 72, 73.

35.   Dobriner argued that the sheer visibility of activities in suburbia, brought about largely by the vastness of the outdoor field of vision in these new communities, led to a peculiarly 'suburban' interaction among its inhabitants. His sample frequently met casually outdoors, *precisely* because they were able to see when others were about. Dobriner, pp. 9, 10.

36.   Betty Friedan's *The Feminine Mystique* (New York: Laurel, 1983 [1963]) remains among the best exposés of the process of this postwar return to domesticity.

37.   The postwar social pressure on young men to marry and begin a family was almost equal to that on the young women. The popular culture

abounded in images and messages that cast young men in domestic situations. Ads for everything from cars to latex paint showed glowing young couples happily participating in some form of domestic activity. Popular music, one of the most universal of languages, was filled with songs of love and marriage specifically aimed at the teenager. Songs like Nat King Cole's "Too Young," for example, insisted that the teenager was not too young for the responsibility of marriage.

The social concern with the unmarried young man as "unsettled" and a potential source of social disruption dates to the onset of industrialization and the rise of wage laborers and other types of "masterless men." Christopher Hill examines the rise of the unattached worker in seventeenth-century England in *The World Turned Upside Down* (New York: Viking Press, 1972). Studies of the early industrialization period in America show a like concern for the disruptive tendencies of young men, especially the unmarried, itinerant day laborer. Marriage and a family are believed to serve as civilizing antidotes to their unbridled power.

The belief in the invulnerability of the unattached male persists in American popular culture. The hero of the cowboy movies was invariably free to move on after he had cleaned up the town for the more settled farmers. *Shane* epitomized this tension between the settled—and therefore vulnerable—family man and the loner who had nothing to lose.

38. See, for example, the Bethpage Realty lease, which demanded the tenant's time and labor, and limited his outdoor activities to those which were approved by the landlord:

10. The tenant agrees not to run or park any motor vehicle upon any part of the premises.

11. The tenant agrees to cut the lawn and remove tall growing weeds at least once a week between April fifteenth and November fifteenth.

39. He further reserved undeveloped land to be sold for schools and churches as the community progressed. Levitt donated three plots to be used for churches. Later congregations had to acquire their own land in order to build their houses of worship. Liell, p. 154.

40. *Successful Subdivisions*, p. 28.

41. For an examination of the social life of blue-collar workers see David Halle, *America's Working Man; Work, Home, and Politics Among Blue Collar Property Owners* (Chicago: The University of Chicago Press, 1984); Mirra Komarovsky, *Blue-Collar Marriage* (New York: Vintage Books, 1967); and Bennett Berger, *Working-Class Suburb: A Study of Auto Workers in Suburbia* (Berkeley: University of California Press, 1968).

See also Dobriner, *Class in Suburbia*, for the school, church and front lawn as the suburban social equivalent of these older establishments.

42. It was also typical for men of the upper-middle class to gather in male-oriented places such as yacht, golf, and country clubs (to which their wives were only admitted as "guests").

43. "Togetherness" as a precept had its origins in the Depression era. At that time, more home-centered activity was advocated in much of the advice aimed at young wives. In part this was an effort to spur the various sectors of the economy that serviced the house and home. Refrigerators, furniture, and other major purchases were more likely to be needed for home-based entertaining, for example. Moreover, the loss of servants among the more affluent had resulted in the "proletarianization" of the upper middle-class women. This, too, resulted in the intensification of home-centered family life. See Ruth Schwartz Cowan, *More Work For Mother* (New York: Basic Books, 1983), pp. 172–91.

However, it was not until the 1950s that the concept had a name: "*McCall's*, by the way, invented the term, 'togetherness'. In the mid-1950s, this was called, 'The Magazine of Togetherness.'" Avodah K. Offit, MD, "The New Togetherness," *McCall's*, March 1986, p. 20.

44. The phrase is that of Christopher Lasch, *Haven in a Heartless World* (New York: Basic Books, 1977).

45. The investment in land accounted for at least 20 percent of the cost of each house. Thus, by adhering to the building code, he could have saved approximately 7 percent on each unit. Moreover, he would have been able to produce an additional 6000 units without investing in any further property.

46. The ready availability of large, undeveloped tracts of land within commuting distance of New York City, coupled with the increased availability of automobiles and consumer credit with which to purchase them, no doubt contributed to the trend toward this type of land use, but it cannot be deemed an economical decision.

47. See note 38.

48. Levitt enforced the lawn mowing among his tenants by inspecting the properties and sending his own landscape crews to mow those lawns which he deemed overgrown. He would then bill the tenant for this service. By 1949, when he had completed the sale of the properties, the Levittown Property Owners Association took over his role as guardian of the community's appearance through their "community appearance committee." See their handbooks under the section "Community Appearance," *Our Town—Levittown*, Levittown Property Owners Association, Second Edition, 1952, p.11.

49. *Work* (The New Basic Readers) showed the series' children painting chairs and tables. *The New We Work and Play*, Second Pre-primer. (Scott, Foresman and Company, 1940/1946/1951), pp 3–10. The actual erection of buildings and even whole towns was encouraged as part of the primary curriculum in the 1940s. See, for example, "Tiny Town" in Leslie W. Irwin, Waid W. Tuttle and Caroline DeKelver, *Growing Day By Day* (Grade II), The Health—Happiness—Success Series (Chicago: Lyons and Carnahan, 1946) pp. 121–24.

50. The promise was somewhat exaggerated; the "after" illustration showed the curtains and furniture in place, the rug down, and the dog sleeping.

51. *Household*, September, 1949, p. 23.

52. Ruth Wyeth Spears: "Jean and Bill Discuss Bedroom Furniture," *Household*, September 1949, p. 42; "To Transform Old Bed," *Household*, July 1948, p.36.

53. This official recognition that two bedrooms was not sufficient reveals yet another pattern of American family life. Two bedrooms were the basic minimum for the postwar house because American children do not, as a rule, sleep with their parents past the toddler stage. Dr. Spock, the childcare expert of the 1940s, held that the child should be "out of the parents' room by 6 months if possible." He continued, "It is preferable that he not sleep in his parents' room after he is about 12 months old." Benjamin Spock, MD, *The Common Sense Book of Baby and Child Care* (New York: Duell, Sloan and Pearce, 1946), p. 100. There is a possibility that this was an intentional move on the part of the Levitts to "Americanize" those among the residents who might have retained their Old World (or urban apartment-induced) willingness to share their bedroom with their children.

See Margaret Mead, *Male and Female; A Study of the Sexes in a Changing World* (New York: W. Morrow, 1949) for "advice" to parents on sexuality; see also Arnold L. Gesell and Frances L. Ilg, *The Child from Five to Ten* (New York: Harper & Brothers, 1946).

54. Kate Simon, in her autobiographical *Bronx Primitive*, points out the urban roots of mixed-gender sleeping quarters. The FHA-sponsored suburban household was not intended to replicate the urban tenement, nor its ethnic idiosyncracies. *Bronx Primitive; Portraits in a Childhood* (New York: Viking Press, 1982).

55. "You may finish attics—Levitt," *Levittown Eagle*, Vol. I, #4, December 18, 1947, pp. 1, 7: "He stressed the fact that any attic construction is done at the tenants' own expense and risk and becomes the property of Levitt and Sons unless the tenant eventually buys the house." (p. 7)

56. The pressure to add onto the basic structure was not simply from within the family unit. The Levitt organization began releasing suggested improvements for the homes almost as soon as they were occupied. In November 1947, he announced the possibility of erecting garages: "The *Eagle* has also learned that permission might be granted to tenants who desire to build garages in Island Trees. The style, construction, placement and other conditions must be approved by the corporation." *Island Trees Eagle*, November 27, 1947, p. 1.

57. The use of the original attic in any event had been strongly discouraged by the third of the bold-type regulations, which stated:

The tenant agrees to assume the responsibility of ensuring that no person shall walk and nothing shall be placed upon the unfinished section of the attic floor. In the event this condition is violated and damage results to such attic floor and/or to the ceiling below, the tenant will pay the cost of repairs, which are estimated at a minimum of $60.00.

(Bethpage Realty Lease, p. 1)

In December, Levitt announced the possibility of finishing the attics (see note 55).

58. Several of my informants spoke of the problems of hanging wash during extended periods of rain. In addition to the attic, many of these women used the living room as drying space when drying family laundry in general, and diapers in particular.

59. The practice of landlords profiting by their tenants' investment was not new; the western Populist writer Hamlin Garland had outlined the tenant's plight in 1898 in his short story "Under the Lion's Paw." *Main Travelled Roads* (New York: Harper & Brothers, 1899).

60. "Levitt May Offer to Sell Homes Next Year to Present Tenants; Will Continue to Rent," *Island Trees Eagle,* December 11, 1947, p. 1.

61. By the end of the month, the company's press releases had begun to use the words "landlord " and "tenant" where before they had used "Mr. Levitt" and "our homes." December 24, 1947, p. 1.

62. Section 505 of the Serviceman's Readjustment Act. The column was written by Robert Hanifin, "a member of the staff of the New York regional office of the Veterans Administration, whose column content is entirely his own." Hanifin, *Levittown Eagle,* December 18, 1947, p. 8.

63. The new increase would begin in October 1948 for the first cohort of tenants, those who had been the earliest arrivals in October 1947.

64. Levitt indicated that a program of "home ownership" had always been the actual goal of his planning, since he did not, "under ordinary conditions," approve of tenancy. He reassured his tenants that although the corporation might, in the future, announce the homes of Levittown for sale, there were no definite plans to that effect. He also assured the existing tenants that in any event, they would be permitted to re-lease on a rental basis for at least another year. *Levittown Eagle,* February 19, 1948, p. 1.

This announcement preceded by several days Truman's message to the Congress calling for continued rent control, another factor in Levitt's move toward disinvestment. "Message from the President of the United States, transmitting a Program for Rent Control and Housing Legislation," February 23, 1948, House document 547, Series 11241, Fiche 141.

65. Many of the Levittown tenants in the first years were not veterans, but military men stationed at nearby Mitchel Field. It would have

been a serious error in judgment for Levitt to have forced these men to purchase. However, even they were "urged" to take advantage of the offer, since Levitt would guarantee to buy back the house, should they be transferred and unable to sell.

66.   The Cape Cod was offered in five models, but the distinctions between them were minor variations in the treatment of the façade. The houses themselves were interchangeable.

67.   Although the women's movement of the sixties has reduced this difference in orientation, the pattern remains only somewhat less true today than in the 1940s.

68.   See, for example, *Popular Science*, which in the late 1940s was offering such articles as H. Sibley's "Furnish Your Garden with Saplings and Staves" (154:195, May 1949); or *Popular Mechanics*, which offered T.L. Johnson's "Take it Easy in This Garden Lounge" (91:206–7, June 1949).

69.   *House and Garden* offered "Summer Look in Winter Rooms," (99:74–77, January, 1951); and *Woman's Home Companion* offered "Tricks with Trimmings" (76:121, September 1951).

70.   No attention was given, for example, to the fact that the Levitt kitchen also served as a major corridor for incoming traffic. In the few instances where traffic pattern was considered, it is an idealized traffic, with Mother moving from stove to table serving dinner. The housewife moving from appliance to table must cross this corridor repeatedly. In a household that includes teenagers, whose coming and going is more autonomous and less predictable, this cross-flow of traffic will interrupt the cooking and serving process repeatedly. Although the tension that results from this interruption of work is often misdirected, the real culprit is not the heedless youth who interrupts his or her mother's efforts, thereby demeaning her work, but the architect who designed a traffic flow for a workplace with no thought to the nature of the work that would take place within it.

71.   This aspect of the marketing strategy was supported by several informants, among whom there was a marked number of instances in which the husbands were the initiators not only in the decision to move, but in the actual choice of the house.

In the nostalgic version the husband came home and proudly announced that he had placed a deposit on the house. This is the scenario used in W. D. Wetherall's short story, "The Man Who Loved Levittown" in Wetherall, *The Man Who Loved Levittown* (Pittsburgh: The University of Pittsburgh Press, 1985). The idea of a companionate shopping for a home is missing from the mythology, if not from the practice, of buying a Levittown house.

Although no quantitative analysis was done, a casual questioning of a number of women in the 60–80-year age bracket revealed an unexpected predominance of instances in which the husband took full initiative for lo-

Redesigned kitchen plans showing improved traffic flow in the post-1949 ranch models. Floor plan CAD sketch. (Author) (a) Kitchen traffic flow, 1947 Cape Cod; A = Incoming traffic. B = Mother's pattern. (b) Kitchen Traffic Flow, Basic 1949 Ranch Model

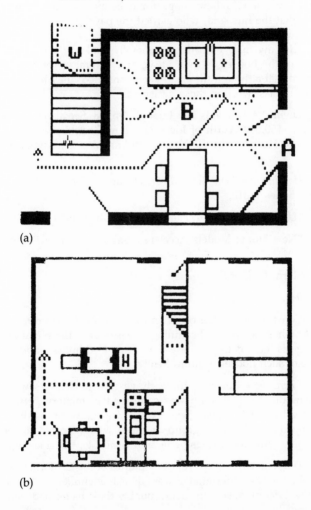

(a)

(b)

cating and acquiring the house. In one instance, the wife did not see the inside of the house until after the closing. This situation was not limited to Levittown or even to GI Bill housing. It may be more related to the contemporary idea that the husband, who earned the paycheck for the family, also earned the sole right to its distribution.

Similarly, my male informants generally spoke of the additions and renovations of the houses as their ideas, and several of the women informants agreed that although they had been consulted, they had had neither the first nor the last word in these decisions.

72.   Levitt, "A House Is Not Enough," p. 68. See also J. Normile and R. M. Jones, "$50,000 Worth of Ideas in a Low-Cost Home; Cape Cottage Brought Up to Date," *Better Homes and Gardens*, Vol. 27, August 1949, pp. 37–41.

73.   *Housing and Rent Act of 1949*, Document No. 35, 81st Congress, 1st Session. Series 11310.

74.   "Up From the Potato Fields," *Time*, July 3, 1950, pp. 67–72.

75.   "New Home Models Accelerate Sales," *American Builder*, March 1949, p. 79.

76.   Stern, *Pride of Place*.

77.   *Ibid*.

78.   Construction of the pools and greens was begun during the period in 1948 when Levitt was beginning to ease out of the rental market by encouraging his tenants to purchase their Cape Cod houses, and by selling the balance of such houses to Junto Realty.

79.   There were others in the early years who clearly saw their stay there as temporary. This group was composed of military personnel stationed at nearby Mitchel Field, who expected to move on as their assignments changed, and another group of those who expected to remain in Levittown only until better housing became available. Dobriner, pp. 89–91.

80.   The term *forty-niner* evokes memories of the California Gold Rush days, and the houses so designated were quickly identified as "ranches." By the time the 1950 models were made public, their name had become the Levittown ranch.

81.   J. Normile and R. M. Jones, "$50,000 Worth of Ideas in a Low-Cost Home," *Better Homes and Gardens*, August 1949, pp. 37–41; Levitt, "A House Is Not Enough," p. 69.

The tendency for Levittown residents to 'move up' by buying a newer model continued throughout the construction of Levittown. *Life* pointed out that one-third of the first 2400 sales of the 1950 models were sold to "people already occupying Levitt houses." "Levitt Adds 1950 Model to His Line," *Life* Magazine, May 22, 1950, pp. 141ff.

82.   *Better Homes and Gardens* pointed out that the plan for the Cape Cods "differed in no important way from the standard FHA low-cost plan." Normile and Jones, p. 38.

83.   "The Utts of Levittown," *Newsday*, October 8, 1949, p. M24.

84.   Full-page ad, "$7990," which ran on 6/17/49 in *The Sun*, *The News*, *Newsday*, and *World Telegram*, and on 6/19/47 in the *New York Herald Tribune* and *The Journal American*. (From an advertising proof kept in the Levitt scrapbook, N.C.M.)

85.   The family income was $275 a month, which represents both Al's salary and a government disability pension. His income, therefore, was slightly higher than average for the area, since many of his neighbors who also worked at Grumman and Republic would not have had the added pension.

The cost of maintaining the house was $92.50 a month: a combined mortgage/tax payment of $64; $9 for heating oil; $6.50 for insurance; $5.00 for telephone; and $8 for electricity.

86.   This transition of a formerly private area to the main public room was resisted by many of the owners, in particular the women. Theodore Robinson, a real estate attorney, noted that among the women whose houses he has closed, the blocking off of the kitchen from the entry was one of the first of the modifications for which they expressed a desire. Interview, Hempstead, New York, November 9, 1987.

87.   Television in 1949 was beginning to provide the rudimentary family situation comedies that would eventually become the staple of prime-time programming. In the home of the television family, the seating is arranged to allow the camera to focus on the faces of the seated. This often results in contrived situations such as a family of four seated along one half of a round table, or sofas set away from the walls to permit traffic to flow behind those seated, but in view of the camera.

88.   "Levitt's Progress," *Fortune*, October 1952, p. 164. Although Wright disdained the Levitt houses as trash, Levitt was fond of pointing out that he had been able to produce the low-cost houses that Wright had only theorized.

89.   Robert C. Twombly, *Frank Lloyd Wright; His Life and His Architecture* (New York: John Wiley and Sons, 1979).

90.   The recognition that it was middle-class housewives, rather than servants, who were doing the housework had been a staple in ads for soaps and household supplies since the 1920s. Cowan, *More Work for Mother*, p. 177.

91.   The new location of the kitchen in the front of the house was a postwar innovation. It appears to be related to the shift in women's work

roles. After several years in the public workforce, many of the women were reluctant to return to the deep privacy of the "backstairs" kitchen. Several commentators have argued that this was merely a practical and economic decision on the part of the builder. That is, a front kitchen provides the shortest line to the utilities, particularly water and waste disposal.

However, at Levittown (as well as several other developments of the period) the right-of-way for the utilities was located at the rear property line between two rows of houses. Here Levitt located both the electric and the telephone lines. Only the water service was located to the front of the house. There was no sewer line; kitchen and bath waste were exhausted to a cesspool located just outside the kitchen wall.

In a comparable Long Island development (Breslau Gardens in West Babylon, c. 1953) the water service was from a shallow well located in the basement of the house, and the cesspool was located in the rear yard, yet here, too, the kitchen was placed in the front of the house.

It would appear, therefore, that the location of the kitchen in the front of the house was a cultural/aesthetic decision that determined the location of the water service and cesspool, rather than the reverse.

By 1960 the location had reverted to the back of the house in comparable development houses and, by 1980, many remodelings included the removal of the kitchen to the rear of the house to provide easy access to patios and decks and to take advantage of the privacy of the garden.

92.   That these needs and desires may have been artificially stimulated by the marketing efforts and advertising campaigns of major manufacturers does not alter the reality that by 1949 they were accepted as needs by a large portion of the consuming public. For a history of the transition from customer to consumer, see Susan Strasser, *Satisfaction Guaranteed; The Making of the American Mass Market* (New York: Pantheon, 1989).

93.   The market change is perhaps best revealed in the fact that in 1950, *Life* noted a sales of 252 houses in the first exhibit weekend for the new model, although there was also a commitment of 1000 sales before the exhibit opened. When the Capes were made available, on the other hand, thousands had lined up for the opportunity to secure one. "Levitt Adds 1950 Model to His Line," *Life*, May 22, 1950, p. 141.

94.   Levitt's original decision not to include garages had been presented as a patriotic affirmation that as long as veterans were homeless, houses for people would take priority over shelter for cars.

In the changed market of 1950, this argument was no longer appropriate; Levitt added the carport to the 1950 model.

95.   Television, in 1950, was still a luxury item for most homeowners. Levitt's inclusion of these two items was clearly a marketing strategy. It provided a status symbol for the homeowners who would pay only $7990 for their homes.

96. Several of the Levittown homeowner-informants have commented that these final models sacrificed construction quality for the superficial appeal of appliances and equipment. The addition of carports, televisions, and spatial expandability without a concomitant addition in the sale price, they claim, necessitated the sacrifice. Yet, despite this, of the original residents interviewed who have remained in Levittown, a high percentage are now owners of the ranch models, usually the 1950/1951 houses, which suggests that this model satisfied some important aspect of the needs and desires of the residents.

97. This memory is expressed by Wetherall's Tommy DeMaria, the man who loved Levittown: "There wasn't anything we couldn't build or fix between us." W. D. Wetherall, "The Man Who Loved Levittown," p. 6.

98. Throughout the period when Levitt's ads addressed themselves to "Mr. Kilroy," there was no comparable ad addressed to Mrs. Kilroy, much less to her factory-working sister, Rosie the Riveter.

99. It is true that in many of these homes heavy labor was provided by the wife—or by the couple. But the two-spouse situation was still necessary, if only to divide the labors.

Chapter 4   The House Becomes a Home

1. A description of the women who attended the congress also reinforces the concept; the women typified the postwar ideal of the American family. For a full analysis of those who attended, see Appendix II.

2. Several topics on the agenda resonated with earlier Levittown architectural decisions: the necessity of a basement, carport, or garage; the suitability of a kitchen-based laundry facility; the kitchen as semiprivate versus semipublic space. In each case, the women's position opposed the design decisions originally made by Levitt and Sons.

3. The peak years of the building boom were between 1950, when there were 1,396,000 housing starts, (of which 1,154,100 were single-family dwellings) and 1955, when there were 1,328,900 housing starts, of which 1,309,500 were single-family dwellings. U.S. Department of Commerce, Series N 106–115. "Permanent Dwelling Units Started in Non-farm Areas," *A Statistical Abstract Supplement; Historical Abstracts of the United States, Colonial Times to 1957* (Washington DC: Bureau of the Census, 1957) p. 393.

4. Sound economics in the 1950s suggested that a house could not be considered an investment until the owner had built up an equity—normally over a ten-year time span. In the case of no down-payment purchases, however, the high interest bite out of the monthly payment probably increased the time needed for equity realization. John Keats, *The Crack in the Picture Window* (Boston: Houghton Mifflin Co., 1956), p. xv.

4.2n

Single-family dwellings starts per year, 1945–1957.

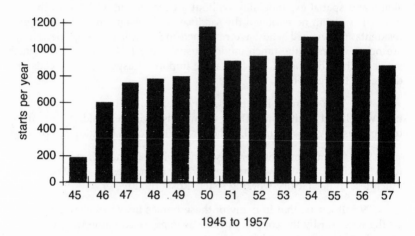

1945 to 1957

Based on Figures in N 106–124, "Permanent Dwelling Units . . . 1889–1957" in *Historical Statistics of the United States; Colonial Times to 1957*, p. 393.

5.   For the nature of those consulted, see U.S. Congress, Joint Committee on Housing, *Report: Housing in America* (Washington, DC: Government Printing Office, 1948).

6.   Annabelle Heath, Introduction, *Report on the First Women's Congress on Housing* (Washington, DC: Housing and Home Finance Agency, 1956) p. 7.

7.   A house identified only as "Levittown" was advertised for $10,490 in the real estate section of *Newsday* on October 16, 1956. A basic Levitt ranch was advertised in the same paper for $10,990. A '51 ranch was advertised "with extras" for $12,500. A "3 bedroom Cape with garage" was advertised in nearby Farmingdale for $12,750, and a "cute" 2-bedroom Cape was offered in Garden City for $24,000.

8.   "Architecture . . . seems to make a physical representation of social relations in the way it organizes people in space. It does this both symbolically—through imagery and 'appropriateness of place' for a particular activity—and in reality through physical boundaries and the spatial relationships made between activities." Jos Boys, "Is there A Feminist Analysis of Architecture?" in *Built Environment*, Vol 10, No. 1, 1984, p. 25.

9.   "The Home of Woman; A View from the Interior," in *Built Environment*, Vol. 10, No.1, 1984, p. 9.

10. Ruth Schwartz Cowan, *More Work for Mother; The Ironies of Household Technology from Open Hearth to the Microwave* (New York: Basic Books, 1983), p. 99.

11. See Cowan, *More Work for Mother*, especially pp. 172–91.

Dolores Hayden, in her examination of alternatives to privatized housekeeping, addresses the rise of the "Taylorized", i.e. efficient, homemaker as part of the move to increase consumption in the late 1920s. *Grand Domestic Revolution* (Cambridge, MA: MIT Press, 1983), p. 275. See also Gwendolyn Wright, "The Model Domestic Environment," in Susan Torre, ed., *Women in American Architecture; A Historic and Contemporary Perspective* (New York: Whitney Library of Design, 1977), pp. 18–31.

12. Even stock characters were remodelled to reflect this new woman. Lurene Tuttle played Effie, Sam Spade's secretary, on the "Sàm Spade" radio program through the forties and fifties. In an interview later, she described the postwar evolution of Effie. "We changed Effie's character. Dashiell Hammett wrote her as hard and wise-cracking as Sam. We made her softer and sweeter. It was more uplifting that way." Posthumous tribute to Lurene Tuttle, WBAI, "Old Time Radio Show," June 7, 1986.

13. Irving Berlin, "The Girl that I Marry" (New York: Irving Berlin Music Company, 1946).

14. Words by Oscar Hammerstein II; music by Richard Rogers. (New York: Williamson Music Inc., 1947). The song was introduced in the Broadway show *Allegro*.

15. This song, which was introduced in 1947 by Vaughan Monroe, was revived in 1955 by Nat "King" Cole. Bob Russell and Carl Sigman (New York: Jefferson Music Company, Inc., 1947).

16. There was some resistance to this segregation by age and gender. Mrs. Fred MacMurray, wife of the movie star, shown in her early American-style home, was quoted as saying, "I like to have the family around me. None of this shutting the children off in one wing and Fred in another. All four of us work and play together. No part of our home is considered out of bounds or off limits." Her comments suggest the degree to which "this shutting off" of the children was being advocated. Quoted in *House Beautiful*, Vol. 88, No. II, July 1946, p. 65.

17. Women were also advised never to let their husbands see them in cold cream or curlers. For socially aware women of lower income, who could not afford a standing appointment at the hair-dressers, this injunction reduced them to spending their days in curlers and bandannas, only to find themselves criticized in the next advice column for going forth looking as if they were ready for bed.

For some of the other contradictory advice given to the young women of the fifties, see Jane Davison, *The Fall of a Doll's House* (New York: Avon

Books, 1980), pp. 141–71. See also Betty Friedan, *The Feminine Mystique* (New York: Laurel, 1963/1983) and Cowan, p. 208.

18. *Household*, September, 1949, p. 61.

19. "Kitchen Marriage" (p.48) and "Custom Build Your Own Storage Walls" (p. 74).

20. "How-to Tips," *American Home*, January 1950, p. 39.

21. *American Home*, February 1950.

22. *Woman's Day*, Vol. 18, No. 4, January 1955, p. 44.

23. D. Sneiger, "New Furniture from Old," *Popular Science*, August 1950, pp. 157–60.
Woman's Day Workshop, William E. Whitlock, Director, "A Room for Two Boys" gave "Directions for constructing boys' room furniture . . . ," *Woman's Day*, Vol. 18, No. 1, January 1955, p. 55.
The "paint and fix" images were not reserved to adult materials. The Scott Foresman reading series relied heavily on images of Father supervising as Dick and Jane (mostly Dick) repaired and painted little red wagons, bird houses, and tricycles.

24. Cary Carson and Lorena S. Walsh, "The Material Life of the Early American Housewife." Paper presented at a Conference on Women in Early America, Williamsburg, Virginia, Nov. 5–7, 1981.

25. Heath, p. 80. The congress was actually unable to create even the economy house for the originally budgeted "$10,000 exclusive of improved plot." Their economy houses contained as minimum "needs" entry foyers at front and rear, dining spaces apart from the kitchen eating area, a basement and/or a carport with storage, and other amenities of which the Levitt houses had been stripped.
When the participants produced diagrammatic layouts, their demands for square footage ranged from a minimum of 1004 square feet (allowing 10 percent for walls, a gross figure of 1104 square feet) to 1324 in the low-cost version. At the 1956 figure of $15 per square foot with which they were working, their "economy house" would have cost $16,560 to build.
At the other end of their range, where they could have "desirable rooms and sizes," their plans varied from 1745 to 2336 square feet. Using the same $15 per square foot, these houses would have cost between $26,175 and $35,040 to produce.
Although the ten years' intervening inflation would have made it impossible to do so, working with Levitt's 1947/1951 figure of $10 per square foot, the Congress would still have had to spend $11,040 for the "economy house" (p. 62ff).

26. See Chapter 1.

27.   Ruth Schwartz Cowan, "The 'Industrial Revolution' in the Home; Household Technology and Social Change in the 20th Century," *Technology and Culture*, 17, (January 1976), pp. 1–42.

28.   A number of studies of both groups in the middle of the twentieth century have found this distinction between intra-familial socializing among the working class and extrafamilial socializing among the middle class. For the home life of the working class, see Bennett Berger, *Working-Class Suburb: A Study of Auto Workers in Suburbia* (Berkeley: University of California Press, 1968); David Halle, *America's Working Man; Work, Home, and Politics among Blue Collar Property Owners* (Chicago: The University of Chicago Press, 1984); Mirra Komarovsky, *Blue-Collar Marriage* (New York: Vintage, 1967/1962); and Lillian B. Rubin, *Worlds of Pain: Life in the Working-Class Family* (New York: Basic Books, 1976).

29.   For a description of the family life of working-class apartment dwellers in the prewar period, see Kate Simon, *Bronx Primitive; Portraits in a Childhood* (New York: Viking Press, 1982); Betty Smith, *A Tree Grows in Brooklyn* (New York: Harper & Brothers, 1943) and *Tomorrow Will Be Better* (New York: Harper, 1948). For contrast, see Sally Benson's story of the life of a middle-class apartment-dwelling family, *Junior Miss* (New York: Random House, 1941).

See also the film *Hester Street* for a visual image of the kitchen as a center of the family life, particularly for first-generation Americans. Second-generation Italian families, even in suburban homes, often create a large cooking/gathering area in their basements that replicates this kitchen.

30.   The role of the boarder in working-class urban homes is analyzed in John Modell and Tamara Hareven, "Urbanization and the Malleable Household: An Examination of Boarding and Lodging in American Families," in Michael Gordon (ed.), *The American Family in Social-Historical Perspective* (New York: St. Martin's Press, 1978), pp. 51–69.

31.   For the lifestyle of the middle class, see Theodore Caplow, Howard M. Bahr, et al., *Middletown Families; Fifty Years of Change and Continuity* (Minneapolis: University of Minnesota Press, 1982); J. R. Seeley, R.A. Sim, and E.W. Loosley, *Crestwood Heights: A Study in the Culture of Suburban Life* (New York: John Wiley & Sons, Inc. 1965/1956); and W. Lloyd Warner and Paul S. Lunt, *The Social Life of A Modern Community* (New Haven: Yale University Press, 1941).

32.   Heath, pp. 5, 14.

33.   Ravitz noted two forces that result in distinct differences in the nature of housing designs in industrial society: "social policy," which derives from building regulations, by-laws, and philanthropic movements, and "market policy," which she defines as "the production of houses that look like better-class dwellings than they really were." "The Home of Woman . . . ," p. 9.

34. Heath, *Report*, p. 82.

35. Larrabee, p. 82.

36. William J. Levitt, "A House Is Not Enough," in Sidney Furst and Milton Sherman (eds.) *Business Decisions That Changed Our Lives* (New York: Random House, 1964), p. 67.

37. At least not to the men who were the providers of the houses; the homeowning men may well have noted—and objected to—the combination of laundry and dining areas, but as we have seen, they were not consulted.

38. In effect, Levitt did make a similar change in the layout of the 1949–1951 ranch kitchen, which had an implied hall along the side wall of the kitchen.

39. Peter De Vries, "Humorists Depict the Suburban Wife," *Life*, Vol. XLI, No.26, December 24, 1956.

In "Suburbia Reconsidered: Diversity and the Creative Life," Dorothy Lee argued that suburban conformity undermined creative fulfillment. Elizabeth Geen, et al., (eds.), *Man and the Modern City* (Pittsburgh: 1963), pp. 122–24.

Suburbia as an incubator for neurosis was the target of such works as Richard E. Gordon, MD, et al., *The Split Level Trap* (New York: 1964), which coined the phrase "Disturbia." See also Reisman, Whyte, and "On the 5:19 to Ulcerville," *Newsweek*, Vol. LIV, No.7, August 17, 1959, p. 32.

For a sympathetic view of the suburban housewife of this period see Davison, *The Fall of a Doll's House*.

For a nostalgic survey of the period with all its purported neuroses, see Thomas Hine, *Populuxe*, (New York: Alfred A. Knopf, 1987), pp. 14–81.

40. Over the years, the residents of Levittown have had a number of complaints. However, it was rarely the houses that drew their fire. In the early decades, Levittown became somewhat infamous for the battles that raged over community standards, particularly within its schools. Accusations of communism, treason, and perversion have greeted those who disagreed with the community's norms for classroom music selections, school library contents, and other "liberal" transgressions.

For a class-based analysis of these battles, see Dobriner, pp. 113–26. See also Joann P. Krieg, "Levittown, L.I.: School For Disharmony." Paper delivered at Metropolitan American Studies Association meeting, 1984; Kay Bartlett, "Long Island School Book Banning is a Serial," *Long Island Sunday Press*, February 20, 1977, p. 11; and Michele Ingrassia, "Island Trees; What's Behind the Infighting?" *Newsday*, December 13, 1976, pp. 4A–5A.

41. The journal's title is a play on the fact that most of the street names in Levittown end in "lane." In the early 1960s, the title changed to *Ideas for the Long Island Home; Levittown's Thousands of Lanes*.

42.   Clarence Dean, citing the Levittown Self-Survey, conducted by Dr. Max Wolff of New York University and some 200 volunteers. "10-Year-Old Levittown Wears the Face of Change," *New York Times*, September 30, 1957, p. 23.

43.   In 1987 the fortieth anniversary committee invited William Levitt, now 82, to serve as grand marshall in their parade. Levitt and his wife later joined the committee at a dinner. The attitude displayed by both committee and onlookers was one of loyalty to the founder and of tearful gratitude for what he had given them. (Interviews with Camille Costanzo, Daphne Rus, Thomas Carroll, members of the Anniversary Committee, and with various onlookers at the parade. Levittown, October 10, 1987.)

44.   William Dobriner found that 61 percent of the Levittown residents of 1960 had been there in 1955 (p. 91); in 1952, Liell had found that 49.5 percent of the owners and 10.5 percent of the tenants expected that Levittown would be a permanent residence (p. 265).

45.   The Cape Cod, at 720 square feet, occupied only twelve percent of the 6000-square foot plot, a fact of which Levitt was very proud. Larrabee, p. 84.

46.   A survey of real estate offerings in *Newsday* in 1957 shows Levitt houses being advertised for anywhere from $10,000 to $18,000, depending upon several factors: location within the community (Wantagh and North Bellmore were higher-priced areas than Island Trees); the condition (many of the early rental houses were being sold by local real estate brokers and were not particularly well maintained); degree of remodeling and expansion; and the model type (the houses were listed in the ads by year and model, i.e., "Levitt '48 Cape" or "Levitt '50 Ranch"). A "'51 ranch" generally had a higher selling price.

47.   Dean, p. 15; Rosenmann, pp. 276, 277.

48.   "The Housing Mess," *Fortune*, Vol. 35, No. 1, January 1947, p. 81. Other critics also focused on the fear that whole subdivisions would eventually be foreclosed, saddling the government with acres and acres of decaying housing stock. Larrabee, p. 85; Liell, p. 344.

Chapter 5   Expanding the American Dream

1.   The story of the transfer of Levitt's rental units to the nonprofit educational institute, Junto, can be found in Appendix I.

2.   Clarence Dean, "10-Year-Old Levittown Wears the Face of Change," *New York Times* Sept 30, 1957, p. 23.
In 1956, John D. Allison found that 48 percent of his Levittown sample worked on Long Island (p. 236). His use of Long Island probably means in Nassau and Suffolk, since he had a separate listing for those who worked in

New York City and Brooklyn. Although Brooklyn is geographically on Long Island, it is politically part of the City of New York. It is unclear whether he considered Queens (also politically part of New York) to be Long Island or New York City, since he does not give it any listing. "An Analysis of Levittown, New York . . . ," diss., New York University, 1956).

In 1960, William Dobriner found that 58.9 percent of the residents worked within Nassau County, whereas only 19.4 percent worked in Manhattan. (By including those who worked within the New York City limits, i.e., Brooklyn, Bronx, and Queens, however, his figures would show more than 35 percent working "in the city."] William M. Dobriner, *Class in Suburbia* (Englewood Cliffs, NJ: Prentice-Hall, Inc., 1963), p.110.

3. The prediction that Levittown would deteriorate into a slum was repeated frequently, if only to prove that it was unfounded:

"[Levittown] stands as a living refutation to the critics of 10 years ago who caustically predicted Levittown would be a gigantic slum of the future." Tony Insolia, "The Levittown Decade." *Newsday*, September 30, 1957, p. 11c.

"Yet two changes that were freely predicted when Levittown was a-borning have not materialized. It has not become a slum, and no fearsome pattern of uniformity is evident among its people." Clarence Dean, p. 1.

"To us, the miracle of Levittown is the surprise we pulled on the 'experts,' who predicted slums here by 1957. Not only have we developed into one of the most beautiful communities on Long Island, but our homes are now being purchased by those same 'experts'—at almost double the original prices!" Elizabeth G. Wannen (ed.), "The Famous Legend of the Potato Fields," *Thousand Lanes*, Vol. IV, No. 1, Fall 1957, p. 4.

Yet the references to the threat of a slum continued:

"But to an awful lot of other people [other than the residents] Levittown was a dirty word, a synonym for suburbia-bound-to-become-slum." Suzanne Gleaves, "Levittown Revisited," *New York*, August 16, 1964, pp. 9–12.

See also Robert A. M. Stern's reference to "sluburbia" in his Public Broadcasting series, *Pride of Place* (Spring, 1986).

There remains a sensitivity about the characterization that touches even those whose homes provide clear evidence to the contrary. The residents whose homes are included in this study also made frequent reference to these early predictions. Regardless of the general acceptance of Levittown as a middle-class community, there is a defensiveness that colors the interviews. One woman, whose remodeled Cape Cod included a 12' by 32' kitchen/dining room, a combination bath-sitting room, a music room, an entertainment room, and two computer rooms, in addition to three bedrooms and a living room, ended the interview at her front door, with a derisive, "And they said this would be a slum!" But earlier in the interview she had also expressed some concern that her parents would have preferred to see her living in a "better" community.

4.   This may have as much to do with the history of the Levitt Cape Cods as with their structure. The 6000 Capes were the ones built originally to serve as rental units. The ranches were always intended for sale. Thus, even well into the 1960s, there were tenants living in Cape Cods. These people would have been far less likely to modify their houses, since they would receive no compensation for their efforts and investment, and might even have faced a raise in their rent as their homes increased in value.

5.   One contractor offered a 30' dormer extension, plus two finished bedrooms, a bathroom and a foyer in the Levitt house for $2590. *Thousand Lanes*, Vol 3, No.3, Spring 1957, p. 3.

6.   Even where no exterior signs existed that alteration was in progress, the tax assessor might be notified that an improvement was pending since contractors generally applied to the town for building permits, as their licenses demanded. However, where the homeowners finished the existing attic themselves, it would be up to them to notify the assessor and request a site inspection and reassessment. Many home-owners simply eliminated this step.

7.   Allison found between 10 and 14 percent of the ranch owners had made this modification by 1956. (He kept separate figures for each of the three ranch models.) Pp. 133, 148.

8.   The squaring of the kitchen could be had professionally for about $170 in 1957. An ad for McLaren & Pfau Contractors, *Thousand Lanes*, Spring 1957 (p. 35) offered to square the ranch kitchen, including tile flooring and spackling, for $169. The same company would enclose the carport for $488, including an overhead door, electricity, a window, and a rear door.

9.   Heath, p. 79.

10.   The nation's youth, particularly 'masterless' young men, have long been a focus of concern in Western civilization. (See, for example, Christopher Hill, *The World Turned Upside Down* (New York: Viking Press, 1972), pp. 32–45). But it was only after the publication of G. Stanley Hall's *Adolescence* in 1904 that the problem of restraining youthful behavior was consciously focused on those whose ages fell between childhood and adulthood.

By the 1920s, there had developed a concerted effort on the part of 'professionals' to reform and standardize the nation's adolescents. The movement was temporarily diverted by the war effort, which needed to harness the energy of the young males. Joseph Kett, *Rites of Passage; Adolescence in America* (New York: Basic Books, 1977). See also Eli Zaretsky, *Capitalism, the Family, and Personal Life* (New York: Harper Colophon Books, 1976).

11.   Philip Wylie's 1942 attack on "Mom" was reissued in 1955 with a scathing running commentary in which he endorsed his earlier position. *A Generation of Vipers* (New York: Holt Rinehart and Winston, 1955).

12. "Responding to normal group activities" in a positive way was an important component of child raising in the 1950s. David Reisman had noted the subtlety of its pervasive role in children's literature. In his analysis of Tootle, an anthropomorphic little engine, Reisman shows the didactic tendency to reward what he terms "other-directed behavior." Tootle learns to conform to society's restrictions when he is forced to return to the green flag of the track by citizens who block his venture into the fields with red flags. Reisman comments,

> [Children] learn that it is bad to go off the tracks and play with flowers and that, in the long run, there is not only success and approval but even freedom to be found in following the green lights. (Reisman, p.130).

13. Yvette Gervey with Mary Graham Bond, "Letter from a Decorator," *Thousand Lanes*, Fall 1961, pp. 26, 27.

14. "As is true of most Levitt homeowners, there are *always* future plans. The small bedroom will be enlarged to make a good-sized den." Mary Graham Bond, "Early American Theme," Spring 1960, pp. 14–15, 36.

"Eventually, the balcony space will include a recreation room for the young people, an extra bathroom, and a den and work area for Mr. Lauricella. Alice St. Aubyn Rossi, "Balcony Adds Lofty Beauty to Levitt Ranch, *TL*, Fall 1960, pp. 12–13.

"'We feel as if we had a real home now,' exclaims Mrs. Kreisher. 'And our children, Judy, 20, and Al, 15, with their own friends and interests, really do appreciate all this extra room.'" "Sunken Living Room Keynotes this Ranch," *TL*, Fall 1963, p. 30.

In many of the remodeling articles that included recreation space, no mention was made of children. Yet each of the houses retained a three-bedroom upper level, which suggests the presence of children. Other references to children are equally abstract. For example, Alice St. Aubyn Rossi uses the term "the family" to refer to those who use the recreation room and its fireplace. Alice St. Aubyn Rossi, "Living Space *Plus* Storage," *TL*, Fall 1960, pp. 26–27.

The omission of children is more common in the 1963 issues. See for example, "Raised Living Room," *Long Island Home, Thousand Lanes*, Fall 1963, pp. 20, 21; "Chinese Serenity," *LIHTL*, Fall 1963, pp. 26–28; and "Up & Down," *LIHTL*, Fall 1963, pp. 30–32. In part this may reflect the fact that the magazine has widened its subject matter to include houses from other suburbs, which may have had different demographics.

15. Juvenile delinquency, like "deviance," was a middle-class construct. The fear that the youth would be subverted through gang affiliation was particularly strong in suburban areas—although the gangs themselves were generally viewed as urban phenomena. This fear may have been linked to a fear of urban behavior as a sympton of downward mobility. For an examination of the 1950s attack on juvenile delinquency, see William

Graebner, "The 'Containment' of Juvenile Delinquency; Social Engineering and American Youth Culture in the Postwar Era," *American Studies*, Volume 27, Number 1, Spring 1986, pp. 81–97.

16.   David Marc, "Comic Visions of the City: New York and the Television Sitcom." Paper delivered at the American Studies Conference, Nov 24, 1987.

17.   The fledgling medium of television was still struggling to find programming.

18.   In the case of Jim Anderson—"Father Knows Best"—they also preached middle-class values. See examples further on.

19.   Jim Anderson was an insurance broker, Donna Reed's husband a physician. Ward Cleaver, occupation unclear, practiced in an office. The image of the mother emerging from the kitchen while drying her hands is used frequently in the "Father Knows Best" series. Variations on this image appear as stock illustrations in many of the reading textbooks of the period. Mother is part of the background, wearing an apron and carrying a bowl and towel.

20.   Plot of "Father Knows Best" rerun, August, 1987.

21.   This effect was achieved by a gradual close-up of Robert Young's face as he spoke earnestly into the camera. The fictive audience was eliminated, and he spoke directly to the viewer.

22.   David Marc tells of one episode of "Father Knows Best" that was funded by the United States Treasury Department in 1959. The episode, "Twenty-four Hours in Tyrant Land," presented the Andersons' home town under communist rule and was designed to convey the message that American values must be protected in order to prevent such a situation. Marc, p. 8.

23.   See, for example, the letter-to-the-editor forum in which the letter of a self-styled "wife of a right-wing extremist" protested the increase in "apathy towards Communism" that she saw in the opposition to the war in Vietnam. Her letter was juxtaposed to one entitled "Fight for Freedom," which countered that the nation was "imposing an alien way [of life and politics] for questionable motives in Vietnam." *Levittown Tribune*, July 13, 1967, p. 6.

24.   During this period there were a number of major battles between Levittown residents and their educational system. Their need to contain costs, for example, resulted in a contretemps in which the American Civil Liberties Union petitioned the State to order the Island Trees School Board to "withdraw a threat to punish teachers who complain about low pay." *Levittown Tribune*, June 15, 1967, p. 8.

25.   Harold Wattel interview, in Selma Greenberg, "The Teachers' Room," video retrospective on Levittown, produced by Charyl Shakeshaft

with the cooperation of the Levittown Teachers' Center and the Hofstra University Telecommunications Center.

26. The school budgets in Levittown have been a persistent issue in Levittown precisely because of the residential quality of the community. The seven-square-mile area is underrepresented in commercial and industrial bases. Therefore, homeowners bear a disproportionate share of the school tax burden, as compared with most other school districts on Long Island. As a result, teachers' salaries, extracurricular activities, and capital improvements are often voted down for economic rather than ideological reasons. However, as Dobriner has shown, the economic origins of the positions are often linked to class and cultural divisions within the community. Dobriner, pp. 100–126.

27. The archetype of the suburban-bashing song was the Monkees' recording of "Pleasant Valley Sunday," which satirized such stereotypical suburban activities as lawn mowing and charcoal barbecues, and the resultant adolescent apathy and parental tranquilizers. By implication, suburbanites were atrophying under the burden of their self-imposed lifestyle.

Janis Ian's recording of "Society's Child" mourned the inability of the young to break with the racial bigotry of their elders.

Other songsters revived the folk music of the Socialist workers' and Labor union movements to protest what they saw as the pervasive injustices of capitalist America: exploitation of the workers, particularly blacks and women, and the steady accumulation of the wealth of the country in the hands of the few.

28. The phrase was coined by Timothy Leary, a former Harvard professor whose experimentation with lysergic acid (LSD) led to his dismissal. He became, along with several others, the *de facto* leader of the hippie movement, and with it, of the drug culture.

A fine survey of the period can be found in Public Broadcasting's study of 1967, "Sergeant Pepper: It Was Twenty Years Ago Today." (PBS, February 24, 1988 et al.).

29. Marilyn French's semiautobiographical novel, *The Women's Room*, paralled the experience of many of these women as they left the kitchen to pursue long-deferred dreams of education and career. Marilyn French, *The Women's Room* (New York: Harcourt Brace Jovanovich, 1977).

30. The *Levittown Tribune* ran a weekly column, "Here, There, and Everywhere," which celebrated the activity of Levittown's young men in the armed services. The headline ironically echoed a song title written by the counterculture's hero, John Lennon.

31. John Liell's follow-up visit to his subjects in 1963 revealed that 80 percent of them no longer lived in the houses in which he had found them in 1951. (There are no data on which of them might have moved within Levittown, rather than out of the community altogether.) Interview, John Liell, Hempstead, New York, June 12, 1987.

32.   But by 1960, Dobriner would find Levittown's population to be slightly more stable than that of either Garden City or Nassau County as a whole. More than 60 percent of Levittown's residents "five years of age and over in 1960" lived in the same house they had in 1955, compared with 57.8 percent for the county and 57.9 percent for Garden City. Dobriner, p. 91.

33.   Advertisement for Levittown Equities, *Thousand Lanes*, Late Spring, 1963, p. 7.

34.   See, for example, Mary Graham Bond, "Trade Your Levitt House? . . . Report on a Growing Trend Among Homeowners," *Thousand Lanes*, Fall 1960, p. 39.

35.   Advertisement for John W. Pergola Real Estate, *Thousand Lanes*, Spring 1966, p. 32.

36.   Supplement to the Spring 1966 issue of *Thousand Lanes*, pp. 31–42.

37.   Ibid.

38.   Lumber and hardware dealers vied with appliance and furniture stores along Hempstead turnpike during the early decades. These have been joined more recently by dealers in "replacement" windows and vinyl siding whose presence serves as a reminder that the houses at Levittown are beginning to show their age.

39.   In the early years, many of the alterations were done by the homeowners themselves, alone or with their neighbors. Others were done by local handymen with varying degrees of skill. The modifications of the FHA loan policies that encouraged home remodeling loans in the 1960s created an economic bonanza for men who wanted to earn extra money. Young men who worked in manual trades found it easy to transfer their skills to home remodeling. In many cases they learned the construction trade through trial and error while remodeling their own homes, and then went into business as contractors. Levittown residents, in particular, who had gained their experience in the remodeling of their own houses, found that the skills were readily transferable to the other houses in the area.

The standard packages these contractors offered included full dormers, half dormers, and a selection of doghouse and shed dormers. The architectural detailing of overhangs, eaves, and reversed gables required more sophistication than many of the contractors could supply. Too often, this resulted in sub-standard workmanship and amateurish architectural design, even in houses with considerable sophistication in terms of interior decoration. In many cases, the extensions were butted up against the original houses with poorly constructed seams, and widespread leaking where the new abuts the old resulted.

Similarly, the relocation of the plumbing core required a high degree of sophistication and experience from the contractor. Even when hiring the

more professional remodelers, homeowners often shied away from relocating the plumbing core because of the expense it entailed. Thus, despite
the extensive remodeling in the Levittown houses, the placement and layout of the original kitchens and baths have been retained to a considerable
degree.

40. *New York Times*, September 30, 1957, p. 1. See also Arnold
Nicholson, "Are You Outgrowing Your House?" in *Saturday Evening Post*,
Jan 10 1959, pp 26–7 and Richheimer ad in *Thousand Lanes*, Vol. 6, No. 2,
Spring 1960, p. 7.

41. *Thousand Lanes*, Vol. 12, No. 2, Spring 1966, p. 13.

42. In addition, FHA-financed renovations were also subject to FHA
approval.

43. Harriet Morrison, "No Longer Like Peas in a Pod," *Today's Living*, October 22, 1961, p. 16.

44. By 1966, *Thousand Lanes*, which had originally been dedicated to
the Levitt houses, had had to branch out. It merged with *Long Island Home*,
and began to include renovations on a variety of house types from other
areas on the Island.

45. See Appendix III for comparative figures.

46. One anecdotal tale, part of the Levittown heritage, has it that a
wealthy dowager from the North Shore had her chauffeur drive her through
Levittown so that she could see what "they are doing for the poor people."

47. Magazines and manufacturers with national markets were quick
to see the marketing value of the owner-redesigned houses of Levittown.
For an analysis of the role of advertising in establishing official approval, see
Michael Schudson's *Advertising, The Uneasy Persuasion*. (New York: Basic
Books, 1984).
     The use of Levittown as a marketing device was begun as early as
1949, when Bendix, York, and General Electric used Levittown in their advertising in such trade journals as *Architectural Record* and *American Builder*.
These early advertisements, however, were primarily aimed at the building
trade, rather than at the consumer.

Chapter 6   A Closer Look

1. Throughout the text, the names of these homeowners have been
changed to protect their confidentiality.

2. The multigenerational use factor came as a surprise. Not only
was it not specified in the original request for houses to survey, but in most
cases, the owners did not appear to consider their households to be exam-

ples of a multigenerational or extended family. The process of adding or adapting the necessary amenities for their parents or their grown children had been an automatic response as the needs had arisen.

These houses do not represent any scientific sampling, and it is premature to generalize about the process. However, the relative affluence of the homeowners in some of the instances suggests that the decision to include members of the extended family was based as much on compassion as on economics. Especially in the case of the older generation, the decision to combine households appears not to have been due to a lack of alternative solutions. Indeed, one such couple eventually placed three of their parents in nursing homes. In the case of the adult children, on the other hand, there appears to be an economic element to the mergers. The young people remain home longer waiting to reach a position of independence, or they return home in order to build a nest egg.

A more focused study concerning the relative importance of economics in the decision to combine households would be useful in determining just how much the limited space of the FHA/GI Bill houses—rather than cultural or social change—generated the dominance of the nuclear family in the postwar years.

3.   This citation, as well as the following references to correspondence relating to the *American Home* contest, were taken from the collection of contest memorabilia of Mr. D. Colmer, winner in the contest.

4.   One year later, the company and the name of Levitt and Sons would be sold to I.T.T. William Levitt continued to operate on Long Island, although no further "Levittowns" could be built.

5.   Alan C. Borg, "Personalizing Development Homes," *American Home*, Vol. 71, No. 4, May 1968, pp. 68–80.

6.   Dennis Colmer, (Levittown homeowner), "Levittown Home Improvement Awards" entry form, p. 1, July 1967.

7.   Neither Mr. nor Mrs. Colmer, however, had been aware of the existence of such a congress until our interview in February 1988.

8.   Personal interview with Mr. and Mrs. Colmer, Hempstead, New York, February 10, 1988.

9.   The Cape Cod model had not come with a fireplace, as had the later Ranch models. The Colmers therefore planned for construction of a fireplace in the center of the exterior sidewall of the newly enlarged living room.

10.   The irony of a building code that "protects the residential nature of the community" while allowing for dishwashing in the bathroom is not lost on Mr. Colmer. However, it is very rare that Mrs. Jenson uses her double-duty sink setup. Since both Mr. and Mrs. Colmer now work outside

the house all week, Mrs. Jensen tends to use their kitchen and dishwasher while they are away. At times, she will also clean up their kitchen for them. Thus, the families are both interactive and independent in their use of the house.

11.   This concern with flexibility in space to allow for change over time was also expressed by the Women's Congress. They recognized the risk of creating age-specific ghettos. This risk has economic as well as social implications. As the bulge in the population matures, housing stock designed specifically for young marrieds loses its resale value. Housing stock designed specifically for empty-nesters, on the other hand, will be unsuitable for young marrieds without considerable alteration and expense.

12.   The fictional account of this process is expressed in W. D. Wetherall's short story, "The Man Who Loved Levittown". *The Man Who Loved Levittown*. (Pittsburgh: University of Pittsburgh Press, 1985). pp. 3–22.

13.   Values for Levittown houses represent typical prices for resales that were listed in *Sunday Newsday*'s real estate section over several months in late 1987 and early 1988.

14.   The decision not to provide a basement under the extension was based on economics. The construction of a basement would have doubled the cost of the extension. Cost was also a factor in deciding to retain the old burner location under the stairs, although Mrs. Taylor feels serious concern about the safety of the location. A burner fire would cut off the second floor of the house from any ready egress.

15.   There is a second computer upstairs in a room that is used as a combination office and exercise room.

16.   The chimney provides an example of the Levittown folklore. It is tilted slightly. The explanation for the tilt is that the chimney was installed first, then the burner, which did not fit directly under the chimney as planned.

17.   An important aspect of the expanding middle class has been the development of standardized products which, by being more readily available, have permitted more people access to symbols of status. This is true not only of the development house, but of the furnishings, fabrics, and accessories available to decorate it. Thus, although a wider population is able to partake of the array of options, the ability to express total individuality is restricted. At the middle-income level, one must choose from among those items which are commercially available. Availability of such products correlates to the profit motive; if a large market can be anticipated, the product will be made.

Thus, whereas the poor have their 'taste' in furnishing imposed upon them from the variety of sources such as thrift shops, charitable organizations, and municipal alms agencies, the middle class can select from an only slightly less restricted pool.

As a result, despite their apparent self-expression, homes like those of Levittown are apt to model the commercially designed rooms and houses that are depicted in the media and the department stores.

18.   The baby boom, which paralleled the suburban revolution, generally refers to the generation born to the returning veterans in the years between 1945 and 1960. This age cohort is now moving out of the childbearing years. Those at the younger end of this generation are the ones who are affected by the changing economies of homeowning.

19.   Like much of the early home remodeling in Levittown, the changes in the spatial arrangements of this house were defined by the limits of the construction workers who undertook them. The original plumbing core was retained, thus limiting the degree of innovation possible in the new kitchens and baths.

The extension has also been damaged by water leakage due in part to the lack of overhanging eaves.

20.   The former garage and the rear extensions are one story in height, which allows for skylights in the living room as well as cathedral ceilings in the dining room and the new master bedroom.

21.   The fact that the sister and her husband are relatives who will remain in the house apparently exempts the Starks from the "absentee" category, despite the fact that they will be fully in residence in New Jersey.

22.   In fact, within months after this visit, the Cotanis' daughter was able to buy a small house—a "handyman's special" about thirty miles east of Levittown—for what was advertised as the "affordable" price of $125,000. With substantial help from her parents, she was able to raise the necessary downpayment. The renovations needed will be spread out over a number of years and will no doubt take the form of a do-it-yourself project.

23.   At some point, a former owner had installed the piping for a second-floor bathroom, but the bathroom was never completed. The room is used as a closet instead. The radiant heating in the floor has been replaced, as has the 12-paned picture window, but in each case it has been because the original equipment wore out, rather than to enhance the original design.

24.   In most areas of the town, even the six-foot fence would be a violation of the building code and would require a special variance.

25.   The history of code evading in suburbia has yet to be written. However, the local papers frequently offer Building Department agendas that include such items as "[Mr. Doe] requests permission to retain an existing extension which encroaches on the building line" or "[Mr. Roe] requests permission for an existing shed." Similarly, the Levittown newspapers and the magazine *Thousand Lanes* published code summaries as reminders to residents of what was—and was not—permissible.

26.   This concern was voiced by the Levittown Property Owners Association in March 1987 at a meeting of the Hempstead Town Board of Zoning Appeals. *Levittown Tribune*, March 12, 1987, p. 7.

Queens County, with its 40' × 100' building lots, was itself considered suburban until the FHA redefined suburban plots in the late 1930s.

27.   Buses in Nassau County are generally routed along the secondary arteries. Except for school buses, they do not travel on residential streets. Although this maintains the suburban atmosphere of the community, it makes reliance on automobiles almost mandatory, particularly in larger suburbs like Levittown, where the distance between those arteries is considerable.

28.   In Suffolk County, several towns have enacted codes that severely restrict overnight parking of any type of vehicles on the street. Other communities prohibit overnight parking of commercial vehicles and trucks anywhere within the residential areas.

29.   Philip S. Gutis, "Levittown L.I. at 40: No Longer a Housing Cure," *New York Times*, September 21, 1987, pp. B1, B6. See also "Waiting for the Word" and "Homeowners Have their Say," both in *Levittown Tribune*, March 12, 1987, pp. 7–8, 12.

30.   Town of Hempstead Zoning Ordinance, Article XV, "The Levittown Planned Residential District."

31.   Several Long Island towns have begun experimenting with limited forms of such housing. Babylon Town grants a temporary permit for a homeowner to rent an apartment, so long as the owner remains in residence and the apartment meets code regulations. As of this writing, Huntington is debating passage of a similar code.

Chapter 7   Myths and Meanings

1.   In his study of semiotics, Jack Solomon expands upon the role of myth as group explanation of a shared and collectively accepted reality. *The Signs of Our Time* (New York: Harper & Row, Publishers, 1988). Among the groundbreaking works in the field of semiotics are Roland Barthes, *Mythologies* (New York: Hill and Wang, 1972) and *Systeme de la Mode* (Paris: Seuil, 1967); and Clifford Geertz, *The Interpretation of Cultures* (New York: Basic Books, 1973). Somewhat related is Walter Abell's *The Collective Dream in Art* (New York: Schocken Books, 1966/1957), which approaches the subject from a psychohistorical perspective.

2.   Tony Insolia, "The Levittown Decade 1957." *Newsday*, September 30 through October 4, 1957. Special section.

3.   Renters who moved on at the end of their lease have not shared similar perceptions of their experiences.

4. Conversation overheard in my office at Hofstra between M. F. Klerk, a colleague, and a graduate student from the People's Republic of China, March, 1988. The irony of describing the pre-Levittown lifestyle to a resident of such a notoriously overcrowded country was lost in the nostalgia of the moment.

5. Originally promoted during the nineteenth century by social reformers, the concept of the private home as providing the correct environment for a democratic, Judeo-Christian society became part of the political credo in the twentieth century. See, for example, Herbert Hoover's statement, "Maintaining a high percentage of individual homeowners is one of the searching tests that now challenge the people of the United States. The present large proportion of families that own their own homes is both the foundation of a sound economic and social system and a guarantee that our society will continue to develop rationally as changing conditions demand." John M. Gries and James S. Taylor Foreword, *How To Own Your Own Home* (Washington, DC: Government Printing Office, 1925).

Franklin Roosevelt repeated the sentiment in a speech before the United States Savings and Loan League in 1942. "[A] nation of homeowners, of people who own a real share in their own land, is unconquerable." Both are quoted in Cleo Fitzsimmons, *The Management of Family Resources* (San Francisco: W. H. Freeman & Co., 1950), p. 38, 39.

6. As recently as April 1989, Jack Kemp, Secretary of Housing and Urban Development, in speaking of the residents of public housing projects he had visited, argued that what they wanted was "the dignity and justice which comes with owning your own home or apartment." Jack Kemp, speaking to the American Legislative Exchange Council, April 28, 1989.

7. W. D. Wetherall, *The Man Who Loved Levittown* (Pittsburgh: University of Pittsburgh Press, 1985), p. 4. This aspect of the story, the 'potato fields to Cape Cods' in Levittown has its parallels in regional expressions such as 'peachtrees to rooftrees' in the South, or 'cornfields to cottages' in the Midwest.

8. This version of life in Levittown formed the framework for two other fictional accounts of suburbia: Marilyn French, *The Women's Room* (New York: Harcourt Brace Jovanovich, 1977), and Gene Horowitz, *The Ladies of Levittown* (New York: Richard Marek Publishers, 1980). Neither work is without strong relationship to the actual Levittown experience; indeed, Horowitz's version is said to be so closely drawn from fact that original residents can readily identify each of his characters.

9. In Wetherall's story, the young DeMaria meets Bill Levitt at the construction site. On learning that DeMaria is a veteran, Levitt accepts De-Maria's $83 instead of the required $100 as down payment for the house. Later in the story, when it becomes clear to DeMaria that he and his fellow old-timers are powerless to stop the changes that are taking place in Levit-

town, he can think of no better solution than to "call Big Bill Levitt up" and enlist his help in "hanging on to our places." Wetherall, p. 19.

10. "Mr. Kilroy's Home," *Time* 48:83, (December 23, 1946); "Their Farmlands Raise Crops of Houses," *Newsday*, May 8, 1948; Joseph M. Guilfoyle and J. Howard Rutledge *Coronet*, "Levitt Licks the Housing Shortage," (September 1948), p. 112ff; Ralph G. Martin, "Life in the New Suburbia," *New York Times Magazine*, (January 15, 1952), p. 16, pp. 40–42; Suzanne Gleaves, "Levittown Revisited," *New York* (August 16, 1964); *Life*, "Nation's Biggest House-builder," August 23, 1948, pp. 75–78; "Leaving Levittown Behind," *Esquire*, April 1987; Arnold Abrams, "Product of the Times," in "Goodbye Levittown; the Early Years," special issue of *Newsday* magazine, October 4, 1987, p. 14.

For media treatments, see, for example, "Our World—1949," American Broadcasting Company series, 1986, which recreated the myth visually as part of its anecdotal coverage of the events of the year 1949. See also the Public Broadcasting System series of Robert A. M. Stern's *Pride of Place*, March 1986, and Long Island Cablevision's Channel 12 News coverage of the fortieth anniversary activities in Levittown, Summer 1987.

11. National Commission on Professional Rights and Responsibilities of the NEA and the Ethical Practices Committee of the N.Y.S. Teachers Association. *Levittown, New York; A Study of Leadership Problems in a Rapidly Developed Community*. (Washington, DC: National Education Association of the United States). But Scott Donaldson, writing in 1969, surveyed the antisuburban literature and argued that the critics were unjustified. He pointed out inconsistencies, as well as outright contradictions, in their positions. He argued that the suburbs were no more dysfunctional than any other aspect of American society—just newer, more visible, and more readily attacked. Isolating the themes of the antisuburban movement, he found that there was an unrealistic urge to recreate a past that had never existed, or one that had only existed for a small minority of the population. It was against this unrealistic standard that the postwar suburbs were being measured and found wanting in the 1950s. Scott Donaldson, *The Suburban Myth*. (New York: Columbia University Press, 1969).

12. Wetherall, p. 7.

13. As Robert Darnton has observed, it is the arcane joke, proverb, or ritual that express the essence of cultural meaning. So, too, with myth. Robert Darnton, *The Great Cat Massacre and Other Episodes in French Cultural History* (New York: Basic Books, 1984), p. 5.

14. Boyden Sparkes, "They'll Build Neighborhoods, Not Houses," *Saturday Evening Post*, October 28, 1944. See also William J. Levitt, "A House Is Not Enough; The Story of America's First Community Builder." In Sidney Furst and Milton Sherman (eds.), *Business Decisions That Changed Our Lives*. (New York: Random House, 1964).

15.   Although it may be possible for a boy to find an unbroken stretch of bicycle pathway in Levittown, he would have to cross a large number of vehicular roadways in order to get to it. The street layout of Levittown is much more like the urban grid than it is like the segregated pathways of Radburn, Sunnyside, and the other prewar "model communities."

16.   In fact, when the houses at Island Trees were built, the postwar inflation had considerably altered the level of pricing. The actual sales price of the "small" houses increased from Levitt's prewar estimate of $4000 to $7500 when the houses were actually built. In comparison, this rate would have raised the price of his Strathmore Vanderbilt houses from their prewar price of $18,000 to prices upwards of $33,500 in 1947.

17.   In this, as in many other characteristics, Levitt's public persona is reminiscent of Henry Ford, who is frequently credited with having invented both the automobile and the assembly line.

18.   *The Town of Tomorrow* (13 brochures showing model houses for the future) (New York: New York World's Fair, 1939); *Lumber-Built Homes* (Chicago: National Lumber Manufacturing Assn, 1939); and *A Man's Home Is His Castle* (New York: Anthracite Industries, Inc., 1936) (for the Pennsylvania exhibit, New York World's Fair of 1939.)
Popular magazines on houses and homemaking featured articles promising maintenance-free materials and modern design. See, for example, "What the G. I. Wants in His Postwar House," *House Beautiful*, Vol. 86, August 1944, pp. 72–75ff, and the responses to it, "A Lady Begs to Differ," *House Beautiful*, Vol. 86, November 1944, pp. 161–63 and "A Lady Sergeant Defends Her Brothers-in-Arms," *House Beautiful*, Vol. 87, May 1945, pp. 132–34).
In addition to the promises for the future, there were also a number of education campaigns generated by such firms as Johns-Mansville, the Gypsum Association, and the Celotex Corporation, which warned against too much optimism. These companies pointed out that although prefabs with 1 1/2"-thick curtain walls of gypsum and Celotex were the method of the future, "outmoded" zoning and building codes would delay their implementation. Sparkes, p. 44.

19.   Both William M. Dobriner, in *Class in Suburbia* (Englewood Cliffs, NJ: Prentice-Hall, 1963) and John T. Liell, in "Levittown: A Study in Community Planning and Development" (unpublished dissertation, Yale University, 1952) refer to the population as "middle class," despite their own socioeconomic data that suggest that it is lower-middle class in both income and in educational level. Peter O. Muller's 1970 study placed the population in the lower-middle category in terms of income and in the blue-collar group in terms of occupation. "Everyday Life in Suburbia," in *American Quarterly*, Vol. 34, Spring 1982, p. 267. A sampling of these figures appears in Appendix III.

7.2n

Income distribution in 1947 divided into fifths.

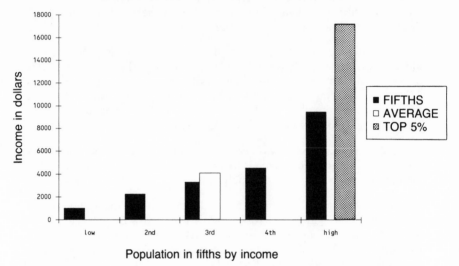

Contrasting columns show average of incomes vs. the middle fifth in income and income of top 5 percent vs. the highest fifth.

Figures based on series G99117, "Family Income Received by Each Fifth and Top 5 Percent of Families and Unattached Individuals: 1929–1957," in *Historical Statistics of the United States, Colonial Times to 1957*, p. 166.

20.   If the population is divided into fifths, the earnings for the middle fifth are considerably lower than the average of the incomes earned by the five groups. For example, the middle fifth of the population in 1947 had average (mean) family income of $3308. The average income for the lowest fifth was $1023, a difference of about $2000. On the other hand, the highest fifth had a family income of $9483, some $6100 more than the middle group. An average of the highest and the lowest fifths would yield a middle income of $5253, whereas an average of the figures for the five fifths comes to $4126. The numerical middle fifth of the population, therefore, earns only 80 percent of the overall average, and just over 60 percent of the numerical middle income. *Historical Statistics of the United States, Colonial Times to 1957*. (Washington, DC: U.S. Department of Commerce, 1958), p.167.

21.   It is the underlying thesis of this book that the redefinition in class which resulted from the housing policies of the FHA and the GI Bill is among the most important contributions of the Roosevelt/Truman years.

22.   For discussion of the politics of housing in the period, see Richard O. Davies, *Housing Reform During the Truman Administration* (Columbia,

MO: University of Missouri Press, 1966) and Davis R. B. Ross, *Preparing for Ulysses, Politics and Veterans during World War II* (New York: Columbia University Press, 1969).

23.   This placed the market for the Levitt houses above the second fifth of the population in income ($2275) but below the third fifth ($3308), that is, roughly the middle of the fourth stanine. In 1947, the median income for two-parent families was $3042. In the same year, the average (mean) family personal income was $4574, according to the Bureau of the Census. *Historical Statistics of the United States, Colonial Times to 1957.* (Washington, DC: U.S. Department of Commerce, 1958), p.167.

24.   Indeed, he originally built only rental units. However, even after he began to sell the houses, the homeowners were more likely to be from a tenant background.

In 1940, statistics for the country as a whole show that 54.3 percent of white Americans lived in rented dwellings. *Statistical Abstract of the United States 1960.* (Washington, DC: U.S. Department of Commerce, 1960), p.766. Levittown's rental population was almost entirely white in 1947, and after the development had been sold, was completely white. See Liell and Dobriner for discussion of racial covenanting in Levittown in 1947–1951.

For urban areas that figure is considerably higher. For example, in New York State the percentage of white households in rental units was placed at 69.7 percent. However, when the figures are narrowed to reflect *urban* areas that rate rises to 75.3 percent. *Sixteenth Census of the United States: 1940: Housing.* Volume II (Washington, DC: U.S. Department of Commerce, 1943), p. 272.

Allison's 1953–54 figures for Levittown homeowners show that 89.1 percent came from within the New York metropolitan area. John D. Allison, "An Analysis of Levittown, New York, with Particular Reference to Demand Satisfaction from Mass-Produced Low-Cost Housing," diss., New York University, 1956, p. 235.

Liell's 1950 figures show 78.1 percent of the population coming from Long Island and the five boroughs of New York (p. 59), and Dobriner shows an even higher rate of metropolitan area natives, 87.7 percent in 1955–60 (p. 90).

Since the target population of Levittown was clearly an urban, lower-income population, it is reasonable to assume that they were predominantly from the tenant class.

25.   Liell, for example, extrapolated from these studies a mean income of $3685 per year. His conclusion was that "No one in the community is rich, no one is poor—although many are getting by, as has been pointed out, 'by the skin of their teeth.'" Liell's figures were drawn from two surveys: Governmental Statistical Corporation, *Municipal Survey for Town of Hemptead, New York: Common School District No. 5 (Jerusalem)* in 1948, and the follow-up *Survey of the Banking Area of Northeastern Hempstead* in 1949. Liell, pp. 203, 204.

See also, Dobriner, *Class in Suburbia*, p. 101.

26. Dobriner, p. 101; Liell, p. 204.

27. Wages such as these were typically earned by head cooks ($3125) or social service workers ($3061) in 1946. *Survey Report of the Salary Standardization Board.* (Albany: New York State Department of Civil Service, 1947), pp. 119, 127.
Larrabee indicates that Levitt's carpenters were earning a "steady" $100 per week throughout the period of construction (p.84).

28. The opposition can be documented only through inference. There were a number of attacks levied by the press against those whom one publication called, "fatuous snobs" who opposed the project. "Slum-gullion," *Newsday*, May 27, 1947, p. 23; "G.O.P. Gazes in Alarm at Levitt-Type Homes, Leases," *Newsday*, October 2, 1947, p. 3.
During the course of this study, this opposition was referred to by long-time residents of the surrounding communities of Valley Stream, Rockville Centre, Baldwin, Garden City, and Hempstead. Many of them had objected to the new project as cheaply built, experimental, and likely to introduce 'a new element' in its tenants. They opposed the subdivision because it would create a low-income ghetto surrounded by middle-class communities, thereby lowering their property values. A few of these residents had not yet changed their opinion.
In its coverage of the tenth anniversary of the community, *Newsday* illustrated the article with a photo of Levittown houses captioned: "Levittown today, 10 years later, with its shrubbery-shrouded homes, well-kept houses and manicured lawns, is far from the 'slum of the future' that had been predicted." Tony Insolia, "The Levittown Decade 1957," *Newsday*, September 30 through October 4, 1957, special section, p. 10.
See also Dobriner, p. 85.

29. In particular, the use of gypsum board for interior walls, and Celotex (asbestos) shingles for the exterior siding came under attack as inferior to traditional—and labor intensive—plaster walls and sheathed exteriors of brick, clapboard or cedar shingles. The radiant heating system, which would eliminate both the need for and the possibility of a basement was another issue that brought serious opposition to Levitt's plans.

30. "Big Rental Housing Job to Start," *Newsday*, May 7, 1947; "Work is Begun on 2000 Homes on Long Island," *Herald Tribune*, May 7, 1947; "2000 Modest Cottages in a Model Community at Island Trees, Some Four Miles East of Hempstead," *New York World Telegram*, June 6, 1947.

31. The fact that over 60 percent of the acreage in the initial Levitt purchase in 1946 and 1947 had been held in speculation by a real estate company since the late 19th century has been little noted. Nor has the importance of the aviation industry to prewar Nassau County been factored into the story. For example, in her comparison of postwar Levittown with the defense housing created for the Kaiser factory at Vanport, Oregon, Do-

lores Hayden commented, "[t]here is no industry in Hicksville except the construction industry." *Redesigning the American Dream*, (New York: W. W. Norton & Co., 1984), p. 6.

Yet, long before the war, Nassau County had been developing a strong manufacturing industry linked to aviation. The defense buildup during the 1940s intensified that link. Between 1939 and 1944 the number of persons working in Long Island's aviation industry alone had risen from 5000 to 90,000. Most of that growth took place within a seven mile radius of Island Trees. Preston R. Bassett, "Early History of the Aviation Industry on Long Island," in Harold Wattel (ed.), *Developing Long Island*. (Hempstead: Hofstra College, 1959), p. 58.

32. A cursory review of the Nassau County phone book yellow pages for the year 1946–1947 shows 50 firms engaged in the sale or production of materials related to the aircraft industry, six firms dealing in electronic equipment and supplies, three chemical manufacturers, and 69 engineers, as well as 10 advertising agencies, all located within the county.

See also Dobriner, p. 86.

33. *Sixteenth Census*, pp. 318, 341.

34. Bureau of the Census, *County Data Book* (Washington, DC: Department of Commerce, 1947), p. 274. United States Department of Commerce, Bureau of the Census, *Sixteenth Census of the United States: 1940; Housing*, Vol II, part 4, p. 379.

35. In the tenth anniversary parade, the potato float played a starring role.

36. *Historical Statistics of the United States, Colonial Times to 1957*, p. 395.

In 1950, 1,154,000 single-family houses were started. Over 42 percent (n = 486,700) of those were funded by mortgages insured under the FHA/GI Bill policies. *Ibid.*, p. 393.

37. The treatment accorded the veterans of World War II was atypical of America's treatment of returning servicemen. In part, that is because they had a well-organized lobby in the American Legion. But even more, it was in the best interests of a number of other groups within the country to provide a package of housing, education, and other benefits at that particular juncture. See, for example, Ross, *Preparing for Ulysses* (New York: Columbia University Press, 1969), and Richard Severo and Lewis Milford, *The Wages of War* (New York: Simon and Schuster, 1989), which traces the treatment of returning servicemen from the Revolution to the Vietnam war. Marc Weiss' study of the real estate industry, especially in the 1930s and 1940s, explores the interplay between real estate developers and public policy: *The Rise of the Community Builders* (New York: Columbia University Press, 1987). See also Joseph B. Mason, *The History of Housing in the U.S. 1930–1980* (Houston: Gulf Publishing Company, 1982) and Ned Eichler, *The Merchant Builders* (Cambridge, MA: The MIT Press, 1982).

38.   It should be noted, however, that among the scholarly analyses, the three studies whose conclusions were most approving were the work of social scientists who were also Levittown residents. Harold Wattel and William Dobriner both lived in the Long Island Levittown that forms the basis of this study, whereas Herbert Gans based his work on the New Jersey Levittown (now called by its original name, Willingboro).

39.   The use of "Levittown" as a generic word for suburbia is also found in the popular culture. In 1986, *Esquire* called for better regional planning with an article entitled "No More Levittowns." Similarly, in an ironic reference to upward mobility, Audrey, the slum-dwelling heroine of *The Little Shop of Horrors*, dreams of a home in a green place—"nothing as fancy as Levittown."

40.   The first such treatment of Levittown was undertaken by Eric Larrabee in 1948. Larrabee examined Levitt's business methods, and the political implications of his techniques in terms of housing codes, housing trades, and economics. Referring to the design of Levitt's house as "rudimentary and inflexible," he criticized the lack of individuality and Levitt's own tendency to subvert expressions of independence among his tenants. Larrabee gave voice to many of the criticisms of the postwar suburbs, but without the rancor that would follow. Eric Larrabee, "The Six Thousand Houses that Levitt Built," *Harper's Magazine*, September 1948, pp. 79–88.

41.   In 1951 John Liell took issue with the popular tendency to link Levittown with the planning ideal. In order to test the concept that Levitt had indeed provided a planned environment, Liell focused on the growth of social community among the people, measuring the impact of their new environment on their familial, social, and economic lives. He concluded, much as Larrabee had, that Levittown was primarily a construction project, which bore little resemblance to the prewar "Garden Cities" model of planned community. Liell, too, predicted that even a minor economic recession would result in massive foreclosures, with the taxpayer picking up the bill. In addition, he linked the specific economics of Levittown and its residents to the rise and fall of the military-industrial complex on Long Island. Thus, Liell argued that, in the absence of a defense buildup, the community would eventually deteriorate even without a national recession. Liell, pp. 345ff.

42.   Taking up the question of whether the new type of suburban communities could or would produce stable communities, David Talmas predicted that the high rate of turnover would result in a rapid deterioration of the housing stock. He based this prediction on John Marshall Miller's opinion that with each change of ownership, maintenance is reduced. In Talmas' words, "pride in one's home (one-family house), considered as the care one takes in his house, in general declines with each successive occupant." David Talmas, "The Levittown Housing Project," unpublished master's thesis, Columbia University, 1950, p. 17.

43. For an overview of the creation of this myth, see Donaldson, *The Suburban Myth*. This approach was based in part on the work of William H. Whyte, Jr. Whyte's study of what he called "the organization man" criticized the new suburbs for a variety of ills, including the tendency to emasculate the men, to isolate the women, to homogenize the neighborhoods, and to force economic overextension in the name of upward mobility. See especially his chapters on "Classlessness in Suburbia" and "Inconspicuous Consumption," pp. 330–364. The Organization Man, (Garden City: Doubleday Anchor Books, 1957).

Although Phillip Wylie's *A Generation of Vipers*, did not single out suburbia, his negative caricature fit neatly with the lifestyle that was being tied to suburbia by its critics. (New York: Holt, Rinehart & Winston, 1955).

44. Herbert Gans, *The Levittowners; Ways of Life and Politics in a New Suburban Community*. (New York: Vantage Books, 1967).

45. Harold Wattel, "Levittown: A Suburban Community," in William M. Dobriner (ed.), *The Suburban Community*. (New York: G. P. Putnam's Sons, 1958), pp. 187–313.

46. Donaldson, *The Suburban Myth*.

47. Lewis Mumford, *The City in History*. (New York: Harcourt, Brace and World, Inc., 1961), p. 509.

48. "Technoburb" was coined by Robert Fishman, *Bourgeois Utopias* (New York: Basic Books, 1987), pp. 182ff.

49. William Levitt actually introduced nothing original in his construction of Levittown. The construction methods Levitt used were developed on the West Coast by David Bohannon and others. This "California Method" was used by many of the large-scale builders during World War II for defense housing. (See Chapter 2). Similarly, the curvilinear roadways, recreational areas, and the ratio of house to lot were mandated in 1939 by the policies of the FHA, which indirectly funded the construction of Levittown. The FHA, in turn, had derived them from the work of nineteenth-century architectural reformers and developers such as Llewelyn S. Haskell, Andrew Jackson Downing, and Ebenezer Howard.

50. In both *The Ladies of Levittown* and *The Women's Room*, this theme is particularly applied to the women who deviate from the cult of domesticity. Those who have ambitions for a future for themselves lose, even when they win. Corinne, in *Ladies*, who had wanted to remain in Greenwich Village and pursue her music, becomes instead a closet drinker in Levittown. Mira, the heroine of *The Women's Room*, gains an education and a professional career, but the narrative ends with her alone and lonely.

51. Dolores Hayden's analysis of suburban houses in the Levittown of 1949–1951, for example, dismisses the builder-delivered Cape Cods as

"awkwardly proportioned," but does not examine the degree to which the residents reshaped those proportions. Her conclusion that "Kaiser's highly praised wartime town [Vanport City, Oregon] lost the public relations battle to Levitt's postwar suburb" reinforces the image of a public duped by the builders and the FHA into accepting inferior housing. More important, it implies that the residents were passive within their environment, victims of it in many cases.

52.   Few studies of the postwar subdivision suburbs have analyzed the implications of the owner-generated redesign of the houses. An important exception is Lois Craig's "Suburbs," *Design Quarterly*, July, 1986. Craig's historical treatment views the twentieth-century suburb through a more positive lens. Acknowledging the limitations in the aesthetics of the built suburban environment, she notes the role of the homeowner, the community, and the passage of time in revisioning it. Craig suggests that the solution to the lack of design in suburbia lies in designers who can engage the suburban environment rather than follow the traditional pattern of disdaining and avoiding it.

53.   In addition to the structured interviews with homeowners that are part of Chapter 5, I have had a number of more casual interviews with Levittown residents who were interested in this project and offered their comments in an off-handed way during other conversations. Levittown residents, present and former, are generally quite eager to share their impressions of the community.

For an outsiders' appraisal see, for example, the segment on Levittown in *I'll Buy That; Fifty Small Wonders and Big Deals That Revolutionized the Lives of Consumers.* (New York: Consumer's Union, 1986). See also "Goodbye, Levittown," special edition of *Newsday* magazine, October 4, 1987, along with the letters to the editor written in response to it.

54.   When the Strathmore Vanderbilt residents published their community pamphlet, William Levitt's role in building the community was given the same coverage—two paragraphs—as the "three red clay tennis courts and two all-weather courts." *Strathmore Vanderbilt; A Great Place to Be* (Manhasset, NY: Strathmore Vanderbilt Civic Association, Country Club, and Women's Club) pp. 5, 9.

55.   None of Levitt's later developments on Long Island contained the type of basic houses that were constructed at Levittown. Country Club Estates at Roslyn and Strathmore at Stony Brook, which he built in the later 1950s and early 1960s, retained many of the innovations of the 1949–1951 Levittown ranches, but were aimed at a more affluent—albeit not wealthy—clientele.

56.   The term was coined by Scott Burns in his seminal work, *The Household Economy; Its Shape, Origins, and Future.* (Boston: Beacon Press, 1975). Burns argues that our understanding of the gross national product is

distorted by our refusal to include the production of homeowners—both male and female—in our assessments.

57. By 1956 more than half of the dwellings in the United States were owner-occupied; we had become a nation of homeowners and—by extension—a nation of the middle class. Bureau of the Census, *Statistical Abstract of the United States, 1960*. (Washington, DC: U.S. Department of Commerce, 1961), p. 766.

Chapter 8   The Politics of House and Home

1. Eric F. Goldman, *The Crucial Decade—and After; American, 1945–1960* (New York: Vintage Books, 1960), esp. Chapter 6. See also Elaine Tyler May, *Homeward Bound; American Families in the Cold War Era* (New York: Basic Books, Inc., 1988).

2. For example, this period also witnessed a marked increase in the membership of the American Legion, along with a steady shift to the political right in that body's political positions. Originally founded after World War I, the Legion was very active during the Depression in veterans' economic affairs, many of which placed the group in an adversarial position vis-a-vis the government. It was the Legion that led the calamitous 1932 Bonus March on Washington, demanding that the government redeem the bonus at the time of greatest need, rather than in 1945, the actual date of maturity. During and after the Second World War, the Legion's agenda changed to one of cooperation and support for the government, accompanied by a strong crusade to oppose "communists," "left-leaners" or their sympathizers, particularly among minority groups. Ross, *Preparing for Ulysses*, pp. 10–33.

3. See, for example, Jim Kemeny's article, "A Critique of Homeownership" in which he cites a "systematic discrimination in favor of homeownership" that restricts the options of the ordinary family as the underlying cause of its apparent popularity. In Rachel G. Bratt, Chester Hartman, and Ann Meyerson (eds.), *Critical Perspectives on Housing* (Philadelphia: Temple University Press, 1986), pp. 272–276.

4. See for example, Peter Marcuse, "Housing Policy and the Myth of the Benevolent State" in Bratt et al., *Critical Perspectives on Housing*. (Philadelphia: Temple University Press, 1986), pp. 248–63. The role of the veterans' programs as a measure to prevent social upheaval among the veterans is also discussed in Ross, *Preparing for Ulysses*.

5. Catharine Beecher and Harriet Beecher Stowe, *American Woman's Home* (Watkins Glen, NY: Library of Victorian Culture, 1979/1869). Andrew Jackson Downing, *The Architecture of Country Houses* (New York: Dover Publications, 1969/1850). George Everston Woodward, *Architecture and Rural Art* (Watkins Glen, NY: American Life Foundation, 1978/1867–68).

The work of the housing reformers is examined in Robert Fishman, *Urban Utopians in the Twentieth Century* (New York: Basic Books, 1977) and Roy Lubove, *Progressives and the Slums*, esp. pp. 21,43. See also Dolores Hayden, *Seven American Utopias* (Cambridge,MA: MIT Press, 1976) and *Grand Domestic Revolution* (Cambridge, MA; MIT Press, 1983). Other examples of the use of the domestic environment for social engineering or control can be found in Stanley Buder, *Pullman: An Experiment in Industrial Order and Community Planning 1880–1930*. (New York: Oxford University Press, 1970); Marcuse, "Housing Policy and the Myth of the Benevolent State" and Sam Bass Warner, Jr. *The Private City; Philadelphia in Three Periods of Its Growth* (Philadelphia: University of Pennsylvania Press, 1968).

6. As early as September 1944, *Fortune* had voiced this possibility in an article entitled "What is the I.L.O.?" In explanation, the article stated, "(The International Labor Organization) has been called 'Revolution Insurance.' Once more it seeks to guide the hopes and desires that, in the wake of war, stir the workers of the world." The author pointed out that the organization, which had been formed in 1919, "when Europe was seething with actual and incipient revolution," was, according to one of its founders, "an alternative to revolution." Its purpose was not to be an organization *of* labor, but rather one which was to deal with "problems concerning labor" (that is, with strikes and unrest). *Fortune* approved the agenda as an important contribution to postwar stability. *Fortune*, Vol. 30, September 1944, pp. 160ff.

In the April 1945 issue of *Fortune*, devoted to housing and the housing shortage, the Hearst newspaper chain ran an ad that chronicled its social contributions for previous years, noting that its editors had "always led the crusade for true SOCIAL PROGRESS." They included supporting anecdotes from past issues, and pointed out that, "In 1945, the Hearst Newspapers lauded labor's amazing record, at the same time deploring the communist-led strikes of a tiny minority." The barely disguised message—that American workers were basically a different breed from those who would change the social order of Europe—carried with it its own form of "revolution insurance" in the form of psychological reinforcement, at least to those workers who read *Fortune*. Vol. 33, April 1946, p. 65.

7. Gallup Poll, December 1945 found that 27 percent of those surveyed believed that the most important problem was "housing," while 10 percent checked the need for an apartment as their most important problem. (Survey #362K). By mid-1946, 27 percent of those surveyed would answer "yes" to whether or not they were affected by the housing shortage. See also Richard O Davies, *Housing Reform During the Truman Administration* (Columbia, MO: University of Missouri Press, 1966).

8. "Tomorrow is Mother's Day, But. . .," Editorial, *Newsday*, May 11, 1946; "Thirty Minutes' Notice," (letter to the editor, *Ibid*.); "Low-Cost Homes Banned by Old Code," *Newsday*, April 29, 1946; Davies, *Housing Reform*, pp. 18–24.

9. Ross, p. 241 [Citation: the testimony of John D. Small, civilian production administrator, before U.S. House, *Patman Bill Hearings* (January 28, 1946), pp. 359–409]. See also Eric F. Goldman, *The Crucial Decade—And After* (New York: Vintage Books, 1960), pp. 22ff.

10. "What is the I.L.O.?" *Fortune*, Vol. 30, September 1944, pp. 160ff.

11. For a comprehensive survey of the means used by the government to avert postwar conflict between veterans and civilians and, by extension, between the citizenry and the body politic, see Davis R. B. Ross, *Preparing for Ulysses; Politics and Veterans During World War II* (New York: Columbia University Press, 1969).

12. Conservatives saw no conflict with their position when private sector construction was built with federal subsidies; it was direct aid to the individual that threatened the social order. Meanwhile, progressives used the fear of subversion to promote their position as well. They were equally careful to invoke American tradition in their defense of housing the American worker, pointing out that "from the social point of view, a supply of good housing, sufficient to meet the needs of all families is essential to a sound and stable democracy." The argument was bolstered with the warning that poor housing would have an adverse effect on the "development of a sound citizenry." Davies, p. 38.

The Taft committee thus echoed the housing reformers of the nineteenth century in linking housing with social control as it pushed for the passage of a "comprehensive bill designed to meet the needs of all citizens." These proponents argued for a national policy that should make clear the obligation of the government to "provide each citizen with an opportunity to enjoy decent housing" while defending such involvement as being fully in harmony with democratic capitalism. The Bill they proposed would include a solidly capitalist-oriented program for "housing research, loans to builders of middle-income homes, the liberalization of FHA lending policies, a new program of yield insurance and the reorganization of the National Housing Agency into a permanent government agency. Davies, p. 27. The quotes are from the report of the Taft subcomitee on housing.

13. Richard O. Davies has detailed the stages by which the housing proposals were revised to eliminate those aspects which constituted direct housing aid to the public. In the first stage, Senator Jesse Wolcott of Michigan—another foe of public housing—had submitted an alternative to the (renamed) Taft-Ellender-Wagner Bill. (With the shift in power to the Republicans after the Congressional election of 1946, credit for the bill's proposal was renamed to reflect the new majority status of the Republicans; thus Taft, the Republican, was the first named).

14. Malvina Reynolds, "Little Boxes and Other Songs" (New York: Oak Publishing Co., 1964).

15. See, for example, Daniel Luria's article "Suburbanization, Ethnicity, and Party Base: Spatial Aspects of the Decline of American Social-

ism," which demonstrates the role of the postwar suburban exodus in undermining the hold of the socialist agenda on the working class. *Antipode* 11 (Fall 1979), pp. 76–79.

The voting patterns in the suburbs remained predominantly conservative and heavily Republican, despite the influx of so many apartment-dwelling urbanites. William H. Whyte, *Organization Man* (New York: Doubleday Anchor 1957), pp. 300–302. Other early studies of political alliances among new suburbanites include Fred I. Greenstein and Raymond E. Wolfinger, "The Suburbs and Shifting Party Loyalties," *Public Opinion Quarterly*, Winter 1958/59, pp. 473–82; Frederick M. Wirt, "The Political Sociology of American Suburbia: A Reinterpretation," *The Journal of Politics*, Vol. 27, (1965), pp. 647ff; and Jerome G. Manis and Leo C. Stine, "Suburban Residence and Political Behavior," *Public Opinion Quarterly*, Winter, 1958/59, pp. 483–89.

Similarly, the suburban factory worker was less likely to organize collectively. For example, Grumman Aerospace, one of Long Island's largest employers, has remained nonunion throughout its 60-year history.

16.   That these policies blatantly discriminated against minorities and women cannot be denied—nor approved. However, that flaw should not blind us to the potential inherent in providing low-cost housing with little or no down payment for large segments of the population.

17.   Vineland was one of the more successful of the model towns. Unlike Pullman, which was tied directly to the Pullman company's need to house its workers, Vineland was originally built as a model community in which a benefactor provided housing for the working class. Where Pullman was pragmatic, Vineland was benevolent. But implicit in both was the controlling interest of the builder/manager. Handlin, *The American Home* (Boston: Little, Brown & Co., 1979), 247–49.

Chapter 9   Postscript

1.   W. D. Wetherall, *The Man Who Loved Levittown*. (Pittsburgh: University of Pittsburgh Press, 1985). Tommy Demaria, the hero of the short story, reluctantly leaves Levittown. The last of the original cohort of residents, DeMaria's final days there revealed to him that the changes he resented were in fact the new reality for Levittown.

2.   Indeed, most of the older couples who presently own Levitt houses could not afford to purchase them either, if they did not already have the economic cushion provided by the inflated equity in their houses.

3.   It is unlikely that the private sector will be the source of any housing reform moves in the near future. As this book goes to print, the savings and loan industry is reeling from a combination of poor investments and outright scandal. Any meaningful funding of high-risk, low-return real estate projects will have to be secured on a widespread, collective basis.

4. This represents a new shift in the living conditions of the American population. In the federal census of 1920, some 54.6 percent of Americans were living in some type of rented living quarters (the number increases to 59.1 percent in nonfarm situations) and 51.4 percent of them were living in cities. By 1956, however, the process had been reversed and more than 60 percent of the population were living in owner-occupied housing. Of the more than 54 million dwellings in the country in 1956, almost 40 million were outside the central cities.

5. Dean, p. 41.

6. Frank Capra, *It's a Wonderful Life*, RKO/Liberty Films, 1946.

7. Eric Larrabee, "The Six Thousand Houses That Levitt Built," *Harper's*, September 1948, p. 84.

8. John McCormick and Peter McKillop, "The Other Suburbia," *Newsweek*, June 26, 1989, pp. 22–24. For an analysis of this process, see Kim Hopper and Jill Hamberg, "The Making of America's Homeless: From Skid Row to the New Poor, 1945–1984" in Rachel Bratt, Chester Hartman, and Ann Meyerson (eds.), *Critical Perspectives on Housing* (Philadelphia: Temple University Press, 1986), pp. 12–40, and Margaret Daly, "Has America Lost Its Commitment to Housing?" *Better Homes and Gardens*, February 1988, pp. 39–41.

See also Tom Morris, "A Boom in Illegal Apts," *Newsday*, November 1, 1988, pp. 3, 27; James Lardner, "Rich, Richer; Poor, Poorer," *New York Times*, April 19, 1989, p. A27; "Home Ownership Drops Among America's Young," *Newsday*, June 23, 1989, p. 45 Business; and Peter Dreier, "Building Low-Income Housing without Profit—or Scandal," *Newsday*, June 25, 1989, p. 4 Ideas.

9. An excellent analysis of these needs and the alternative housing forms that address them can be found in Dolores Hayden, *Redesigning the American Dream* (New York: W. W. Norton, 1984), pp. 3–16.

Appendix I   The Sale of the Rental Units

1. "How the Levitts Played Safe," *Business Week*, March 18, 1950, p. 25.

2. *Ibid.*, p. 26.

3. At the time of the Levitt transaction, Junto had only $10,000 in its treasury. "High Finance; Whence Comes the Dew?" *Time*, March 13, 1950, p. 65.

4. "High Finance: Whence Comes the Dew?" p. 66.

5. *Ibid.*, p. 66.

Appendix II   The Women's Congress on Housing

1. Annabelle Heath, *Report from the Women's Congress on Housing* (Washington, DC: Housing and Home Finance Agency, 1956), p. 3.

2. Heath, p. 82.

3. William M. Dobriner, *Class in Suburbia*, (Englewood Cliffs, NJ: Prentice-Hall, Inc., 1963), p. 98.

4. Dobriner, p. 96.

Appendix III   Comparative Social Statistics on Levittown over Time

1. Long Island Association, *Long Island, The Sunrise Homeland.*

2. *County and City Data Book*, p. 878.

3. William M. Dobriner, *Class in Suburbia*, (Englewood Cliffs, NJ: Prentice-Hall, Inc., 1963), p. 99.

4. County and City Data Book (Washington, DC: U.S. Department of Commerce, 1983), p. 878.

5. *Ibid.*, p. 97.

6. *County and City Data Book*, p. 878.

7. Sources: County and City Data Book (Washington, DC: U.S. Department of Commerce, 1983). State and Metropolitan Area Data Book (1986).

8. *Ibid.*

9. Dobriner, p. 97.

10. County and City Data Book pp. 878–879.

11. Dobriner, p. 97.

12. Source: *1980 Census Population General Social and Economic Characteristics.* (Washington, DC: Bureau of the Census, 1983), Table 129.

13. This figure includes 835 "teachers, librarians, counselors," which occupations, although demanding professional educations, do not command salaries commensurate with other professionals such as attorneys, physicians, engineers.

Bibliography

Primary Sources

Books and Pamphlets

Artley, A. Sterl, and Lillian Gray. *We Three*. Reading for Independence. Curriculum Foundation Series. Chicago: Scott, Foresman and Company, 1947.

———. *What Next?* Reading for Independence. Curriculum Foundation Series. Chicago: Scott, Foresman and Company, 1947.

Atlas of Queens and Nassau Counties. New York: Hagstrom, 1942; 1946.

Beecher, Catharine, and Harriet Beecher Stowe. *The American Woman's Home; Or, Principles of Domestic Science, Being a Guide to the Formation and Maintenance of Ecnomical, Healthful, Beautiful, and Christian Homes*. New York: J. B. Ford & Co., 1869. Watkins Glen, NY: Library of Victorian Culture, 1979.

Benson, Sally. *Junior Miss*. New York: Random House, 1941.

Burris-Meyer, Elizabeth. *Decorating Livable Homes*. New York: Prentice-Hall, 1947.

Child, Georgie Boynton. *The Efficient Kitchen; Definite Directions for the Planning and Equipment of the Modern Labor-Saving Kitchen—A Practical Book for the Homemaker*. New York: McBride, Nash & Co., 1914.

Cleaveland, Henry W., William Backus, and Samuel D. Backus. *Village and Farm Cottages*. Ed. David Schuyler. New York: D. Appleton and Company, 1850. Watkins Glen, NY: American Life Foundation, 1982.

Colean, Miles L. *Housing for Defense*. The Twentieth Century Fund Housing Survey. New York: The Twentieth Century Fund, 1940.

Dean, John. *Home-Ownership, Is It Sound?* New York: Harper and Brothers, 1945.

Downing, Andrew Jackson. *The Architecture of Country Houses*. New York: D. Appleton & Co., 1850. New York: Dover Publications, 1969.

Eastlake, Charles L. *Hints on Household Taste in Furniture, Upholstery and Other Details*. New York: Dover Publications, 1969.

Elson, William H. and William S. Gray *Elson-Gray Basic Readers, Book One,* Curriculum Foundation Series. Chicago: Scott, Foresman and Company, 1930/36.

Fitzsimmons, Cleo. *The Management of Family Resources.* San Francisco: W. H. Freeman & Co., 1950.

French, Marilyn. *The Women's Room.* New York: Harcourt Brace Jovanovich, 1977.

Garland, Hamlin. *Main Travelled Roads.* New York: Harper & Brothers, 1899.

Genauer, Emily. *Modern Interiors Today and Tomorrow.* New York: Illustrated Editions Company, Inc., 1939.

Gesell, Arnold L., and Frances L. Ilg. *The Child from Five to Ten.* New York: Harper & Brothers, 1946.

Gordon, Richard E. *The Split Level Trap.* New York, 1964.

Horowitz, Gene. *The Ladies of Levittown.* New York: Richard Marek Publishers, 1980.

Irwin, Leslie W., Waid W. Tuttle, and Caroline DeKelver. *Growing Day by Day.* Grade II. The Health—Happiness—Success Series. Chicago: Lyons and Carnahan, 1946.

Jefferson, Thomas. *Notes on the State of Virginia.* New York: Furman and Loudon, 1801.

Keats, John. *The Crack in the Picture Window.* Boston: Houghton Mifflin Co., 1956.

Kennedy, Robert Woods. *The House and the Art of Its Design.* New York: Reinhold Publishing Co., 1953.

Kilmer, Joyce. *Trees and Other Poems.* Garden City: Doubleday, Doran & Company, Inc., 1914.

Lee, Ruth W., and L. T. Bolender. *Fashions in Furnishings.* New York: McGraw-Hill Co., Inc., 1948.

Levitt, William J. "A House Is Not Enough." *Business Decisions That Changed Our Lives.* Ed. Sidney Furst and Milton Sherman. New York: Random House, 1964.

Levittown Property Owners Association. *Our Town—Levittown.* Levittown: Levittown Property Owners Association, 1952.

Link, David E. *Residential Designs.* Boston: Cahners Publishing Company, Inc., 1974.

The Long Island Home Builders Institute, Inc. "The Long Island Story." Reprinted from the pages of *Practical Builder* Mar. 1951: 1–16.

Lumber Built Homes Chicago: National Lumber Manufacturing Assn. (for the New York World's Fair, 1939.

A Man's Home Is His Castle New York: Anthracite Industries, Inc. (for the Pennsylvania exhibit, New York World's Fair of 1939) 1936.

Mead, Margaret. *Male and Female: A Study of the Sexes in a Changing World.* New York: W. Morrow, 1949.

National Commission on Professional Rights and Responsibilities of the NEA and the Ethical Practices Committee of the N.Y.S. Teachers Assn. *Levittown, New York; A Study of Leadership Problems in a Rapidly Developed Community.* Washington, DC: National Education Association of the United States, 19.

O'Donnell, Mabel. *Down the River Road.* The Alice and Jerry Books; Reading Foundation Series. Evanston, IL: Row, Peterson and Company, 1938.

Palliser, Palliser & Co. *Palliser's Model Homes.* Bridgeport, CT: Palliser, Palliser & Co., 1878. Watkins Glen, NY: American Life Foundation [n.d.].

Reisman, David. *The Lonely Crowd; A Study of the Changing American Character.* Garden City, NY: Doubleday Anchor Books, 1953.

Rosenman, Dorothy R. *A Million Homes a Year.* New York: Harcourt, Brace and Co., 1945.

Scott, Frank J. *Victorian Gardens; The Art of Beautifying Suburban Home Grounds.* Ed. David Schuyler. New York: D. Appleton & Co., 1870. Watkins Glen, NY: American Life Foundation, 1982.

Simon, Kate. *Bronx Primitive; Portraits in a Childhood.* New York: Viking Press, 1982.

Smith, Betty. *Tomorrow Will Be Better.* New York: Harper, 1948.

———. *A Tree Grows in Brooklyn.* New York: Harper & Brothers, 1943.

Spock, Benjamin, MD. *The Common Sense Book of Baby and Child Care.* New York: Duell, Sloan and Pierce, 1946.

The Town of Tomorrow (13 brochures showing model houses for the future) New York: New York World's Fair, 1939.

Wetherall, W. D. *The Man Who Loved Levittown.* Pittsburgh: The University of Pittsburgh Press, 1985.

Wheeler, Gervase. *Homes for the People in Suburb and Country.* New York: Charles Scribner, 1855. New York: Arno Press, 1972.

Whyte, William H. Jr. *The Organization Man.* Garden City, NY: Doubleday-Anchor Books, 1957.

Wilson, Sloan. *The Man in the Gray Flannel Suit.* New York: Simon and Schuster, 1955.

Woodward, George E. *Woodward's Country Homes.* New York: George E. Woodward, 1865. Watkins Glen, NY: American Life Foundation, 1976.

————. *Architecture and Rural Art.* New York: George E. Woodward, 1867. Watkins Glen, NY: American Life Foundation, 1978.

————. *The Architecture of Country Houses.* New York: George E. Woodward, 1850. New York: Dover Publications, 1969.

Work. The New We Work and Play. The New Basic Readers. 1940/1946. New York: Scott, Foresman and Company, 1951.

Wylie, Phillip. *A Generation of Vipers.* New York: Holt, Rinehart & Winston, 1955.

Articles and Professional Papers

"1000 of 2000 Houses Rented as Work Begins." *New York Herald Tribune* 9 May 1947: 5.

"2000 Modest Cottages in a Model Community . . . ." *New York World Telegram* 6 June 1947.

"2600 Acres Made Useless by Nematode." *Nassau Daily Review Star* 16 Apr. 1947: 1.

Abrams, Arnold. "Product of the Times." In "Goodbye Levittown; The Early Years" special section in *Newsday* 4 Oct. 1987.

Adams, Elizabeth M. "Woman to Woman." *Island Trees [Levittown] Tribune* 29 Jan. 1948: 6.

Bartlett, Kay. "Long Island School Book Banning Is a Serial." *Long Island Sunday Press* 20 Feb. 1977: 11.

Benge, Jean Griffith. "Stepping Stones to Happiness." *Household* May 1948: 7;80.

"Big Dave Bohannon; Operative Builder by the California Method." *Fortune* Apr. 1946: 145–90.

"Big Rental Housing Job to Start." *Newsday* 7 May 1947.

Borg, Alan C. "Personalizing Development Homes." *American Home* May 1968: 68–80.

Boroff, David. "Suburbia—Levittown, Long Island." *New York Post* Apr. 14–20, 1958, sec. M.

"Charge Housing Gyp Conspiracy." *Newsday* 9 May 1947.

Childs, Richard T., and George A. Kramer, appraisers. Appraisal of 4,028 Dwellings Located at Levittown in the Town of Hempstead, Nassau County, New York. December, 1949. Mineola, New York, 1949. 1–19.

"Citizen Joe Writes on Americanism." *Long Island Press* 2 May 1947: 1.

"College Dean Sees Hysteria in War on A[merican] Y[outh] [For] D[emocracy]." *Long Island Press* 2 May 1947: 1.

"A Complete House for $6900." *Architectural Forum* May 1947: 70.

"Construction and Obstruction." *Newsday* 7 May 1947.

Corbett, Scott. "Just One Big Happy Family." *Better Homes and Gardens* Nov. 1946: 170.

"Custom Build Your Own Storage Walls." *American Home* Dec. 1949: 74.

D.M.C. "No Room at the Inn." *Newsday* 27 May 1947.

Davenport, Russell. "A Round Table on Housing." *Life* 31 Jan. 1949: 73.

De Vries, Peter. "Humorists Depict the Suburban Wife." *Life* 24 Dec. 1956.

Dean, Clarence. "10-Year-Old Levittown Wears the Face of Change." *New York Times* 30 Sep. 1957: 23.

Dobson, Meade C. "Long Island Family Buying Power Far Above National Average." *The Long Island Builder*. Spring, 1948.

"Everyone's Making Rugs Today!" *American Home* Feb. 1950: 34.

"Fight for Freedom." Letter. *Levittown Tribune* 13 July 1967: 6.

Fisher, Berni. "Board Okays Cellarless Houses." *Newsday* 28 May 1947.

———. "Plywood Or Sheathing? Battle Stalls 4,000 Rental Job." *Newsday* 25 June 1947, 2.

"G.O.P. Gazes in Alarm at Levitt-Type Homes, Leases." *Newsday* 2 Oct. 1947: 3.

"Garden City Is Part of Big Tract Sold to Merchant 90 Years Ago." *New York Times* 4 Oct. 1959.

Gilbert, James. "Confusing Young Rebels with Their Cause." *Newsday* 17 June 1986: 65.

Gleaves, Suzanne. "Levittown Revisited." *New York* 16 Aug. 1964: 9–12.

Guilfoyle, Joseph M., and J. Howard Rutledge. "Levitt Licks the Housing Shortage." *Coronet* Sep. 1948: 112.

Gutis, Philip S. "Levittown L. I. At 40: No Longer a Housing Cure." *New York Times* 21 Sep. 1987, sec. B: 1;6.

Hanifin, Robert, "Veterans Advisor." *Island Trees Eagle* 18 Dec. 1947: 8.

Herbert, Elizabeth Sweeney. "This Is How I Keep House." *McCalls* Apr. 1949: 41–44.

"Here, There, and Everywhere." *Levittown Tribune* 1967.

Holton, James L. "Levitts Halt Sales for Low-Cost Homes . . . ." *World Telegram* 14 Aug. 1947.

———. "New Levitt Project to House 2000 Vets." *World Telegram* 9 May 1947.

"Home Models Accelerate Sales." *American Builder* Mar. 1949: 79.

"Homeowners Have Their Say." *Levittown Tribune* 12 Mar. 1987: 12.

"The Housing Mess." *Fortune* Jan. 1947: 81.

"How the Levitts Played Safe." *Business Week* 18 Mar. 1950: 25–26.

"How-to Tips." *American Home* Jan. 1950: 39.

Ingrassia, Michele. "Island Trees; What's Behind the In-fighting? *Newsday* 13 Dec. 1976, sec. A: 4–5.

Insolia, Tony. "The Levittown Decade 1957." *Newsday* 30 Sep. through 4 Oct. 1957, sec. C.

Johnson, T. L. "Take It Easy in This Garden Lounge." *Popular Mechanics* June 1949: 206–7.

Jones, Bob. "Operative Building—One Way Out." *Better Homes and Gardens* Oct. 1946: 53–54.

"A Kitchen Makes a Wonderful Nursery." *American Home* Jan. 1950: 88.

"Kitchen Marriage." *American Home* Dec. 1949: 48.

"A Lady Begs to Differ." *House Beautiful* Nov. 1944: 161–63.

"A Lady Sergeant Defends Her Brothers-In-Arms." *House Beautiful* May 1945: 132–34.

Larrabee, Eric. "The Six Thousand Houses That Levitt Built." *Harper's* Sep. 1948: 79–88.

"Leaving Levittown Behind." *Esquire* Apr. 1987.

Lee. Dorothy. "Suburbia Reconsidered: Diversity and the Creative Life." *Man and the Modern City.* Ed. Elizabeth Geen. Pittsburgh: University of Pittsburgh Press, 1963. 122–24.

"Levitt Adds 1950 Model to His Line." *Life* 22 May 1950: 141.

"Levitt May Offer to Sell Homes Next Year . . . ." *Island Trees Eagle* 11 Dec. 1947: 1.

"Levitt's Progress." *Fortune* Oct. 1952: 164.

Levitt, Abraham. "Fruit Is Fine for Little Gardens." *American Home* Jan. 1950: 72.

———. "Welcoming Message from the Founder." Editorial. *Island Trees Tribune* 12 Dec. 1947: 1.

Levitt, Alfred. "A Community Builder Looks at Community Planning." *Journal of the American Institute of Planners* Spring (1951): 80–88.

Levittown Property Owners Association. "What Makes Levittown a Miracle Community?" *Levittown Tribune* 27 June 1947.

"Levitts Quit Low Priced House Field." *World Telegram* 10 Aug. 1947.

"Low Cost Homes Banned by Old Code." *Newsday* 29 Apr. 1946.

"Made Over for Fun." *American Home* Jan. 1950:39.

Martin, Ralph G. "Life in the New Suburbia." *New York Times Magazine* 15 Jan. 1952: 16–42.

"May Day Parade Photos Taken to Cite Army Men for 'Treason'." *New York Herald Tribune* 4 May 1947: 1.

"May Park Cars on Lawns During Three Snow Months." *Island Trees Eagle* 27 Nov. 1947: 1.

Meinz, Howard W. "What! Decadence in Nassau." Letter. *Newsday* 9 May 1946.

"A Modern Embroidered Screen." *Woman's Day* Jan. 1955: 44.

"Monsignor Sheen Offers Plan to Curb Reds." *New York Herald Tribune* 4 May 1947: 34.

Moorsteen, Betty. "Long Island Builder Mass-Producing Homes to Rent at $60 Per Month." *Newsday* 22 May 1947.

Morrison, Harriet. "No Longer like Peas in a Pod." *Today's Living* 22 Oct. 1961: 16.

"The Most House for the Money." *Fortune* Oct. 1952: 165.

"Mr. Kilroy's Home." *Time* 23 Dec. 1946.

Murray, Mrs Helen. Letter. *Newsday* 9 Oct. 1947.

"Nation's Biggest Housebuilder." *Life* 23 Aug. 1948: 75–78.

"New Home Models Accelerate Sales." *American Builder* Mar. 1949: 79.

Nicholson, Arnold. "Are You Outgrowing Your House?" in *Saturday Evening Post*, Jan. 10, 1959 pp. 26–7ff.

"No Island Trees Communist Party." *Levittown Eagle* 4 Mar. 1948: 1.

Noeth, Fred. "Current Comments." *The Enterprise Pilot* 4 Dec. 1947.

Normile, J., and R. M. Jones. "$50,000 Worth of Ideas in a Low-Cost Home; Cape Cottage Brought Up to Date." *Better Homes and Gardens* Aug. 1949: 37–41.

"OK on 2000 Rent Homes up to Town Law Change." *Newsday* 8 May 1947.

Offit, Avodah K., MD "The New Togetherness." *McCalls* Mar. 1986; 20.

"On the 5:19 to Ulcerville." *Newsweek* 17 Aug. 1959: 32.

"A One-Room Camp You Can Build Yourself." *American Home* Feb. 1950: 24.

Patterson, A. Holly. "Welcome." Editorial. *Island Trees Eagle* 20 Nov. 1947: 1.

"Pick-Up Work." *Household* Sep. 1949: 61.

"Pride and Prejudice." *Newsday* 2 Oct. 1947: 3.

"A Rent $ Value in Small Homes." *Practical Builder* June 1947: 8–9.

Robinson, Ann. "Levittown, U.S.A.; A Biased Sociological Study." Thesis, New York University, 1958.

Ryttenberg, Madeline. "See $6500 'Prefabs' Answer to Housing." *Newsday* 27 Mar. 1946: 12.

"Should the Home-Starved Vet Be Forced to Build? We Say No?" *Better Homes and Gardens* Nov. 1946: 10.

Sibley, H. "Furnish Your Garden with Saplings and Staves." *Popular Science* May 1949: 195.

"Slumgullion." Editorial. *Newsday* 27 May 1947: 23.

Sneiger, D. "New Furniture from Old." *Popular Science* Aug. 1950: 157–60.

Sparkes, Boyden. "They'll Build Neighborhoods, Not Houses." *Saturday Evening Post* 28 Oct. 1944; 11;43–46.

"Summer Look in Winter Rooms." *House and Garden* Jan. 1951: 74–77.

"Survey 362K; Housing." *Gallup Poll* Dec. 1945.

"Text of the New Law Extending Rent Controls . . . ." *New York Times* 1 July 1947, sec. L: 2.

"Their Farmlands Raise Crops of Houses." *Newsday* 8 May 1948.

"They Have So Much Enthusiasm." Editorial. *Island Trees Eagle* 4 Dec. 1947: 2.

"Thirty Minutes Notice." Letter. *Newsday* 11 May 1946.

"Tomorrow Is Mother's Day, But . . . ." Editorial. *Newsday* 11 May 1946.

"Tricks with Trimmings." *Woman's Home Companion* Sep. 1951: 121.

"Truman's Rent Bill Message." *New York Herald Tribune* 1 July 1947: 16.

"Twenty People to a Bathroom." *Better Homes and Gardens* Sep. 1946: 25.

"Up from the Potato Fields." *Time* 3 July 1950: 67–68.

"The Utts of Levittown." *Newsday* 8 Oct. 1949, sec. M: 2.

Vitello, Paul. "Home Is Where High Taxes Aren't." *Newsday* 25 June 1989: 6.

"Waiting for the Word." *Levittown Tribune* 12 Mar. 1987: 7–8.

Wannen, Elizabeth G. "The Famous Legend of the Potato Fields." *Thousand Lanes* Fall 1957: 4.

"What Is the I. L. O.?" *Fortune* Sep. 1944: 160ff.

"What the G. I. Wants in His Postwar House." *House Beautiful* Aug. 1944: 72–75ff.

"Whence Comes the Dew?" *Time* 13 Mar. 1950: 65–66.

Whitlock, William E. "A Room for Two Boys." *Woman's Day* Jan. 1955: 55.

Wife of a Right Wing Extremist. "Apathy Towards Communism." Letter. *Levittown Tribune* 13 July 1967: 6.

"Will Raise Rents to $65 at End of Lease." *Levittown Eagle* 19 Feb. 1948: 1.

"Work Is Begun on 2000 Homes on Long Island." *Herald Tribune* 7 May 1947.

"You *Have* a Sewing Room." *American Home* Feb. 1950: 33.

"You May Finish Attics—Levitt." *Levittown Eagle* 18 Dec. 1948: 1.

Newspapers

Better Homes and Gardens. 1946–1950.

Fortune. 1944–1950.

House Beautiful. 1944–1950.

Household. 1939–1955.

Island Trees Eagle. 1947–1948.

Island Trees Tribune. 1947–1948.

Levittown Eagle. 1948–1967.

Levittown Tribune. 1948–1967.

Long Island Daily Press. 1959.

New York Herald Tribune. 1947–1951.

New York Journal American. 1947–1951.

New York Times. 1947–1967.

New York World Telegram. 1947–1948.

Newsday. 1945–1967.

Woman's Day. 1937–1957.

Popular Music

Berlin, Irving. "The Girl That I Marry." New York: Irving Berlin Music Co., 1946.

Hammerstein, Oscar, and Richard Rodgers. "A Fellow Needs a Girl." New York: Williamson Music Inc., 1947.

Ian, Janis. "Society's Child."

Reynolds, Malvina. "Little Boxes." *Little Boxes and Other Handmade Songs.* New York: Oad Publishing Co., 1964.

Russell, Bob, and Carl Sigman. "Ballerina." New York: Jefferson Music Co. 1947.

The Monkees. "Pleasant Valley Sunday."

Media and Film

[Dean, James]. *Rebel Without a Cause.* Warner Brothers, 1955.

[Grant, Cary]. *Every Girl Should Be Married.* R.K.O. Films, 1947.

Greenberg, Selma, and Charyl Shakeshaft, producers. *The Teacher's Room.* Hempstead, NY: The Levittown Teachers Center and Hofstra University Communications Center, 1988.

"Our World—1949" American Broadcasting Company. 1986.

[Reed, Donna]. "The Donna Reed Show." Nickelodeon Television, August 1987 (rerun).

[Robert Young]. "Father Knows Best." Nickelodeon Television, August, 1987 (rerun).

"Sergeant Pepper; It Was Twenty Years Ago Today." Public Broadcasting System. 1988.

Stern, Robert A. M. *Pride of Place*. Public Broadcasting System. 1986.

Government Publications

Department of Commerce. *1956 National Housing Inventory; Components of Change 1950 to 1956*. 1956. Vol. 1. Washington, DC: U.S. Government Printing Office, 1956.

———. *How to Own Your Own Home*. 1925. Washington, DC: U.S. Government Printing Office, 1925.

———. Bureau of the Census. *Census Population; General Social and Economic Characteristics*. 1980. Washington, DC: Bureau of the Census, 1983.

———. Bureau of the Census. *County and City Data Book*. 1983. Washington, DC: Department of Commerce, 1983.

———. Bureau of the Census. *County Data Book*. Washington, DC: Government Printing Office, 1947.

———. Bureau of the Census. *Historical Statistics of the United States; Colonial Times to 1970*. Washington, DC: Department of Commerce, 1975.

———. Bureau of the Census. *Sixteenth Census of the United States: 1940 Housing*. Washington, DC: Government Printing Office, 1943.

———. Bureau of the Census. *State and Metropolitan Data Book*. 1986. Washington, DC: Department of Commerce, 1986.

———. Bureau of the Census. *Statistical Abstract of the United States*. 1960. Washington, DC: Government Printing Office, 1961.

———. Bureau of the Census. Social Science Research Council. *Statistical Abstract Supplement; Historical Abstracts of the United States, Colonial Times to 1957*. Washington, DC: U.S. Government Printing Office, 1957.

Eightieth Congress. *United States Statutes at Large* . . . . 1947. Part I, Public Laws, Reorganization Plans, Proposed Amendment to the Constitution. Vol. 61. Washington, DC: Government Printing Office, 1948.

Federal Housing Administration. *Eleventh Annual Report*. 1944. Washington, DC: Government Printing Office, 1945.

———. *Fourteenth Annual Report*. 1947. Washington, DC: Government Printing Office, 1948.

———. *Land Planning Bulletin no. 1*. "Successful Subdivisions Planned as Neighborhoods for Profitable Investment and Appeal to Homeowners." Washington, DC: Government Printing Office, 1940.

———. *Land Planning Bulletin no. 4*. "Neighborhoods Built for Rental Housing." Washington, DC: Government Printing Office, 1947.

———. *Minimum Construction Requirements for New Dwelling Located in the Counties of Queens, Nassau, and Suffolk*. 1939. Washington, DC: Government Printing Office, 1939.

———. *Tenth Annual Report*. 1943. Washington, DC: Government Printing Office, 1944.

———. *Thirteenth Annual Report*. 1946. Washington, DC: Government Printing Office, 1947.

———. *Twelfth Annual Report*. 1945. Washington, DC: Government Printing Office, 1946.

Housing and Home Finance Agency. Women's Congress on Housing. *Report on the First Women's Congress on Housing*. 1956. Washington, DC: Housing and Home Finance Agency, 1956.

New York State. Department of Civil Service. *Survey Report of the Salary Standardization Board*. 1946. Albany: New York State, 1947.

———. Department of Commerce. *Zoning in New York State; A Guide to the Preparation of Zoning Ordinances*. 1959. Albany: State of New York, 1959.

Town Board. *Zoning Ordinance*. Article XV, "The Levittown Planned Residential District." Hempstead, NY: Town of Hempstead, 1951.

Town of Babylon. Building and Zoning Department. *Building Zone Ordinance*. 1953. Babylon, NY: Town of Babylon, 1953.

Town of Hempstead. Building and Zoning Board. *Zoning Ordinance*. 1930. Hempstead, NY: Town of Hempstead, 1930.

U.S. Department of Housing and Urban Development. *HUD Statistics Yearbook 1966*. 1968. Washington, DC: U.S. Government Printing Office, 1968.

U.S. Congress. *Housing and Rent Act*. 81st Cong., 1st sess. 35. 1949. Washington, DC: Government Printing Office, 1949.

———. House. *Message from the President of the United States, Transmitting a Program for Rent Control and Housing Legislation*. 80th Cong., 2nd sess. H. Rep. 547. 1948. Washington, DC: Government Printing Office, 1948.

———. House. Committee on Banking and Currency. *Housing and Rent Control Act.* 80th Cong., 2nd sess. H. Rep. 1611. 1948. Washington, DC: Government Printing Office, 1948.

———. House. Committee on Banking and Currency. *Report to Accompany S.B.2182 Housing and Rent Act of 1948.* 80th Cong., 2nd sess. H. Rep. 1560. 1948. Washington, DC: Government Printing Office, 1948.

———. House. The President of the United States. *Protect Small Home Owners from Foreclosures.* A request for legislation to protect small home owners from foreclosure and to relieve them of a portion of the burden of excessive interest and principal payments incurred during the period of higher values and higher earning power. 73rd Cong., 1st sess. H. Doc. 19. 1933. Washington, DC: Government Printing Office, 1933. Referred to the Committee on Banking and Currency, April 13, 1933.

———. Joint Committee on Housing. *Final Majority Report.* 80th Cong., 2nd sess. Rep. 1564. 1948. Washington, DC: Government Printing Office, 1948.

———. Joint Committee on Housing. *Report: Housing in America.* 80th Cong., 1948. Washington, DC: Government Printing Office, 1948.

———. Joint Committee on Housing. *"Views on Public Housing," Housing in America.* 80th Cong., 2nd sess. 1948. Washington, DC: Government Printing Office, 1948.

———. Senate. Committee on Banking and Currency. *Hearings before the Committee on Banking and Currency.* 80th Cong., 1st sess. S. Rept. 866. 1947. Washington, DC: Government Printing Office, 1947.

Personal Interviews

Atkinson, William P. Builder and developer, Midwest City, Oklahoma. Personal interview. Midwest City, 1 Aug. 1986.

Colmer, Mr and Mrs D. Levittown Homeowners/renovators. Personal interview. Hempstead, New York. 10 Feb. 1988.

Kelly, Paul. President, Kelcon Construction. Personal interview. Babylon, Long Island, 11 Dec. 1986.

Klerk, M. F. Former Levittown resident. Personal interview. Hempstead, New York, 18 Jun. 1986.

Levittown Historical Society. Discussion with members of the Historical Society at their meeting, December, 1989.

Long Island Studies Council. Discussion with audience members, former residents of Levittown, October 9, 1986.

"The Paint Pots." Meeting with six members of the "Paint Pots," home-makers who gathered weekly during Levittown's early days to develop their skills in various forms of art. January 11, 1991.

Robinson, Theodore. Hempstead, N.Y., November 9, 1987.

Trivilino, Armand, commander. Nassau County American Legion. Personal interview. 22 Jan. 1986.

Secondary Sources

Books and Pamphlets

Abell, Walter. *The Collective Dream in Art*. 1957. New York: Schocken Books, 1966.

Allison, John D. "An Analysis of Levittown, New York, with Particular Reference to Demand Satisfaction from Mass-Produced Low-Cost Housing." Diss. New York University, 1956.

Baritz, Loren. *The Good Life; The Meaning of Success for the American Middle Class*. New York: Alfred A. Knopf, 1989.

Barthes, Roland. *Mythologies*. New York: Hill and Wang, 1972.

———. *Systeme de la Mode*. Paris: Seuil, 1967.

Bellah, Robert N., Richard Madson, William N. Sullivan, et al. *Habits of the Heart; Individualism and Commitment in American Life*. Berkeley: University of California Press, 1985.

Berger, Bennett. *Working-Class Suburb: A Study of Auto Workers in Suburbia*. Berkeley: University of California Press, 1968.

Bratt, Rachel G., Chester Hartman, and Ann Meyerson, eds. *Critical Perspectives on Housing*. Philadelphia: Temple University Press, 1986.

Buder, Stanley. *Pullman; An Experiment in Industrial Order and Community Planning 1880–1930*. New York: Oxford University Press, 1970.

Burns, Scott. *The Household Economy; Its Shape, Origins, and Future*. Boston: Beacon Press, 1975.

Caplow, Theodore, Howard M. Bahr, et al. *Middletown Families; Fifty Years of Change and Continuity*. Minneapolis: University of Minnesota Press, 1982.

Caro, Robert. *The Power Broker*. New York: Alfred E. Knopf, 1978.

Carr, Lowell J., and James E. Stermer. *Willow Run; A Study of Industrialization and Cultural Inadequacy*. New York: Harper and Brothers, 1952.

Clark, Clifford E., Jr. *The American Family Home, 1800–1960*. Chapel Hill: University of North Carolina Press, 1986.

Condit, Carl W. *The Rise of the Skyscraper*. Chicago: University of Chicago Press, 1952.

Consumer's Union. *I'll Buy That; Fifty Small Wonders and Big Deals That Revolutionized the Live of Consumers*. New York: Consumer's Union, 1986.

Cott, Nancy F. *The Bonds of Womanhood*. New Haven: Yale University Press, 1977.

Cowan, Ruth Schwartz. *More Work for Mother; The Ironies of Household Technology from Open Hearth to the Microwave*. New York: Basic Books, 1983.

Darnton, Robert. *The Great Cat Massacre and Other Episodes in French Cultural History*. New York: Basic Books, 1984.

Davies, Richard O. *Housing Reform During the Truman Administration*. Columbia, MO: University of Missouri, 1966.

Davison, Jane. *The Fall of a Doll's House*. New York: Avon Books, 1980.

Dean, John. *Home-Ownership, Is It Sound?* New York: Harper and Brothers, 1945.

Deetz, James. *In Small Things Forgotten; The Archaeology of American Life*. Garden City, N.J.: Anchor Books, 1977.

Dobriner, William M. *Classes in Suburbia*. Englewood Cliffs, NJ: Prentice-Hall, Inc., 1963.

———. *The Suburban Community*. New York: Putnam, 1958.

Dolkart, Andrew S., and Sharon Z. Macosko. *A Dream Fulfilled; City and Suburban's York Avenue Estate*. New York: Coalition to Save City and Suburban Housing, Inc., 1988.

Donaldson, Scott. *The Suburban Myth*. New York: Columbia University Press, 1969.

Eichler, Ned. *The Merchant Builders*. Cambridge, MA: The MIT Press, 1982.

Ewen, Stuart. *Captains of Consciousness: Advertising and the Social Roots of the Consumer Culture*. New York: McGraw-Hill, 1976.

Fishman, Robert. *Bourgeois Utopias*. New York: Basic Books, 1987.

———. *Urban Utopians in the Twentieth Century; Ebenezer Howard, Frank Lloyd Wright, LeCorbusier*. New York: Basic Books, 1977.

Fitch, James Marston. *American Building; The Forces Which Shaped It*. Boston: Houghton Mifflin Co., 1948.

Foley, Mary Mix. *The American House*. New York: Harper and Row, 1980.

Fox, Kenneth. *Metropolitan America*. Jackson, MS: University Press of Mississippi, 1986.

Freeman, John C. *Furniture for the Victorian Home*. Watkins Glen, NY: Century House, 1968.

Friedan, Betty. *The Feminine Mystique*. New York: Laurel, 1983.

Gans, Herbert. *The Levittowners; Ways of Life and Politics in a New Suburban Community*. New York: Vintage Books, 1969.

Geen, Elizabeth, et al., eds. *Man and the Modern City*. Pittsburgh: University of Pittsburgh Press, 1963.

Geertz, Clifford. *The Interpretation of Cultures*. New York: Basic Books, 1973.

Giedion, Sigfried. *Space, Time, and Architecture; The Growth of a New Tradition*. Cambridge, MA: MIT Press, 1949.

Glassie, Henry. *Folk Housing in Middle Virginia: A Structural Analysis of Historic Artifacts*. Knoxville: University of Tennessee Press, 1975.

Goldman, Eric F. *The Crucial Decade—and After*. New York: Vintage Books, 1960.

Gordon, Michael, ed. *The American Family in Social-Historical Perspective*. New York: St. Martin's Press, 1978.

Gowans, Alan. *The Comfortable House; North American Suburban Architecture, 1890–1930*. Cambridge, MA: MIT Press, 1986.

Green, Harvey. *The Light of the Home*. New York: Pantheon Books, 1983.

Griffith, Robert. *The Politics of Fear; Joseph McCarthy and the Senate*. Rochelle Park, NJ: Hayden Book Co., 1970.

Halle, David. *America's Working Man; Work, Home, and Politics Among Blue Collar Property Owners*. Chicago: The University of Chicago Press, 1984.

Handlin, David. *The American Home*. Boston: Little, Brown & Company, 1979.

Hayden, Dolores. *Grand Domestic Revolution*. Cambridge, MA: MIT Press, 1983.

———. *Redesigning the American Dream*. New York: W. W. Norton, 1984.

———. *Seven American Utopias; The Architecture of Communitarian Socialism, 1790–1975*. Cambridge, MA: MIT Press, 1976.

Hill, Christopher. *The World Turned Upside Down*. New York: Viking Press, 1972.

Hine, Thomas. *Populuxe*. New York: Alfred A. Knopf, 1987.

Jackson, Kenneth. *The Crabgrass Frontier*. New York: Oxford University Press, 1985.

Jardim, Anne. *The First Henry Ford; A Study in Personality and Business* Cambridge, MA: MIT Press, 1970.

Komarovsky, Mirra. *Blue-Collar Marriage*. New York: Vintage Books, 1967.

Kron, Joan. *Home-Psych; The Social Psychology of Homes and Decoration* New York: Clarkson N. Potter Publishing Co., 1983.

Lane, Barbara Miller. *Architecture and Politics in Germany*. Cambridge: Cambridge University Press, 1968.

Larson, Paul, Phillip Larson, and Dean Swanson. *Prairie School Architecture in Minnesota, Iowa, Wisconsin*. St. Paul, MN: Minnesota Museum of Art, 1982.

Lasch, Christopher. *Haven in a Heartless World*. New York: Basic Books, 1977.

Lewis, Cyril A. *Historical Long Island Paintings and Sketches*. Westhampton Beach, NY: Long Island Forum, 1964.

Liell, John. "Levittown: A Study in Community Planning and Development." Diss. Yale University, 1952.

Lubove, Roy. *The Progressives and the Slums*. Pittsburgh: University of Pittsburgh Press, 1962.

Marchand, Roland. *Advertising the American Dream*. Berkeley: University of California Press, 1985.

Mason, Joseph B. *The History of Housing in the U.S. 1930–1980*. Houston: Gulf Publishing Company, 1982.

May, Elaine Tyler. *Homeward Bound; American Families in the Cold War Era*. New York: Basic Books, Inc, 1988.

Mitchell, J. Paul, ed. *Federal Housing Policy and Program: Past and Present*. New Brunswick, NJ: Rutgers University, 1985.

Mollenkopf, John F. *The Contested City*. Princeton, NJ: Princeton University Press, 1983.

Moore, Charles, G. Allen, and D. Lyndon. *The Place of Houses*. New York: Holt, Rinehart & Winston, 1974.

Mumford, Lewis. *The Brown Decades*. New York: Harcourt, Brace and Company, 1931. New York: Dover Publications, 1971.

———. *The City in History*. New York: Harcourt, Brace and World, Inc., 1961.

Nevins, Allan. *Ford* (New York: Scribner, 1954).

Perin, Constance. *Everything in Its Place.* Princeton, NJ: Princeton University Press, 1977.

Rosenberg, Charles E. *The Cholera Years.* Chicago: University of Chicago Press, 1962.

Ross, Davis R. B. *Preparing for Ulysses; Politics and Veterans During World War II.* New York: Columbia University Press, 1969.

Rubin, Lillian B. *Worlds of Pain: Life in the Working-Class Family.* New York: Basic Books, 1976.

Rudofsky, Bernard. *Behind the Picture Window.* New York: Oxford University Press, 1955.

Rybczynski, Witold. *Home; A Short History of an Idea.* New York: Viking Penguin, Inc., 1986.

Schaffer, Daniel. *Garden Cities for America; The Radburn Experience.* Philadelphia: Temple University Press, 1982.

Schudson, Michael. *Advertising, the Uneasy Persuasion.* New York: Basic Books, 1984.

Sclare, Lisa, and Donald Sclare. *Beaux-Arts Estates; A Guide to the Architecture of Long Island.* New York: The Viking Press, 1980.

Scully, Vincent J., Jr. *The Shingle Style and the Stick Style.* New Haven: Yale University Press, 1971.

Seeley, J. R., S. A. Sim, and E. W. Loosley. *Crestwood Heights: A Study in the Culture of Suburban Life.* 1956. New York: John Wiley & Sons, 1965.

Severo, Richard, and Lewis Milford. *The Wages of War.* New York: Simon and Schuster, 1989.

Skolnick, Arlene. *The Intimate Environment.* Boston: Little, Brown & Co., 1983.

Smith, Mildred. *The History of Garden City.* Manhasset, NY: Channel Press, 1963.

Smith, Nila Banton. *American Reading Instruction.* Chicago: Silver, Burdett and Company, 1934. Newark, DE: International Reading Association, 1965.

Solomon, Jack. *The Signs of Our Time.* New York: Harper & Row, Publishers, 1988.

Steinberg, Peter L. *The Great "Red Menace"; United States Prosecution of American Communists.* Westport, CT: Greenwood Press, 1984.

Stevenson, Katherine Cole, and H. Ward Jandl. *Houses by Mail; A Guide to Houses from Sears, Roebuck and Company*. Washington, DC: The Preservation Press, 1986.

Strasser, Susan. *Satisfaction Guaranteed; The Making of the American Mass Market*. New York: Pantheon Books, 1989.

Strathmore Vanderbilt Civic Assn. *Strathmore Vanderbilt; A Great Place to Be*. Manhasset, NY: Strathmore Vanderbilt Civic Assn., Country Club, and Women's Club, 1983.

Taylor, Robert, *The Word in Stone*. Berkeley: University of California Press, 1974.

Thernstrom, Stephan. *Poverty and Progress; Social Mobility in a Nineteenth-Century City*. Cambridge, MA: Harvard University Press, 1964. New York: Atheneum, 1975.

Torre, Susan, ed. *Women in American Architecture; A Historic and Contemporary Perspective*. New York: Whitney Library of Design, 1977.

Twombly, Robert C. *Frank Floyd Wright: His Life and His Architecture*. New York: John Wiley & Sons, 1979.

Viemeister, August. *An Architectural Journey Through Long Island*. New York: Kennikat Press Corp., 1974.

Walker, Gina Luria & Associates, ed. *The City and Suburban Homes Company's York Avenue Estate: A Social and Architectural History*. 3 vols. New York: Kalikow 78/79 Company, 1990.

Walker, Lester. *American Shelter*. Woodstock, NY: The Overlook Press, 1981.

Warner, Sam Bass Jr. *The Private City; Philadelphia in Three Periods of Its Growth*. Philadelphia: University of Pennsylvania Press, 1968.

———. *Streetcar Suburbs*. Cambridge, MA: Harvard University Press, 1963.

———. *The Urban Wilderness*. New York: Harper & Row, 1972.

Warner, W. Lloyd, and Paul S. Lunt. *The Social Life of a Modern Community*. New Haven: Yale University Press, 1941.

Weiss, Marc A. *The Rise of the Community Builders*. New York: Columbia University Press, 1987.

Wiebe, Robert. *The Search for Order*. New York: Hill and Wang, 1967.

Wiedenhoeft, Ronald. *Berlin's Housing Revolution: German Reform in the 1920s*. Ann Arbor: UMI Research Press, 1985.

Wolfe, Tom. *From Bauhaus to Our House*. New York: Farrar, Straus & Giroux, 1981.

Wood, Robert C. *Suburbia, Its People and Their Politics*. Boston: Houghton Mifflin Company, 1958.

Wright, Gwendolyn. *Building the Dream*. New York: Pantheon Books, 1981.

———. *Moralism and the Model Home*. Chicago: University of Chicago Press, 1980.

Zukowsky, John, and R. P. Simson. *Hudson River Villas*. New York: Rizzoli, 1985.

Articles and Professional Papers

Bassett, Preston R. "Early History of Aviation on Long Island." *Developing Long Island*. Ed. Harold Wattel. Hempstead, NY: Hofstra College, 1959.

Beckham, Sue Bridwell. "The American Front Porch: Women's Liminal Space." *Making the American Home: Middle-Class Women and Domestic Material Culture, 1840–1940*. Ed. Marilyn Ferris Motz and Pat Browne. Bowling Green, OH: Bowling Green State University Popular Press, 1988. 69–89.

Blair, Alex. "'Women Wake Up'; The Struggle for Equal Pay in the U. E. And the I. U. E." Paper Delivered at the Annual Conference of the Organization of American Historians. Philadelphia, 1986.

Bledsoe, Richard. "The Founding of Midwest City." Unpublished manuscript for the University of Oklahoma Department of History. May 1967.

Boys, Jos. "Is There a Feminist Analysis of Architecture?" *Built Environment* 10.1 (1984): 25.

Buhr, Jenni. "Levittown as a Utopian Community." *Long Island; The Suburban Experience*. Ed. Barbara M. Kelly. Hempstead, NY: Long Island Studies Institute, Hofstra University, 1990. 67–78.

Carson, Cary, and Lorena S. Walsh. "The Material Life of the Early American Housewife." Paper delivered at the Conference on Women in Early America. Williamsburg, VA. 1981.

Clark, Clifford E., Jr. "Domestic Architecture as an Index to Social History." *Journal of Interdisciplinary History* 7.1 (1976): 33–56.

Cowan, Ruth Schwartz. "The 'Industrial Revolution' in the Home; Household Technology and Social Change in the 20th Century." *Technology and Culture* 17 (1976): 1–42.

Craig, Lois. "Suburbs." *Design Quarterly* Summer 132 (1986).

Daly, Margaret. "Has America Lost Its Commitment to Housing?" *Better Homes and Gardens*, February 1988, pp. 39–41.

Dreier, Peter. "Building Low-Income Housing without Profit—or Scandal," *Newsday*, June 25, 1989, p. 4 Ideas.

Fifield, Michael. "Transitional Spaces: Design Considerations for a New Generation of Housing." *Suburbia Re-examined*. Ed. Barbara M. Kelly. Westport, CT: Greenwood Press, 1989.

Graebner, William. "The 'Containment' of Juvenile Delinquency; Social Engineering and American Youth Culture in the Postwar Era." *American Studies* 27.1 (1986): 81–97.

Greenstein, Fred I., and Raymond E. Wolfinger. "The Suburbs and Shifting Party Loyalties." *Public Opinion Quarterly* Winter 1958/59: 473–82.

"Home Ownership Drops Among America's Young," *Newsday*, June 23, 1989 p. 45 Business.

Hopper, Kim and Jill Hamberg. "The Making of America's Homeless; From Skid Row to the New Poor, 1945–1984" In Rachel Bratt, Chester Hartman, and Ann Meyerson (ed.), *Critical Perspectives on Housing* Philadelphia: Temple University Press, 1986 pp. 12–40.

Jennings, W. W. "The Value of Home Owning as Exemplified in American History." *Social Science* 1 (1938): 13. Cited in John P. Dean, *Homeownership; Is It Sound?* p. 4.

Jordy, William H. "The Aftermath of the Bauhaus in American History." *Perspectives in American History* (1968).

Kelly, Barbara M. "The Story of Beaver Pond." *Long Island Forum* Feb. 1980: 24–28.

Kemeny, Jim. "A Critique of Homeownership." *Critical Perspectives on Housing*. Ed. Rachel G. Bratt, Chester Hartman, and Ann Meyerson. Philadelphia: Temple University Press, 1986. 272–76.

Krieg, Joann. "Levittown, L.I.; School for Disharmony." Paper delivered at the MASA-NCASA Conference. Omaha, 1984.

Lardner, James. "Rich, Richer; Poor, Poorer," *New York Times*, April 19, 1989. p. A27.

Luria, Daniel. "Suburbanization, Ethnicity, and Party Base: Spatial Aspects of the Decline of American Socialism." *Antipode* 11 (1979): 76–79.

McCormick, John and Peter McKillop. "The Other Suburbia," *Newsweek* June 26, 1989 pp. 22–24.

Manis, Jerome G., and Leo C. Stine. "Suburban Residence and Political Behavior." *Public Opinion Quarterly* (1958/59): 483–89.

Marc, David. "Comic Visions of the City; New York and the Television Sit-com." Paper delivered at the annual conference of the American Studies Association, Nov. 24, 1987.

Marcuse, Peter. "Housing Policy and the Myth of the Benevolent State." *Critical Perspectives on Housing.* Ed. Rachel G. Bratt, Chester Hartman, and Ann Meyerson. Philadelphia: Temple University Press, 1986. 248–76.

Modell, John, and Tamara Hareven. "Urbanization and the Malleable Household." *The American Family in Social-Historical Perspective.* Ed. Michael Gordon. New York: St. Martin's Press, 1978.

Morris, Tom. "A Boom in Illegal Apts," *Newsday*, November 1, 1988, pp. 3, 27.

Muller, Peter O. "Everyday Life in Suburbia." *American Quarterly* 34 (1982): 273.

Orzack, Louis, and Irwin T. Sanders. "A Social Profile of Levittown, New York." Unpublished manuscript. Department of Sociology and Anthropology. Boston University. Boston, MA. (Copy on File at the Levittown Public Library, Levittown Collection)

Pleck, Elizabeth, H., and Ellen K. Rothman. "Legacies: A History of Women and the Family in America, 1607–1870." The Annenberg/CPB Project for Public Television, 1987.

Ravitz, Alison. "The Home of Woman: A View from the Interior." *Built Environment* 10.1 (1984): 9.

Rose, Marc. " 'There Is Less Smoke in the District.' " *Journal of the West* 25.1 (1986): 44–54.

Scime, Joy. "Public Policy and the Married Working Woman in the Great Depression." Paper delivered at the Conference of the Organization of American Historians. Philadelphia, PA. Spring, 1986.

Silverman, Arnold. "Defense and Deconcentration." *Suburbia Re-examined.* Ed. Barbara M. Kelly. Westport, CT: Greenwood Press, 1989.

Soren, Josh. "The History of Levittown." Talk and slide presentation sponsored by the Levittown 40th Anniversary Committee. Levittown Public Library. 27 Sep. 1987.

Talmas, David. "The Levittown Housing Project." Unpublished master's thesis. Columbia University, 1950.

Wattel, Harold. "Abraham Levitt." *Dictionary of American Biography.*

———. "Levittown: A Suburban Community." *The Suburban Community.* Ed. William M. Dobriner. New York: Putnam, 1958. 287–313.

Weiss, Marc. "The Rise of the Community Builders; The American Real Estate Industry and Urban Land Planning." *Suburbia Re-examined*. Ed. Barbara M. Kelly. Westport, CT: Greenwood Press, 1989.

Welter, Barbara. "The Cult of True Womanhood." *American Quarterly* 18 (1966): 151–74.

Wirt, Frederick M. "The Political Sociology of American Suburbia: A Reinterpretation." *The Journal of Politics* 27 (1965): 647.

Wright, Gwendolyn. "The Model Domestic Environment." *Women in American Architecture; A Historic and Contemporary Perspective*. Ed. Susan Torre. New York: Whitney Library of Design, 1977. 18–31.

Index

Adolescence: and house design, 107–108; and juvenile delinquency, 106, 228n.15; concept in history, 227n.10
American Character, 22, 42
American Civil Liberties Union, 229n.24
American Dream: and Arcadian setting, 71; and suburban houses, 167; as reward for military service, 16; home ownership as emblem of, 12; Levittown as expression of, 44, 65, 149–151
American Legion, 247n.2
American values: and generation gap, 113; and home ownership, 22; and social class, 94; reflected in houses, 14
Anniversary: Tenth, 100, 103, 148, 157, 242n.28, 243n.35; Twentieth, 120; Fortieth, 160, 169, 206n.11, 225n.43; open house, 100
Automobile, importance in postwar suburbs, 15, 86
Authoritarianism in Levittown, 62
Aviation industry in Nassau County, 242n.31

Baby boom, 235n.18
Bank of Buffalo, 47
Bank of Manhattan Company, 47
Barkley, Mrs. Alben, in *McCalls*, 65
Bethpage Realty Company: 32, 192n.36; divestiture of Cape Cods, 74; lease terms, 210n.38, 212n.57; sold to Junto, 173

Boarders, in working class homes, 95, 223n.30
Building boom, 219n.3
Building codes: in suburbia, 235n.25; Town of Babylon, 205n.83, 236n.31; Town of Hempstead, 29, 124, 146, 235n.24, 236n.30; violations of, 144
Building permits, 227n.6

Cape Cod style house, lack of marketability of, 47
"Capitalist Realism," 199n.35; Levittown as an expression of, 47
Carport: added to Ranch model, 85; implications, 86
Chimney in Levittown folklore, 234n.16
City Housing Corporation, 44
Collective facilities, absence of, 65, 208n.24
Collectivity among Levittown men, 70
Colmer house: and family life, 120–127; as two-family dwelling, 128; Jensen apartment, 123–124; remodeling, 127; streetscape, 121–123
Communism: in "Father Knows Best," 229n.22; opposition to, 206n.8, 229n.23
Communist Party, in Levittown, 201n.53
Community Associations in Levitt-built developments, 51
Conformity, 60–62; as mental health, 207n.17; David Reisman on, 228n.12